International Entrepreneurship

International Entrepreneurship

Theoretical Foundations and Practices

Antonella Zucchella

and

Paolo Scabini

First published in 2007 by
PALGRAVE MACMILLAN
Houndmills, Basingstoke, Hampshire RG21 6XS and
175 Fifth Avenue, New York, N.Y. 10010
Companies and representatives throughout the world.

PALGRAVE MACMILLAN is the global academic imprint of the Palgrave Macmillan division of St. Martin's Press, LLC and of Palgrave Macmillan Ltd. Macmillan® is a registered trademark in the United States, United Kingdom and other countries. Palgrave is a registered trademark in the European Union and other countries.

ISBN-13: 978–0–230–51547–5 hardback
ISBN-10: 0–230–51547–9 hardback

This book is printed on paper suitable for recycling and made from fully managed and sustained forest sources. Logging, pulping and manufacturing processes are expected to conform to the environmental regulations of the country of origin.

A catalogue record for this book is available from the British Library.

A catalog record for this book is available from the Library of Congress.

Printed and bound in Great Britain by
CPI Antony Rowe, Chippenham and Eastbourne

Contents

List of Figures

List of Tables

Acknowledgements

The authors would like to acknowledge the financial support of the Italian Ministry for Education, Universities and Research (FIRB, Project RISC – RBNE039XKA: 'Research and entrepreneurship in the knowledge-based economy: The effects on the competitiveness of Italy in the European Union').

Foreword

Many years back, arriving in a new city to start a new business education, I was 'hijacked' by some students and business managers with the purpose of making me understand the importance of entrepreneurship. Indeed, they managed and an entrepreneurship programme was launched. Since then I have been a great friend of entrepreneurship, basically believing it is as much a matter of attitudes as of intellectual skills. Now I am happy to see entrepreneurship research making such a strong inroad into traditional domains of international business and strategy: a new area of knowledge has been born – International Entrepreneurship, leaving the authors of this book to grapple with definitions.

This volume is a timely one, integrating previous knowledge from Strategic Management, International Business and Entrepreneurship, helping to shape the contours of our new area of research and, hopefully, education. I believe the book is timely, as I share the view that 'old Europe' risks lagging behind the rapid development in other parts of the world. It is great to see what is effectuated in China and India, for example, but we in Europe need to improve on our 'international entrepreneurship skills' to stay competitive.

I believe the authors of this book are making a welcome contribution to research, education and management.

JAN-ERIK VAHLNE
Professor of International Business
University of Göteborg

Introduction

International Entrepreneurship represents an evolving and promising field both for research and for practitioners. The interest in the topic arises from the consideration that there is a potential connection between the entrepreneurial posture of the firm and its long run performance (Knight, 2000; Zahra and Garvis, 2000). The entrepreneurial posture is on the one hand, expressed through its internationalization strategy and, on the other, it is fed by it, which unfolds wider and more diversified growth opportunities. In fact, 'International Entrepreneurship is the discovery, enactment, evaluation, and exploitation of opportunities – across national borders – to create future goods and services' (Oviatt and McDougall, 2003).

'In short, firms with entrepreneurial postures are risk taking, innovative and proactive' (Covin and Slevin, 1991, p. 7). This definition supports the idea that entrepreneurship is also a firm-level attribute (and not just a personal trait) and may be understood through the above mentioned dimensions. Moreover, 'entrepreneurial strategic posture and international diversification strategy have been suggested as key factors to help firms succeed in the global marketplace' (Thoumrungroje and Tansuhaj, 2005, p. 55).

Research in International Entrepreneurship has grown over the past decades, and it is distinguished by a multiplicity of approaches. A major issue in the International Entrepreneurship field is the lack of a commonly agreed and comprehensive theoretical framework, even though a tendency towards a growing integration of approaches and models has been observed (Shane and

Venkataraman, 2000; Jones and Coviello, 2005). This area seeks delimitation of its boundaries and demarcation of its key theoretical aspects, as International Entrepreneurship is typically considered one of the main areas of interest in International Business, Entrepreneurship and Strategic Management studies. Both entrepreneurship and international business are fields of research which have seen an increasing number of studies during the last decade (McDougall and Oviatt, 1997; Oviatt and MacDougall, 2000; Zahra and Garvis, 2000).

Attention to the topic of International Entrepreneurship has grown in connection with the surge in international new ventures, one of the effects (and causes) of market globalization. From the 1990s researchers paid attention to the motivations and the patterns of internationalization shown by new ventures, a phenomenon which partially contrasts with the idea that firms engage gradually in international activities. Born-Global firms are defined as 'business organizations that from inception seek to derive significant competitive advantages from the use of resources and sale of outputs in multiple countries' (Oviatt and McDougall, 1994). Born-Global firms or International New Ventures (INVs)have been considered as an expression of International Entrepreneurship.

A second literature stream focuses on companies of different age and size showing entrepreneurial attitude as they venture into international markets (Zahra and Garvis, 2000). They have highlighted the entrepreneurial behaviour in order to define the research field of International Entrepreneurship, suggesting that even corporate entrepreneurship and venture should be included.

A third literature stream is represented by the studies of entrepreneurship in multinational firms, which received considerable attention in recent International Business research (Bartlett and Ghoshal, 2000; Birkinshaw, 1997) and could provide additional insights into the domain of International Entrepreneurship.

The first purpose of this book is to identify the foundations of International Entrepreneurship, which are found at the intersection of International Business, Entrepreneurship and Strategic Management studies. A better understanding of these and their rich and diversified foundations might help in developing a general framework for International Entrepreneurship. The aim of this work is to propose a simplified theoretical model as applicable to international ventures,

in order to evaluate their entrepreneurial posture. The research question underlying this work is the following: what are the resources and capabilities at the individual and organizational level which support International Entrepreneurship?

The field of observation is defined by International Entrepreneurial Organizations (IEOs). Literature typically addresses to two special cases of the latter, that is, International New Ventures and Multinational Enterprise (MNE) subsidiaries: the former are represented by new firms that engage in international markets, the latter are represented by established subsidiaries that compete entrepreneurially in the market. The intersection between the two dimensions of these firms – type of firm in terms of age and the governance – permits the identification of two other typologies of entrepreneurial international firms, which although consistent with the International Entrepreneurship literature, have been less considered by researchers (Figure A).

Despite the fact that INVs have traditionally been at the centre of International Entrepreneurship studies, other contributions point out the need to expand boundaries to the study of established firms. The motivations for, and effects of, internationalization in these companies have been explored from economic and organizational perspectives; however, they have rarely been viewed through the lenses of entrepreneurship. The latter perspective is essential since the turbulence of the current international business environment emphasizes the importance of considering entrepreneurship in established and large firms.

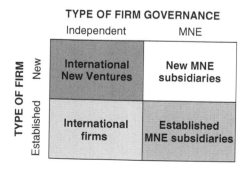

Figure A Field of observation

This work aims at highlighting the various forms of IEOs, through both a theoretical and a case studies research approach. It is applied to three very different firms representing alternatives to International Entrepreneurship, namely an International New Venture or Born-Global firm, identified as a new venture showing a fast process of internationalization, a multinational subsidiary and an established medium-sized firm. These firms demonstrate attributes of proactiveness, innovativeness and risk taking, that is, the capacity to identify and select opportunities and to assume risks on an international scale. The listed attributes are considered by different authors to be the core attitudes of entrepreneurship, and they can characterize individuals, entrepreneurs, management teams and their organizations. The objective is to verify if some specific resources and capabilities are commonly used and developed in these very different kinds of firms, responding to the research question of this work.

Ability to coordinate and to integrate internal and external resources, to reconfigure the firm's asset structure in terms of product portfolio and/or internal processes and personal or organizational experience, together with personal or organizational networking, seem to be the most important resources and capabilities able to define and identify IEOs.

After reviewing the International Entrepreneurship literature, and its foundations in International Business, Entrepreneurship and Strategic Management studies, in order to identify its main themes, the research gap is discussed. The different theoretical approaches and models considered in the literature review are then examined to select and build the theoretical framework adopted.

The qualitative case studies approach enables the assessment of the process of internationalization, the role of entrepreneurs, the features of IEOs and the search for driving forces that lead firms towards international operations (Marshall and Rossman, 1999). Results from the case studies enable us to refine the theoretical model and to draw conclusions on which (if any) are the common resources and capabilities supporting international entrepreneurial organizations belonging to different conceptual categories.

1
Theoretical Foundations of International Entrepreneurship

The difficulty of considering International Entrepreneurship as an effective domain of academic research is reflected by the lack of a general and widely accepted definition of the subject. Nevertheless, the meaning and scope of the term 'International Entrepreneurship' has evolved during the last decade and academic interest in the topic has grown.

Early definitions mostly considered new ventures, while other definitions include individuals, groups and established organizations, in order to include areas such as corporate entrepreneurship, entrepreneur characteristics and general economic development initiatives without giving a defining characteristic of firm size and age. The definition of International Entrepreneurship (IE) is a matter of continuing debate, which will evolve as new perspectives and new areas of research are proposed by academics and researchers.

Despite the absence of a generally agreed definition of the domain, International Entrepreneurship represents an important research field. This is witnessed by a growing number of papers, articles and contributions, which have been published throughout the 1990s up to the present time. On the other hand, this growing body of literature is still rather fragmented and calls for more robust theoretical frameworks (Oviatt and McDougall, 2000) and methodologies (Jones and Coviello, 2005). Above all, a holistic and interdisciplinary approach to research in IE is needed (Dana, Etemad and Wright, 1999). For this reason our analysis of the field starts from a review of both the definitions and drivers of IE and of the main literature foundations of the subject from a multi-disciplinary perspective.

1.1   Definitions of International Entrepreneurship

Morrow (1988) introduced the term 'International Entrepreneurship' in describing the evolving technological and cultural international environment which was opening previously untapped foreign markets to new ventures. From the beginning of the 1990s studies on the subject have had an impressive growth, ranging from contributions on the role of national culture (McGrath, MacMillan and Scheinberg, 1992; Thomas and Mueller, 2000; Wright and Ricks, 1994; Zahra and Schulte, 1994), to the practice of alliances and inter-firm cooperation (Li and Atuahene-Gima, 2001; Steensma, Marino, Weaver, and Dickson, 2000), with a dominant emphasis on the internationalization of Small and Medium-Sized Enterprises (SMEs) (Lu and Beamish, 2001), on the entrepreneurial posture and background of top management teams (Reuber and Fischer, 1997), and on the role of venture financing (Roure, Keeley and Keller, 1992).

One of the first empirical studies in the International Entrepreneurship area was McDougall's (1989) work on new ventures' international sales. This study has provided important insights into the differences between these firms and those that did not start out on an international scale. McDougall (1989) defined International Entrepreneurship 'as the development of international new ventures or start-ups that, from their inception, engage in international business, thus viewing their operating domain as international from the initial stages of the firm's operation'.

In the early 1990s, McDougall and Oviatt further developed the study on the so-called 'born-global ventures' defined as '... a business organization that, from inception, seeks to derive significant competitive advantage from the use of resources and sale of outputs in multiple countries'.

The definition of the boundaries of International Entrepreneurship has been discussed by many researchers: while some authors identify its domain in new ventures, others emphasize the construct of entrepreneurial behaviour, which can be observed in very different kinds of organizations. Zahra (1993), for example, suggested that the study of International Entrepreneurship should encompass both new firms and established companies, defining International Entrepreneurship as 'the study of the nature and consequences of a firm's risk-taking behaviour as it ventures into international markets'. Wright and

Ricks (1994) suggested that International Entrepreneurship is observable at the organizational behaviour level and focuses on the relationship between businesses and the international environments in which they operate. In addition, other authors recognize that a firm's business environment plays an important role in influencing the expression of entrepreneurial activities (Zahra 1991, 1993) and their returns (Zahra and Covin, 1995). The importance of national cultures as 'loci' for different expressions of International Entrepreneurship and the specific influence of the business environment emphasize the need for comparative studies as one of the areas of interest in International Entrepreneurship.

In 2000 Oviatt and McDougall introduced a broader definition of International Entrepreneurship including the study of established companies and the recognition of comparative (cross-national) analysis. They defined this field as 'a combination of innovative, proactive, and risk-seeking behaviour that crosses or is compared across national borders and is intended to create value in business organizations'. This definition considers Miller's (1983) definition of entrepreneurship as a phenomenon at the organizational level that focuses on innovation, risk taking and proactive behaviour. It also focuses on the entrepreneurial behaviour of these firms rather than studying only the characteristics and intentions of the individual entrepreneurs. The key dimensions of entrepreneurship – innovativeness, proactiveness and risk propensity – can be found and developed at the organizational level.

Innovativeness reflects a tendency to support new ideas, experimentation and new processes, while *proactiveness* refers to the capacity to anticipate and act on future needs and desires. Lastly, *risk-taking* conduct indicates the will to commit large amounts of resources, fully aware that the potential for failure may be high.

Including established companies in the study permits us to make the assumption that well-established companies can also be innovative and risk-taking, correcting an oversight in the entrepreneurship field. Many highly regarded well-established companies work hard to foster innovation, support venturing and encourage risk taking.

The process supporting international entrepreneurial orientation is described by Shane and Venkataraman (2000) as a process of discovery, and this seems to correspond to what Weick (1995) describes as enactment. Consequently, the McDougall, Oviatt and Shrader

Table 1.1 Some International Entrepreneurship definitions

International Entrepreneurship is defined in this study as the development of international new ventures or start-ups that, from their inception, engage in international business, thus viewing their operating domain as international from the initial stages of the firm's operation.

(McDougall, 1989)

The study of the nature and consequences of a firm's risk-taking behaviour as it ventures into international markets.

(Zahra, 1993)

.... a business organization that, from inception, seeks to derive significant competitive advantage from the use of resources and sale of outputs in multiple countries.

(Oviatt and McDougall, 1994)

New and innovative activities that have the goal of value creation and growth in business organization across national borders.

(McDougall and Oviatt, 1996)

A combination of innovative, proactive, and risk-seeking behaviour that crosses or is compared across national borders and is intended to create value in business organizations.

(Oviatt and McDougall, 2000)

It is associated with opportunity seeking, risk taking, and decision action catalysed by a strong leader or an organisation.

(Knight, 2000)

International entrepreneurial orientation reflects the firm's overall proactiveness and aggressiveness in its pursuit of international markets.

(Knight, 2001)

International Entrepreneurship is the discovery, enactment, evaluation, and exploitation of opportunities – across national borders – to create future goods and services.

(McDougall, Oviatt and Shrader, 2003)

... [an] evolutionary and potentially discontinuous process determined by innovation, and influenced by environmental change and human volition, action or decision.

(Jones and Coviello, 2005)

definition (2003) will be adopted in this book: 'International Entrepreneurship is the discovery, enactment, evaluation, and exploitation of opportunities – across national borders – to create future goods and services.' According to this definition it follows that International Entrepreneurship examines and compares how, by whom, and with what effects those opportunities are pursued and exploited across national borders.

According to the McDougall, Oviatt and Shrader definition (2003), the International Entrepreneurship arena includes both the study of entrepreneurial activities that cross national borders and the comparison of domestic entrepreneurial activities in multiple countries. A comparison among different definitions of IE over the last 15 years (Table 1.1) permits observation of the gradual enlargement already mentioned of the research field in terms of object of analysis (kinds of firms), but it also discloses an emerging perspective, which considers:

- both entrepreneurial attitude and action
- both events and processes
- both individual and organizational resources and capabilities

Consequently, the areas of academic study which have shown an interest in the topic and more frequently come into contact with it are International Business, Entrepreneurship and Strategic Management studies.

1.2 Factors affecting International Entrepreneurship

International Entrepreneurship is not in itself a novel orientation of firms and entrepreneurs. Schumpeter (1934) underlined the entry in new markets – also in geographic terms – as an expression of entrepreneurship. The evolution in the definitions of IE proposed by different authors suggests that an expression of International Entrepreneurship is not the entry *per se* in a foreign market but it is a combination of attitudes at the individual and organizational level (proactiveness, innovativeness, risktaking) and of actions over time, along an evolutionary and potentially discontinuous process.

The growing interest in the subject is related to the fact that the recent evolution of market conditions and business responses seem

10

Table 1.2 Key drivers of International Entrepreneurship: a literature review

	Context		Drivers		
	Global environment	**Business-specific**	**Location specific (clusters and districts)**	**Networking attitude**	**Entrepreneur-specific**
Literature issues	1. Shrinking transportation and communication costs (Holstein, 1992) 2. Better accessibility to knowledge, enhanced knowledge creation and exploitation (Czinkota and Ronkaininen, 1995; Evans and Wurster, 1999; Dunning, 2000) 3. Role of ICT (Kobrin, 1991; de la Torre and Moxon, 2001; Dunning and	1. From industries to spaces where myriads of born-global niches either exist or can be created by entrepreneurs (see also entrepreneurial drivers) (Hamel and Prahalad, 1994) 2. Knowledge intensive industries and high tech businesses as natural arena of born global behaviour (Livak, 1990; Lindquist, 1991;	1. The role of local networking (Johanisson, 1994; Lindmark, 1994) 2. Co-location effects and local clusters as drivers of fast international growth (Solvell and Zander, 1995; Dunning, 2000; Markusen, 1996; Porter, 1998; Brown and Bell 2001; Porter, 1990; Enright, 1998; Servais and Rasmussen, 1999) 3. Industrial districts as a natural locus for	1. The role of international networking (both personal and inter-organizational) in internationalization (Rasmussen, Madsen and Evangelista, 1999; Nooteboom, 2004; Petersen, Pedersen and Sharma, 2002; Chetty, Eriksson and Hohenthal, 2002; Beamish and Makino, 1999) 2. The role of partnering with global customers (Majkgård and Sharma, 1998)	1. Key features in international entrepreneurship (Cavusgil, Tamer and Naor, 1987; Sahlman and Stevenson, 1991; Venkataraman, 1997; Brush, Greene and Hart, 2001; Andersson, 2003) 2. The role of the entrepreneur in born global firms (Madsen and Servais, 1997; Rasmussen, Madsen and Evangelista, 1999; Bloodgood, Sapienza and

Wymbs, 2001;
Nayyar and Bantel,
1994)
4. Enhanced
opportunities to
create value and to
manage
international value
chains
(Brandenburger,
and Nalebuff, 1998;
de la Torre and Moxon,
2001)
5. Enhanced speed
of growth and value
creation processes
(Nayyar and Bantel,
1994; Eisenhardt,
Martin, 2000;
Zaheer and
Zaheer Manrakhan,2001)

Preece, Miles
and Baetz, 1998)
3. Growing
niche orientation
both in mature
and in innovative
businesses
(McKinsey
& Co., 1993;
Zucchella,2001;
Madsen and
Servais, 1997)

international
entrepreneurial
orientation
(Storper, 1992;
Sopas, 2001;
Saxenian, 1994;
Leamer and
Storper, 2001;
Maccarini, Scabini
and Zucchella,
2003)

Almeida, 1996;
Kandsaami, 1998;
Harveston, Kedia
and Davis, 2000);
and governance
issues in
international
entrepreneurial
firms (Oviatt,
McDougall,1994;
Preece, Miles and
Baetz, 1998;
Larimo, 2001;
Kedia and
Harveston, 1998;
Kuemmerle,
2002; Arenius
and Autio, 2002)

Source: Adapted from Zucchella, A., 'Non-sequential internationalisation processes between competition and co-operation: A tentative re-conciliation of alternative approaches'. In T. Morrow, S. Loane, J. Bell and C. Wheeler (eds), *International Business in an enlarging Europe*, Basingstoke: Palgrave Macmillan, 2005.

to highlight the need for an entrepreneurial approach to foreign markets. This paragraph aims at analysing the main factors which drive this orientation, which are summarized and related to literature in Tables 1.2 and 1.3.

The relevant changes that occurred in the worldwide economy and its markets from the 1980s are due to the interplay of the globalization of markets, with the facilitating role of ICTs; the emergence of global segments and global customers in a growing number of businesses; and the advent of a number of technological innovations and developments characterized by a pervasive nature and capable of modifying business and conditions in established markets/industries and/or to create new markets and industries on an international or global scale.

Such changes led to reactive rather than proactive strategies by both established and new/infant firms, which more and more frequently assumed the form of core business focusing, product specialization and niche orientation, and so on. Markets and industries in a number of cases turned progressively into wider competitive spaces where different industries converged (luxury space, digital space, entertainment space, etc.), which broke down in a myriad of niches, typically global or at least continental ones (the smaller the segment, the larger the geographic scope) (Zucchella, Palamara, 2006).

The evolving competitive environment highlights the role of entrepreneurial and managerial factors, which are also changing rapidly: a new generation of entrepreneurs and managers recently joined the economic scene, characterized by higher education than the former ones and stronger international vision (thanks to intense ICT use, frequent travel, studies abroad and better knowledge of foreign languages). Moreover, in the last two decades emerging entrepreneurs experienced more opportunities to access the 'international markets/customers knowledge capital' embedded in local clusters and districts, and in other forms of inter-firm network relationships/strategic alliances. This is a form of tacit knowledge, typically embedded in given contexts and having access to it enables new firms to venture early and rapidly into foreign markets. Similar considerations hold also for the role of international networks, where the social networks established by entrepreneurs and managers support opportunities discovery and exploitation through foreign markets expansion.

Table 1.3   Influence of organizational factors on International Entrepreneurship

Variable	Dimension	Findings
Top management team	Foreign work experience	• Case analyses showed that new ventures led by managers with foreign work experience were able to quickly internationalize their operations and do so successfully (Oviatt and McDougall, 1995; McDougall and Oviatt, 1996). • Positive and significant association between managers' foreign work experience and degree of new venture's internationalization (Bloodgood et al., 1996; Burgel and Murray, 1998). • A higher percentage of managers of companies that internationalized worked for a foreign company at home (Burgel and Murray, 1998).
	Education	• Positive (not significant) relationship between managers' receiving education outside the USA and new ventures' international expansion (Bloodgood et al., 1996). • A higher percentage of managers of companies that interionalized received education abroad than those of start ups that did not internationalize (Burgel and Murray, 1998).
Resources	Background	• Firms with principal founders drawn from managerial parental backgrounds were significantly more likely to export than firms with other types of founders (Westhead et al.,1998).
	Global vision	• Case analyses suggested that new ventures by managers with global visions were able to internationalize quickly and successfully (Oviatt and McDougall, 1995).

Continued

Table 1.3 Continued

Variable	Dimension	Findings
	Unique assets	• Case analyses suggested that new ventures with unique intangible assets were able to internationalize quickly and successfully (Oviatt and McDougall, 1995). • Companies that international- ized their operations had products that required signifi- cantly less customization and maintenance than those that did not (Burgel and Murray, 1998). There were no differences between the two groups in the amount of installation or training required to use their products. • Start up companies that did not intenationalize were more likely to describe their products as being less innovative (Burgel and Murray, 1998).
	R&D spending	• Positively (not significantly) related to internationalization status, speed or degree (Zahra et al., 2000b). • Start-ups that internationalized their operations had higher R&D-to-sales ratios (Burgel and Murray, 1998). • Start-ups that internationalized their operations had higher ratios of employees who worked 50% or more of their time on new product development as a percentage of sales than those that did not (Burgel and Murray, 1998).
	Network	• Positively (not significantly) related to internationalization status,speed or degree (Zahra et al., 2000b).

Continued

Table 1.3   Continued

Variable	Dimension	Findings
		• Start-ups that internationalized their operations had higher R&D-to-sales ratios (Burgel and Murray, 1998).
		• Start-ups that internationalized their operations had higher ratios of employees who worked 50% or more of their time on new product development as a percentage of sales than those that did not (Burgel and Murray, 1998).
	Reputation	• A reputation for technological superiority is positively associated with status, speed and degree of internationalization. This effect is higher for status and degree of internationalization in new firms with high R&D spending (Zahra et al., 2000a). Interaction of reputation and R&D is not significant in the case of speed.
Firm-related variables	Size	• Venture size is positively associated with degree of internationalization (Bloodgood et al., 1997).
		• Venture size (time 1) was negatively (not significantly) associated with relative market share in time 2 (McDougall and Oviatt, 1996).
		• Venture size was positively (not significantly) associated with internationalization status, speed or degree (Zahra et al., 2000a).
		• Company size is negatively associated (not significantly) with degree of internationalization (Reuber and Fischer, 1997).

Continued

Table 1.3 Continued

Variable	Dimension	Findings
	Age	• High-tech start ups that internationalized were significantly larger in sales and employment than firms that did not internationalize (Burgel and Murray, 1998). • There was no significant difference in employment of exporters vs. non-exporters (Westhead et al., 1998). • Age was negatively (not significantly) associated with ROI in time 2 (McDougall and Oviatt, 1996). • Age is positively associated with degree of internationalization in one equation but negatively (not significantly) in another (Reuber and Fischer, 1997). • Age is positively associated with degree of internationalization (Denicolai et al., 2005). • Venture age was positively (not significantly) associated with internationalization status or degree (Zahra et al., 2000a). Speed of internationalization was not explored in the analysis.
	Location	• There was no significant difference between firms that exported and those that did not in rural vs. urban location (Westhead et al., 1998). • National culture influences the formation of technology alliances by entrepreneurial firms (Steensma et al., 2000). Being located in a cluster is positively associated with

Continued

Table 1.3 Continued

Variable	Dimension	Findings
		speed and degree of internationalization (Urban, Vendemini, 1992; Beamish, 1999; Majkgård and Sharma, 1998).
		• Being located in a district is positively associated with speed and degree of internationalization (Maccarini et al., 2003).
	Growth orientation	• Firm growth orientation was positively associated with average absolute annual international sales growth (Autio et al., 1997).
	Environmental scanning	• Average amount of environ mental scanning was positively and significantly associated with international collaborative relationships which, in turn, was positively and significantly associated with average absolute annual international sales growth (Autio et al.,1997).
		• Analyses indicated that limited global information gathering capabilities limited companies' internationalization (Karagozoglu and Lindell, 1998).
	Financial Strength	• ROE was positively (but not significantly) associated with internationalization status, positively and marginally significant ($p < 0.10$) with speed and degree of sales international- ization (Zahra et al., 2000a).
		• Leverage was positively (not significantly) associated with degree of internationalization (Bloodgood et al., 1996).

Source: Adaptation based on S. A. Zahra and G. George, 'International Entrepreneurship: The current status of the field and future research agenda'. In M. Hitt, D. Ireland, D. Sexton and M. Camp (eds), *Strategic Entrepreneurship: Creating an Integrated Mindset*, Strategic Management Series, Oxford: Blackwell, 2002.

Table 1.3 focuses on the drivers at the firm level, and in particular on the crucial role of firm resources, among which the top management team plays a relevant part. The characteristics of the latter significantly affect firms' strategic decisions (Finkelstein and Hambrick, 1996), such as internationalization (Calof and Beamish, 1994; Carpenter and Frederickson, 2001). In Table 1.3 it is possible to identify the importance of previous international experience, foreign education and the vision of the management team. Senior managers' international experience is positively related to some indicators of firm performance (Carpenter, Sanders and Gregersen, 2001; Daily, Certo and Dalton, 2000).

The resource-based view offers a theoretical background to the analysis of the different factors affecting International Entrepreneurship at the firm level of analysis (Barney, 1991). Unique organizational assets and knowledge bases can influence International Entrepreneurship (Oviatt and McDougall, 1995). On the other hand, entry into foreign markets enhances the firm's learning and gives it access to a wider set of opportunities (Zahra, Dharwadkar and George (2000).

A Resource-Based View approach appears rich and potentially conclusive in empirical findings, but remains too static. According to the process view of International Entrepreneurship, dynamic factors are important as well. As a consequence human resources – especially at the entrepreneur/Top Management Team (TMT) level – are crucial, and the process of organizational learning is fundamental as well. Through the latter, unique attitudes and skills are 'transferred' to the organization and 'transformed' into organizational routines. In this process, a shift from individual to organizational entrepreneurship is attained. This is one of the relatively neglected areas in the study of International Entrepreneurship, as applied to organizations, both new and established.

1.3   Research gap

Distinct streams have already emerged in the International Entrepreneurship literature (Oviatt and McDougall, 2000). One stream focuses on international new ventures: start-ups that are international from inception. A second stream considers MNEs subsidiaries and another one looks at the internationalization of

established firms. Yeung (2002) extended the notion of entrepreneurs to government-linked firms operating abroad.

Although International Entrepreneurship researchers have mainly focused on two typologies of firms (Born-Globals and MNE subsidiaries), there are also other entities which have received less attention but might also be considered as relevant expressions of the phenomenon.

An important evidence of the existence of other international entrepreneurial entities is given by some companies, especially small to medium-sized firms that show typical entrepreneurial characteristics, but they are neither Born-Globals because they do not develop international activities from their foundation, nor subsidiaries because they are not linked to any Multinational enterprise. An example is represented by born-again global firms (Bell, McNaughton and Young, 2001). They are firms that have been well established in their domestic markets, with apparently no prior motivation to internationalize, but which have suddenly embraced rapid and dedicated internationalization.

Dimitratos, Lioukas and Carter (2004) found that older firms in mature and low-technology industries can show international entrepreneurial behaviour. These firms demonstrate proactive behaviour, and show a receptive attitude to international opportunities, which are all common characteristics of the two other typologies of international entrepreneurial firms. These characteristics are found also in other established firms, where the attributes of proactiveness, innovativeness and risk-taking behaviour are present, as far as foreign markets and their opportunities are concerned.

We could thus conclude that 'IE has the potential to distinguish activities of all private and public organizations transcending national borders, regardless of age, size or industrial sector' (Dimitratos and Jones, 2005, p. 121) Consequently, the definitions of IE and the object of analysis tend to move from specific subjects (given typologies of firms along with their industries and markets and their international behaviour) to personal and organizational attributes, grounded on entrepreneurship literature, firm resources and capabilities. The McDougall, Oviatt and Shrader (2003) definition makes it difficult to recognize International Entrepreneurship in terms of easily observable factors (age, size, industry) and imposes a deeper understanding of firm resources, processes and behaviour. The enlarging

field of research in IE leads us to adopt the term 'International Entrepreneurial Organizations' (IEO). The latter construct needs to be developed in terms of internal consistency of resources and capabilities, environmental fit, and differentiation from other kinds of organizations.

From this point of view the construct of IEO reveals a research gap, to which this work addresses. In particular the areas where the gap is more consistent are the following ones, namely:

- Digging into the theoretical foundations of International Entrepreneurship and their interplay. An enlarged definition, which encompasses the resources, capabilities and behaviour of both individuals and organizations calls for a larger theoretical base and for the understanding of inter-relationships among different theoretical streams (entrepreneurship, strategic management, international business).
- Opening the black box, which means analysing which internal resources, processes and capabilities support international entrepreneurial orientation in different organizations. In fact this is the new level at which both the analysis and the construct validity of IE need to be developed, and not at the level of firm age, size, industry.
- Developing a dynamic perspective of IE, because the latter is a process and not a single decision or event (e.g., foreign market entry). In a highly competitive and dynamic environment, International Entrepreneurship must become a process in time, where processes of organizational learning from multi-domestic experience take place, routines and capabilities are adapted/reconfigured to changing market conditions and to the need for coping with new worldwide opportunities. For this reason a dynamic capabilities approach will be proposed to complement other traditional approaches to the understanding of IEOs.

As mentioned above researchers have mainly focused on the firm's resources as a factor influencing International Entrepreneurship, particularly – at the individual level – on the entrepreneurial characteristics and attitudes, and – at the firm level – on how the firm's unique assets (product innovativeness, intangible assets such as reputation, local and global networking) can influence the speed and degree of internationalization. Issues such as discovery, evaluation,

exploitation and exploration of opportunities have also been examined in order to explain the entrepreneurial process in a firm's internationalization. Less attention has been paid to the dynamic variables affecting International Entrepreneurship over time, in process perspective (Jones and Coviello, 2005). In particular, a relatively unexplored field is represented by the development of organizational capabilities, which can support IE over time.

A research gap exists in International Entrepreneurship in the area of organizational learning and dynamic capabilities. The knowledge-creation process in International New Ventures (INVs) and/or in SMEs is developed from the entrepreneur's/TMT experience, attitudes, skills and background, but the linkages between individual and organizational learning are not always clear and the core organizational processes which are more relevant in the case of IEOs are rarely considered in literature. The identification of such processes and dynamic capabilities could permit the analysis of different categories of IEOs (INVs, MNEs subsidiaries, SMEs and established entrepreneurial firms in general) adopting a common theoretical framework.

1.4 Foundations of International Entrepreneurship: from personal to organizational, from static to dynamic variables

Due to the variety of fields which have given attention to International Entrepreneurship over the years, academics have considered this area of research from different perspectives in order to better understand the phenomenon. It is worthwhile to outline the areas of study trying to utilize the frameworks and the concepts already established in literature, highlighting the most relevant aspects. In order to better understand this framework, Figure 1.1 includes the main influential fields which will be analysed in more depth later on.

International Business studies have been considerably used in literature to describe and to explain the internationalization process and although they have been criticized over the years, they are relevant to the theoretical framework for International Entrepreneurship. For example, Internalization and the Transaction Costs Theory tends to emphasize variables such as costs, investments, risk and control

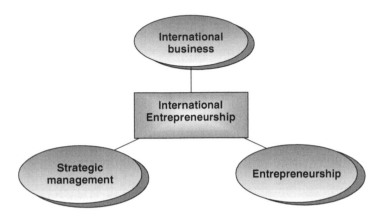

Figure 1.1   International Entrepreneurship foundations

as business decision-making criteria, focusing on economics-based factors influencing internationalization. On the contrary, frameworks such as the Dunning Eclectic Paradigm, the Network Theory or in general the organizational learning approaches, describing the behavioural process that underlines internationalization are considered more consistent with the field of International Entrepreneurship and seem to fit better within its domain. For example, Dunning's (1991) ownership-specific or location-specific advantages that are considered as a source of competitive advantage seem to recall the characteristics of an entrepreneurial firm's unique resources, assets and the propensity of this typology to set their business activities in high-value and strategic locations. Furthermore, the 'international among others' typology of firms by Johanson and Mattson Network Theory (1988) recalls the importance to an international entrepreneurial firm of being part of a network where it is possible to gain advantages, thanks to the greater interdependency of the internationalized network.

In light of the most relevant assumptions of International Business Theories, this work examines the theories on 'entrepreneurship and economic development', enabling basic understanding both of the entrepreneur as an economic agent and what causes entrepreneurs to achieve successful growth in an international environment. Indeed, classic entrepreneurship theories consider the role of the entrepreneur

in terms of innovation and firm growth but also in terms of transaction costs and internalization decisions (Kirzner 1973; Knight, 1921; Schumpeter, 1934). Moreover, the importance of entrepreneurs has been dealt with in many studies and the findings reveal a positive relationship between entrepreneurs' international attitude, orientation, experience and network, and positive international development (Andersson, 2003; Ibeh and Young, 2001; Kuemmerle, 2002; Preece, Miles and Baetz, 1998; Westhead, Wright and Ucbasaran, 2001).

Finally, since researchers suggest that entrepreneurial companies lead to higher performances and a stronger competitive advantage and profitability, Strategic Management analyses the key factors of the entrepreneurial process: opportunities, resources, strategic processes, organizational capabilities and their sequence in terms of temporal evolution, which is often discontinuous. The environmental changes, which can be both internal and external to the firm, originate new opportunities that the entrepreneur might exploit to develop successful and innovative outcomes. The process is proactive and needs the commitment of resources that are both tangible and intangible, but it also requires a suitable organizational structure characterized by permeable boundaries able to establish and manage international points of contact in order to enhance a firm's resource and knowledge base. The entrepreneur's main characteristics and role in discovering, accessing and combining resources in order to exploit a market opportunity and generate innovation are consistent with the body of literature that regards the Resource-Based approach in combination with the network approach in International Business studies.

This focuses on unique and idiosyncratic assets and capabilities. The ownership and development of such assets and capabilities might explain successful growth abroad. The importance of internal capabilities is rooted in evolutionary economics. This means that the ability to sustain innovation and create new knowledge leads to the development of capabilities, consisting of competences and organizational routines. The knowledge accumulation, the capabilities, financial resources, the equipment and other physical resources are the main drivers that older firms can draw on to perform well in foreign markets, but which young firms lack. They rely upon intangible knowledge-based capabilities in approaching foreign market entry. Moreover, capabilities-based resources are particularly important to SMEs, because they are poor in tangible resources and they deal with

different environments in different countries around the world (Knight and Cavusgil, 2004).

From another perspective, long-run performance depends not only on a firm's resources and capabilities *per se* but – most importantly – on some core processes, that is, dynamic features as opposed to the static resources and capabilities-based ones. Among the former, this work outlines in particular the capacity to mobilize and combine dynamically external and internal resources, to pursue incremental as well as radical innovations (including foreign market entry) at different units of analysis, to reconfigure and transform capabilities continually in non-imitable configurations (dynamic capabilities, Teece, Pisano and Schuen, 1997).

These capabilities emerge from and are a source of learning. Learning mechanisms through which capabilities arise consist in experience accumulation, knowledge articulation and codification (Zollo and Winter, 2002). Researchers in the international learning area have mostly investigated the determinants of the acquisition of international market knowledge for organizations that internationalize incrementally and for those that internationalize from inception. In the former, learning through a firm's own experience is considered critical to the internationalization process (Johanson and Vahlne, 1977): only the acquisition of international market knowledge through experience and/or learning from networks can reduce the firm's uncertainty. In new organizations, international market diversity, mode of market entry, top management's previous experience, entrepreneurial orientation and social capital all have a positive influence on the different forms of learning, notably international learning. International market diversity and high-control mode of market entry have a positive effect on technological learning, with the relationship being stronger when firms implement knowledge integration activities (Zahra, Dharwadkar and George, 2000). Top management's prior experience moderates the effect of international diversity on learning (Yeoh, 2004). In contrast, a firm's age at first international entry has a negative relationship with its international learning effort (Sapienza et al., 2005). Thus, the younger the firm is when it internationalizes, the more learning about internationalization occurs.

Finally, a firm's entrepreneurial orientation and social capital also have a positive impact on learning about international

markets (Sapienza, Clercq and Sandberg, 2005; Yli-Renko, Autio and Tontti, 2002). Some studies report that these firms display learning characteristics that may allow them to internationalize rapidly and successfully, related to development of a proactive learning approach during the internationalization process (Autio, Sapienza and Almeida, 2000). Moreover, they may not have yet developed organizational routines comparable to those of older and established firms. Other forms of learning are the acquisition of experiential knowledge through hiring knowledgeable staff (Bengtsoon, 2004; Saarenketo, Puumalainen, Kuivalainen and Kylaheiko, 2004); imitation of other firms that have internationalized successfully; searching for international market knowledge; and congenital learning,that is, learning brought to the organization by founders (Bengtsoon, 2004; Saarenketo et al., 2004). In SMEs and in new international firms, the process by which personal learning and knowledge evolves into an organizational one through interpretation, distribution and institutionalization of knowledge is crucial.

1.5 A comparison among different theoretical frameworks

The firm's competitive advantage is a highly dynamic one, and requires continuous innovative reconfiguration as well as resource mobilization, given path dependence and market positions (Leonard-Barton, 1992; Teece, Pisano and Shuen, 1997).

Theories of multinational enterprise argue that some enterprises are multinational because of certain firm-specific capabilities and routines that they possess and accumulate (Kogut, 1984; Leonard Barton, 1992). Theories of International Entrepreneurship, on the other hand, argue that some firms become international because of entrepreneur-specific capabilities (Bloodgood, Sapienza and Almeida, 1996; Knight and Cavusgil, 1995; McDougall and Oviatt, 1996).

The main argument of this work is that the latter is not an alternative but a complementary vision to the first one, since entrepreneur-specific capabilities influence the strategic management and the organizational architecture of firms, originating a progressive sedimentation of capabilities and organizational routines, stemming from the resources mobilization and integration led from the new venture's start up by the entrepreneur.

Table 1.4 A comparison among different theoretical frameworks

Theoretical frame	Resource-based	Dynamic capabilities	Entrepreneurship	International Entrepreneurship	International Entrepreneurship in a dynamic capabilities frame
Level of Analysis	Organizations	Organizations	Entrepreneurs, intrapreneurs, new ventures	International entrepreneurs, intrapreneurs, international ventures	*International entrepreneurial organizations*
Unit of analysis	Resources	Processes Positions Paths	Attributes and behaviour of entrepreneurs and entrepreneurial organizations	Resources and attributes of entrepreneurs, intrapreneurs and international ventures	*Processes, positions and paths of international entrepreneurial organizations*
Core activity	Resources mobilization, integration and coordination	Resources mobilization and reconfiguration transformation Development and reconfiguration of capabilities	Opportunity discovery and evaluation Resources mobilization, integration and coordination	Opportunity scanning and selection Opportunities exploitation through resources mobilization, integration and coordination on international scale	*Opportunity scanning and selection Opportunities exploitation through resources mobilization, integration and coordination on international scale Reconfiguration of capabilities over time through international learning processes*

From these perspectives the Resource-Based view (Barney, 1991; Penrose, 1959; Peteraf, 1993; Wernerfelt, 1984), Dynamic Capabilities (Teece, Pisano and Shuen, 1997) and the entrepreneurship approaches (Dana and Wright, 2004; Etemad, 2004; Venkataraman, 1997) share the common issue of resource mobilization and combination as fundamental activities that must be renewed over time to explore new opportunities and to create a dynamic stock of resources difficult to imitate (Table 1.4).

The Resource-Based view variables, indeed, contribute significantly, since entrepreneurial firms exhibit the possession of unique resources and a diverse and particular acquisition, usage and organization of them. Entrepreneurial organizations are also able to dynamically reconfigure their capabilities, creating 'waves' of innovation in terms of products, processes and markets (IEOs). These resources and capabilities are considered as most influential contributors to the firm's competitive advantage and success abroad, since they are one of the means by which the entrepreneur might reach a significant international competitive advantage. In this sense entrepreneurial dynamic capabilities play a key role in the explanation of entrepreneurial success.

Another useful view examines the recent developments in entrepreneurship theory, which have turned to the phenomenon of social and industrial networks. In such a context, alliances and partnerships are at the same time vehicles to not only initiate activities abroad in conditions of scarce resources but also effective organizational settings. Indeed, the entrepreneur with his/her personal relationships might help the business to find assets, resources and knowledge to start and develop the business, but at the same time networks are effective organizational answers to a dynamic and evolving environment where flexibility is a source of competitive advantage.

It appears that the area of intersection in research at the internationalization and entrepreneurial level is progressively expanding, and represents a very interesting field to explore further since it reflects the common theoretical bases in both frames. Moreover a research gap has been identified in the area of dynamic capabilities and processes supporting International Entrepreneurship.

The following chapters are devoted to deepening the core theoretical foundations of International Entrepreneurship, in order to better define such a gap and to elaborate a multi-disciplinary theoretical framework.

2
International Business Studies

Both entrepreneurship and international business are fields of research that have seen an increasing number of studies during the last decade (McDougall and Oviatt, 1997, 2000; Zahra and Garvis, 2000). Entrepreneurship and international business are strictly interrelated because entering and venturing into foreign markets are viewed as entrepreneurial activities for the firm (Ibeh and Young, 2001; Lumpkin and Dess, 1996; Zahra and George, 2002).

The Internationalization phenomenon has been studied for a long time and a series of meanings and definitions have been attributed. In general, internationalization is the growth of the firm out of its national boundaries and more precisely it is concerned with growth and development in foreign markets. This phenomenon does not imply only the normal business activities of an enterprise abroad or, on the other hand, the influence that a firm has to maintain in its environment regarding that of being a foreign firm's business; but also a partial mitigation of cultural differences. From an enterprise point of view, it means a growing standardization of product characteristics and operational procedures which leads managers all over the world to run their business in an increasingly similar way.

In this context internationalization theories were introduced before the development of International Entrepreneurship as an academic field of research. This theoretical background is important for several reasons including the fact that it provides a frame of reference in understanding the evolutionary aspects of International Entrepreneurship, and thus gives an explanation of its emergence; it

is also relevant in checking the applicability of these theories to new international business phenomena. Finally, it is worthwhile to highlight the most significant aspects of each theory, in order to make assumptions regarding the creation of an integrated framework of analysis of international business.

The modern theory of the internationalization of the firm can be dated back to the 1960s, when an increased number of researchers started to analyse the subject of the international development of firms from different points of view. Nevertheless, it must be remembered that the first theoretical frameworks about international business have their roots first in the study of Adam Smith and David Ricardo later on.

In 1776 Adam Smith, premising that human needs cannot be totally satisfied since resources are scarce, underlined specialization as an element of advantage. Even though he focused his attention on a nation-based view instead of a firm-based one, at an international level each nation should specialize in the production of goods in which it demonstrates better competence and more resources, exporting part of that production and receiving in exchange other goods it cannot manufacture efficiently.

David Ricardo (1817), building on Smith's theory of absolute advantage, put forward the concept of comparative advantage: each nation possesses a particular advantage (comparative advantage) in the production of goods that it can produce more efficiently than others. According to Ricardo, a country should focus resources on the goods in which it has a greater comparative advantage and import the goods in which its comparative advantage is lower. Smith and Ricardo focused their attention on entire nations, while today the question is why firms trade and how they adopt different policies for foreign direct investment, licensing or exporting. In this sense, a growing interest about the firm and its involvement in international markets gained ground after the 1960s.

Theoretically, theory in business administration was at that time dominated by *economic-based* models, followed in the 1970s by *behavioural* theories and models. The former theories were proposed in order to understand the reasons why firms enter international markets. The latter theories try to explain the process of international expansion in terms of learning and related decisional patterns.

Consequently, traditional theories in the field of international business can be divided into two groups: the economic decision-based approaches to internationalization and the evolutionary behavioural approaches to internationalization (Benito and Welch, 1994). In this sense the first and most important economic-based theories, which formed main streams, are the market power approach (Hymer, 1976), the Product Life Cycle approach (PLC) (Vernon, 1966, 1974), the Internalization and Transaction costs theory, the Eclectic paradigm (Dunning, 1988).[1] These theories are dominated by cost issues, as the driver of punctual internationalization decisions (static perspective). On the other side, behavioural and evolutionary models build on the issues of firm resources (including knowledge base) and capabilities (state aspects) and on learning processes and new knowledge creation and exploitation (dynamic aspects). Among these streams, where models prevail over theories, we can mention the Uppsala model (Johanson and Vahlne, 1977), the Innovation model and the Network approach. The knowledge-based theory (Kogut and Zander, 1993) complements these streams.

The following paragraphs summarize – even though not exhaustively – the international theories proposed by the literature.

2.1 Economic decision-based approaches to internationalization

In this section are included the traditional theories and models of internationalization. They are primarily cost-related models applied to large-sized companies that deal with monopolistic advantage theory and oligopolistic theory.

---

[1] It must be mentioned that academics and theorists have given different classification and higher or lower consideration to the theories published over the years. Cantwell, for example using a distinction between different levels of analysis grouped the main theories into four groups: the market power or Hymer theory of the firm, the internalization or Coasian theory of the firm, the macroeconomic approach and the last one is based on the analysis of comparative firm growth in competitive international industries. Nevertheless in this work it has been considered more appropriate to give a brief description of the most well-known and acknowledged theories (as listed above) also keeping in mind the aim of the work in itself.

2.1.1 Hymer's approach

Stephen Hymer through his PhD thesis in 1960[2] tried to find a perspective on the internationalization process, based on an internal control of the firm, and attempted to explain the composition of foreign direct investment. It was the earliest articulation of a theory of international production separate from the theory of international trade and capital movements (Cantwell, 1995).

According to Hymer the search for new opportunities motivates internationalization since the goal of the firm is profit maximization through efficient resource allocation and utilization. The drivers of foreign expansion encompass scarce exchange opportunities and excessive competition in domestic markets, firm-specific advantages or industry maturity. Once an organization has developed its firm-specific advantages, it can try to exploit them in international markets even if at additional costs compared to the home territory. Hymer started his theory considering the existence of several limits, which an enterprise might face operating abroad.[3] He maintained that foreign firms have to face unfavourable market conditions in comparison to the national ones. The latter already know the market conditions, the language, the legal system and consumer habits. For these reasons, foreign enterprises must expend greater effort to reach their competitors' level, which means supporting higher costs added to the existing direct ones; for example, communication costs.

Last, but not least, governmental and consumer discrimination is the ultimate element of a series which put the multinational enterprise in a position of disadvantage compared to the local firms. Nevertheless, firms go abroad, often finding it economically convenient: the main idea is that in the early stage of growth, firms increase their presence in the domestic market so raising industrial concentration and market power. However, the firm reaches a stage where it is no longer easy to increase concentration in the local market and thus the profits shared among a few monopolistic companies are then invested abroad where the same stages will be followed.

Being located in diverse environments (i.e., being multinational/international) offers many advantages: the access to resources not available to

---

[2] Published in 1976.
[3] Of an enterprise of one nationality over those of another.

competitors; scale economies; exclusive ownership of intangible assets; the exploitation of different skills and knowledge compared to home-based competitors.

Beyond the presence of market power, to explain how this is possible the author considers the existence of market imperfections; all these advantages instead of being sold to local firms, are used internally and the reason lies in the possibility of generating innovations and ideas and retaining the exclusive right to their use under the control of the firm (Dunning, 1995). Thus internationalization is a process of the rational identification of exchange opportunities in both domestic and foreign markets.

This theory is based on several assumptions: market position established at home, the ownership of the firm, resources and capabilities in order to collect and evaluate information about foreign markets, and finally, it assumes that the firm must be of a sufficient size.

2.1.2 The international Product Life Cycle (Vernon)

Vernon (1966) proposed the Product Life Cycle model from an international perspective. This model is based on the logic of the international trade between different parts of the world, in particular focusing on, and trying to explain, the flows between the United States and Europe. Moreover, he tries to explain why firms sharing a common background develop a high level of innovation and how they exploit it in international markets by means of foreign direct investments. Generally, the location of new products is carried out in the developing countries, as for the United States in Vernon's case. In the 1960s, when he elaborated his theory, the American economy was characterized by high levels of income and high labour cost. The former meant an increase in consumer needs, which gave US industry the opening to introduce new products in order to satisfy the internal demand, while the latter forced American firms to choose innovative labour-saving technology for production.

According to Vernon, there are four stages that the product goes through: the first one is the introduction; the second is the growth stage, then maturity, and finally decline.

During introduction the production is home-based, which means that there is no need to go abroad for either sales or production. The reason behind this is the monopoly the firm gains in selling a completely new product with a high growth margin at a price fixed

by a non-competitive logic. The price elasticity of demand for the output is in fact low. The only effort made now is linked to the advertisement of the product.

In the second stage (growth), the product is better accepted by consumers, which keeps sales rising not only in the domestic market but also abroad. Export is the means by which the production can reach new markets.

In the maturity phase, exporting is no longer convenient; market conditions have changed. In fact, attracted by the high demand, new local competitors have entered the marketso that the exporters have to face a new threat. The best solution is to start the production closer to the market, investing directly in production facilities abroad, betting on the proximity and standardization, and selling at low prices, which is possible thanks to the existence of economies of scale.

In the decline of the product, it has lost its novelty and the firm has lost its status of monopolistic player; it tries to find a new economically convenient location to produce at low costs, to differentiate or abandon the production.

During the seventies Vernon already knew the model was going to be obsolete: international markets were seeing the emergence of new economies such as Japan and in the European area, moreover most of the new technologies were coming from different countries and not only from the United States.

The last limit was the change of approach used by the multinational companies which had served markets differently, according to their different characteristics and cultures.

2.1.3   Product Life Cycle: a modified version

As the original Product Life Cycle model was losing its explanatory capacity in 1974 Vernon suggested a modified version, which introduced oligopolistic considerations.

In the new model there are now three stages, after the initial innovatory phase the market is characterized by the presence of an oligopolistic competition as the product matures; locating the production abroad, in fact, is no longer a matter of profit maximization but the emphasis is shifted towards risk minimising strategies, in order to avoid price wars within a mature market where the low level of competition is due to high barriers to entry. On the assumption of

an industry characterized by economies of scale on production, marketing and logistics, security became a more important consideration rather than profitability, which led firms to localize their production in markets where competitors were active.

The last stage Vernon calls *senescent oligopoly*, in which enterprises try to differentiate their offers, barriers to entry are no longer important and are no longer due to economies of scale. In this scenario several firms will leave the market, unable to face the price competition politics adopted by the few enterprises still inside the market, which will localize the activity in areas where the cost of the production is low.

Two other very important approaches to the internationalization topic which have been exposed to the attention of practitioners and academics are the Transaction Costs approach and the Eclectic Paradigm (Dunning). The latter cannot really be called a general theory of international growth; it in fact synthesizes and combines elements of different theories, giving it the ability of being applied to diverse aspects of the internationalization phenomenon.

2.1.4 The Internalization and Transaction Cost approaches

In these approaches costs are taken as the main variable in relation to the international growth of a firm. In particular it analyses how transaction costs affect the decisions of the firm and how management reacts to minimize these costs.

The Transaction Cost approach in fact has its roots in the work of Coase (1937), who first defined 'transaction costs'. He argued that due to the transaction costs of foreign activities, it is more efficient for a firm to internalize export transactions, by substituting them with foreign direct investments (FDIs). Enterprises carry on various activities to achieve the result of profitable production of goods and services. However, these activities are possible not only through flows of other intermediate products, but also of knowledge and of expertise. According to Coase (1937), because of imperfections in intermediate products markets, there is an incentive to avoid these markets transactions and create an internal one within the company. Therefore, activities which were previously linked by the market mechanism are brought under the control of the firm hierarchy. In this sense the firm and the market are alternative methods of organizing exchanges.

The internalization theory suggests that a firm internalizes a transaction whenever the costs of using markets are higher than those of organizing internally. The higher efficiency of an internal market, compared to that of the market exchanges, derives from lower internal costs of coordination within the firm: where the transaction costs of a controlled exchange are lower than those of a market exchange, the market is internalized and efficiency is increased. 'Apart from the existences of economies of scope across activities, the direct coordination of transactions may reduce the costs, associated with information impactedness, opportunism and uncertainty' (Caves, 1982, p. 36). Market structure is indeed important when analysing transaction costs: in perfect markets the large number of sellers and buyers makes transaction costs close to zero and makes market outcomes efficient since competition is strong and agents are provided with the information necessary to reach optimal decisions. Nevertheless, transaction costs are generally found because markets are rarely perfectly competitive: consequently, internalization is likely to be an efficient choice.

From this theoretical perspective, according to Williamson (1975), the goal of the firm is to reach a suitable grade of efficiency by decreasing risk and uncertainty by means of defensive assets. Williamson's contribution to the theory is connected to analysis of the reasons supporting the internalization decision, which also depends on limited rationality, opportunistic behaviour and firms' resources specificity. These three factors enhance the efficiency of internalization when compared to market transactions and their costs.

Building on the mentioned framework of Transaction Costs theory, Buckley and Casson (1976) and Hennart (1982) in particular developed the understanding of FDIs across different countries. Buckley and Casson identified different factors determining the internalization decision, which does not depend only on market imperfections but also on the organizational capabilities of the multinational company, especially in terms of internal market organization and coordination. They also considered the role of knowledge – as one the most imperfect markets – in driving foreign investments decisions as opposed to market transactions.

2.1.5 The Eclectic Paradigm (Dunning)

During the 1980s John Dunning developed this general framework, which draws on a variety of theoretical approaches, with the aim of

creating common ground by stressing points of contact among them as well as areas of disagreement; however, it cannot be considered as a general theory, because it is itself a combination of quite different approaches to international production and also, as noted by the author: 'Precisely because of its generality, the eclectic paradigm only has limited power to explain or predict particular kinds of international production, and even less power to explain the behaviour of individual enterprises' (Dunning, 1988, p. 1). The goal of the author is therefore to combine different theoretical threads into a single model in order to explore international production and to examine foreign direct investments decisions.

According to Dunning national firms have various growth avenues: they can diversify horizontally into new products or vertically into new activities, proceed with mergers or acquisition or expand towards new markets. Choosing the last option they become international enterprises, which are defined as firms servicing foreign markets.

According to the Eclectic Paradigm, a firm, to develop transactions abroad conveniently, has to rely on one or more of the following three conditions: ownership-specific advantages (O advantages), location-specific advantages (L advantages) or internalization incentive advantages (I advantages).

Ownership-specific advantages.   The first condition is the possession of assets, meant as anything capable of generating a future income (Johnson, 1970), which competitors do not possess. Dunning defines these kinds of assets as ownership advantages, and according to his own description these are: 'advantages that stem from the exclusive privileged possession of or access to particular generating income assets' (Dunning, 1988, p. 2). MNCs utilize these advantages in establishing production on sites that are attractive due to their local advantages. Ownership advantages can be divided into two types: asset ownership advantages arise from the proprietary ownership of specific assets by MNEs; transactional ownership advantages mirror the capacity of MNE external markets to exploit the benefits in transactions, arising from the common governance of a network of these assets, located in different countries (Table 2.1).

Asset ownership advantages. These are available to every firm, but are specific in their origin at particular locations and have to be used in that

location. They can be either material or immaterial, such as firm-specific technology, natural resources, kinds of labour, proximity to markets, but also market structure, particular laws or policies that may give the company an advantage. Certainly, this typology of advantage is an asset which a firm can take advantage of, independently from the internationalization process.

Table 2.1 Ownership-specific advantages

(a) Property rights and/or intangible asset advantages (Oa): Product innovations, production management, organizational and marketing systems, innovatory capacity, non-codifiable knowledge: 'bank' of human capital experience; marketing, finance, know-how, etc.
(b) Advantages of common governance, i.e. of organizing Oa with complementary assets (Ot):
• advantages that branch plants of established enterprises may enjoy over *de novo* firms. Those due mainly to size, product diversity and learning experiences, e.g., economies of scope and specialization. Exclusive or favoured access to inputs, e.g., labour, natural resources, finance information. Ability to obtain inputs on favoured terms (e.g., due to size or monopsonistic influence). Ability of parent company to conclude productive and cooperative inter-firm relationships, e.g., like those between Japanese auto assemblers and their suppliers. Exclusive or favoured access to product markets. Access to resources of parent company at marginal cost. Synergistic economies (not only in production, but in purchasing, marketing, finance, etc.);
• advantages which specifically arise because of the multinationality. A phenomenon which enhances operational flexibility by offering wider opportunities for arbitrating, production shifting and global sourcing of inputs. It creates more favoured access to and/or better knowledge about international markets, e.g., for information, finance, labour, etc., ability to take advantage of geographic differences in factor endowments, government intervention, markets, etc. A multinational nature generates ability to diversify or reduce risks, e.g., in different currency areas, and creates a range of options and/or political and cultural scenarios. It provides the opportunity to learn from societal differences in organizational and managerial processes and systems. Balancing economies of integration with an ability to respond to differences in country-specific needs and advantages.

Source: J. H. Dunning, 'The eclectic paradigm of international production: A restatement and some possible extension', *Journal of International Business Studies*, 19(1), 1988.

Table 2.2   Location-specific variables

- Spatial distribution of natural and created resource endowments and markets.
- Input prices, quality and productivity, e.g., labour, energy, materials, components, semi-finished goods.
- International transport and communication costs.
- Investment incentives and disincentives (including performance requirements, etc.).
- Artificial barriers (e.g. import controls) to trade goods.
- Societal and infrastructure provisions (commercial, legal, educational, transport, and communication).
- Cross-country ideological, language, cultural business, political, etc. differences.
- Economies of centralization of R&D production and marketing.
- Economic system and policies of government: the institutional framework for resource allocation.

Source: J. H. Dunning, 'The eclectic paradigm of international production: A restatement and some possible extension', *Journal of International Business Studies*, 19(1), 1988.

Transactional ownership advantages. These arise from the governance of a network of assets spread throughout various locations. In this sense transactional ownership is a kind of advantage over competitors which develops, thanks to the international operations, differently from the first type mentioned above. Examples are the ability to create new technology or organizational skills, to take advantage of economies of scale or synergies in production, purchasing, marketing, research, finance and transportation.

Location specific advantages. These are assets specific to a certain location which a firm might find convenient to exploit. International growth, from this point of view, originates from the research of location advantages which are the availability of low cost production factors such as labour, energy or materials; they may also result from easier market access, because of import restrictions or high transport costs which hamper exports to the foreign market (Table 2.2).

Internalization incentive advantages.   The third condition deals with the benefit of undertaking and setting some relevant activities inside the organization. According to Dunning, Ownership and Internalization advantages are closely interrelated with each other. Internalization

Table 2.3   Internalization incentive advantages

- Avoidance of search and negotiating costs.
- To avoid costs of moral hazard, information asymmetries and adverse selection; and to protect reputation of internalizing firms.
- To avoid costs of broken contracts ensuing litigation.
- Buyer uncertainty (about nature and value of inputs [e.g., technology] being sold).
- When the market does not permit price discrimination.
- Need of seller to protect quality of intermediate or final products.
- To capture economies of interdependent activities.
- To compensate for absence of future markets.
- To avoid or exploit government intervention (e.g., quotas, tariffs, price controls, tax differences, etc.).
- To control supplies and condition of sale of inputs (including technology).
- To control market outlets (including those which might be used by competitors).
- To be able to engage in practices such as cross-subsidization predatory pricing, leads and lags, transfer pricing, etc, as a competitive (or anti-competitive) strategy.

Source: J. H. Dunning, 'The eclectic paradigm of international production: A restatement and some possible extension', *Journal of International Business Studies*, 19(1), 1988.

advantages arise when the potential returns from the O advantages are higher if they are transferred across borders within the firm's organization rather than if they are sold in the external market. Foreign production is so utilized whenever the transaction costs of using the market to exchange products across borders exceed the cost of coordinating the production and the exchange of these products within the firm (Table 2.3).

Firms undertaking foreign production internalize their O advantages in foreign markets but, by doing so, they may also generate new O advantages and increase the benefits of internalising.

2.2   Behavioural and evolutionary approaches to internationalization

The behavioural and evolutionary approaches refer to two different models: the organizational learning schools or stage theories and the network approach. Both models form their methodological basis on

a key concept related to market knowledge. According to both of them, firms assimilate experience gained from the foreign marketplace in order to translate it into knowledge.

The stage theory is based on progressive experiential knowledge, obtained through incremental international commitment that reduces the firms perception of market uncertainty. The network theory indicates that the development of cooperative relationships with customers, suppliers or other business partners may drive the internationalization process of the firm.

2.2.1 The Uppsala model

The Uppsala model is based on the behavioural theory of the firm, found in particular in the works of Aharoni (1966) and Johanson and Vahlne (1977) who describe internationalization of the firm as a process whereby firms gradually increase their international involvement. The foundations of the model can be dated back to 'The theory of the growth of the firm' edited by Penrose in 1959,[4] who considered knowledge as an asset to be gained mainly through experience.

Johanson and Vahlne, observing some Swedish companies, elaborated a dynamic model in 1977 suitable to explain the international involvement of the firms, seen as a process that can influence the pattern and the pace of internationalization. According to this behavioural theory, the main hypothesis is that companies are supposed to improve their business abroad through a gradual process, which takes place in incremental stages and over a relatively long period of time.

This process is based on an interaction between the development of new knowledge about foreign markets and a consequent commitment of resources to these markets as far as knowledge improves and uncertainty is reduced; the central issue of the model is the learning

---

[4] The theory by Penrose does not explicitly take the internationalization process into account. According to Penrose firms are collections of productive resources that are organized in an administrative framework. As they go along with their productive operations, firms obtain knowledge; the result of such a learning process is the expansion of firm's 'productive opportunity set' which managers can take advantage of, and secondly, the release of managerial excess resources that can be used in other related business areas. The general effect will be that more resources will be committed to the development of foreign markets activities.

process of the firms and how this learning affects their international behaviour. More precisely, on one side the model focuses on gradual acquisition through experience and use of knowledge about foreign markets, the lack of which is considered a great obstacle to the establishing of international operations. While on the other side, it analyses how the increased commitment of resources is invested into foreign markets. As indicated above, the authors have used a dynamic model to explain all the steps in the internationalization process, where the output of one decision becomes the input of the next and so on.

The Uppsala model builds on the issue of risk avoidance, where risk and uncertainty related to foreign markets are influenced by psychic distance and by experience. Psychic distance is defined as 'the distance between the home market and a foreign market resulting from the perception and understanding of cultural and business differences' (Evans, Treadgold and Mavondo, 2000, p. 377). Differences in languages, culture, and business practices can be considered as examples able to negatively influence the establishment of the firm internationally. The model shows that firms begin their operation abroad in psychically close markets and only later do they gradually penetrate more distant markets.

In summary, according to this model gradualism in the internationalization process refers to two dimensions: widening and deepening. They respectively represent a geographical/cultural dimension where the establishments move from culturally close to more distant markets (widening), and a 'commitment' dimension (deepening), where the form of market operation becomes steadily more demanding. Exporting is usually the first step along the internationalization path, which begins casually in most cases – and only after the firm is established in the domestic market – and grows with the firm's size and experience. Exporting is then followed by more committed forms of internationalization.

The commitment to engage in operations in a specific foreign market develops according to the so-called 'establishment chain', which is a sequence of stages that are made in small incremental steps, extending commitment with every new step. Johanson and Wiedersheim-Paul (1975) distinguished four different steps: Non-Regular export activities; Export via representatives (agents); Sales subsidiary; Production subsidiary.

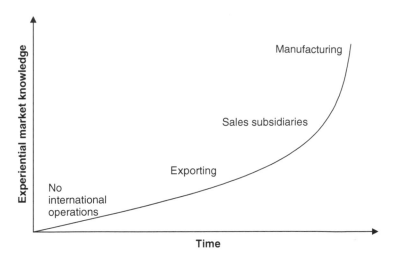

Figure 2.1   The establishment chain and stages of the Uppsala model

Source: P. Arenius, *Creation of Firm-Level Social Capital, its Exploitation, and the Process of Early Internationalization*, PhD Thesis, Helsinki University of Technology, Espoo, 2002.

The second pattern of the model shows that firms begin their operations abroad, in psychically close markets and only gradually penetrate more distant markets. Consequently, the less a firm knows a foreign market the greater the uncertainty perceived. Thus, firms will enter markets they can understand better and where they feel uncertainty is low, and, as explained before, the best way to minimize the risk and to find new opportunities is through experiential knowledge (Figure 2.1). This is the reason for incremental steps and sequential engagement in foreign markets.

In the Uppsala model two core concepts are expressed: State and Change aspects (Figure 2.2). The state aspects are resource commitment to the foreign markets and foreign market knowledge. Change aspects are the current business activity and commitment decisions. Both the state and the change aspects mutually affect themselves. Market commitment is comprised of the amount of resources and the degree of commitment. The amount of resources is described as the size of the investment, which may include marketing, organization or personnel. The degree of commitment, on the other hand becomes higher the more the resources are integrated with other parts of the

organization and when their value is derived from this integration (Johanson and Vahlne, 1977).

Market knowledge consists of general knowledge and market-specific knowledge. Both knowledge dimensions are needed when entering a market. The latter can mainly be acquired through experience in the specific market, while the former can be transferred from one market to another. More precisely, general knowledge concerns marketing methods and knowledge of certain characteristics of customers, while market knowledge is about the characteristics of each foreign market and encompasses its market structures, business habits, cultural patterns and, in particular, characteristics of the individual customer firms and their personnel.

There is also a distinction between how the firm gains this knowledge. The Uppsala model, moving from the Penrose distinction between objective knowledge, which can be taught, and experiential knowledge that can only be learned through personal experience, emphasizes the latter one, assuming that this kind of knowledge makes it possible to achieve good results and to perceive international opportunities.

The change aspects are current activities and commitment decisions, which both affect the state aspect. According to the authors, current business activities are important for several reasons. First, there is often a lag between the activities and the consequences,

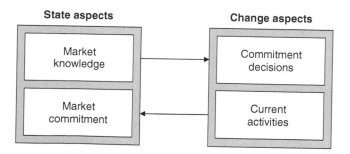

Figure 2.2   The basic mechanism of internationalization – state and change aspects

Source: J. Johanson and E. Vahlne, 'The internationalization process of the firm: A model of knowledge development and increasing foreign market commitment', *Journal of International Business Studies*, 8, 1977.

for example, marketing activities. The expected consequences may not be realized unless the activities are performed continuously over a long period of time. Furthermore, the longer the lag, the more resources are needed and consequently the higher the commitment is.

Another reason is that through these activities the firm gets its main source of experience. And as stated above, it is through experience that the firm can perceive opportunities that may lead to market commitments. However, the firm can gain experience by the hiring of personnel with experience or consultants from outside the firm. The fact is that the needed experience is very hard to get hold of, the firm has to acquire it through a learning process connected with its current business activities. This is one of the reasons why internationalization is a slow process.

Finally, if the activities are highly production-oriented, or if there is a low need for interaction between the activities and the market environment, the easier it will be to start new operations which are not incremental additions to the current activities. It will also be easier to substitute advice from outside and from hired personnel (Johanson and Vahlne, 1977).

The second change aspect is commitment decisions, which are decisions to commit resources to a market. It is assumed that decisions are made in response to problems and opportunities in the market on the one hand while, on the other hand, awareness of these problems and opportunities is assumed to be dependent on experience from activities carried out in the specific market. The decisions are also dependent on the existing market risk and the existing market uncertainty, that is, the decision-maker's inability to estimate the present and future market and market influencing factors, perceived by the firm.

The existing market risk is composed of existing market commitment and existing market uncertainty. The firm will make incremental commitments to the market until its maximum tolerable risk is reached; these commitments are made incrementally due to market uncertainty (Johanson and Vahlne, 1977). The more the firm/decision-maker knows about the market the lower the uncertainty and the market risk will be. This fact can mitigate the need of an incremental approach to commitment.

The Uppsala Internationalization model has gained support in many studies, but there has also been criticism: it has been argued

that the model is too deterministic and it might be valid only in the early stages of internationalization when lack of market knowledge and resources are limiting factors. Later, these issues are not always a problem. There has also been criticism over the psychic distance concept, arguing that companies today can enter directly into markets that are neither close nor similar to their home country. Nowadays, lack of market knowledge is not always a problem: the general internationalization of industries and markets gives every firm the chance easily to gain access to knowledge about international markets. Lastly, many authors stated that the Uppsala model does not take into consideration the interdependencies between different markets: companies do not necessarily view different countries as totally separate from one another.

All these considerations are consistent with recent discussion about the applicability of the model to accelerated International Entrepreneurship phenomena such as Born-Globals and International New Ventures. Those firms typically face market conditions that require immediate knowledge of how to sell products in different environments. Therefore the Stages theory is unable to explain the emergence of Born-Globals and International New Ventures because those firms skip the establishment chain described in the model and enter distinct markets at an earlier stage. The internationalization process of Born-Globals can be seen as a case of 'leap-frogging' in internationalization processes. Another weakness of the Uppsala model is that it does not include the figure of the entrepreneur: nowadays, many researchers agree on the importance of considering the individual level when analysing the international behaviour of firms.

All these issues found empirical confirmation: McDougall, Shane and Oviatt (1994) conducted research on 24 Born-Globals and none of these firms followed the traditional stages of internationalization. Moreover, Moen in 2001 carried out an analysis of a sample of Norwegian firms classified as Born Globals, showing that 74 per cent of these firms had their most important single market outside the Nordic countries, in places which are not geographically and culturally similar to Norway. The same conclusions have been reached by many other authors over the years, pointing out the scarce adaptability of the Uppsala model to the new typology of firms.

Later on, in response to criticism such as being deterministic (Reid, 1981; Turnbull, 1985) and only being applicable to the early stages of

internationalization, Johanson and Vahlne (1990) attempted to extend the explanatory power of the model by developing its theoretical basis to embrace new concepts and approaches. It is argued that experience could be gained alternatively through the hiring of personnel with experience, or through advice/consulting from people with experience. To clarify the role of these sources in the process of internationalization, they have distinguished between firm experience and market experience, both of which are essential.

First, they related the internationalization model to direct investment theory by building on the eclectic paradigm. Thus, the purpose of the model has been modified and defined as: 'explaining the pattern and mode of establishing marketing-oriented operations (including manufacturing for the local market)' (Johanson and Vahlne, 1990, p. 16). Therefore, with respect to the 'location', they took into account not only psychic distance but also assumed that the firm would enter where demand for its products exists. Regarding the second variable – 'mode of entry' – 'uncertainty avoidance' is assumed as the influential factor. Thus, not only lack of experiential knowledge of the foreign market, but also lack of established relationships with various parties, especially customers, in the foreign market (which makes it possible to calculate costs and risks) are considered as explanatory variables.

Second, some other deficiencies are discussed by relating the process model to the concept of the industrial network. In response to the developing role of the network of business relationships among firms, Johanson and Vahlne (1990) argue that business relationships and industrial networks are subtle phenomena that are not easily observed by outsiders. These relationships can only be understood through experience brought about from inside interaction; therefore, regarding the internationalization process model, it can be assumed that ' "market" (i.e., network) knowledge is based on experience from current business activities, or current business interaction' (1990, p. 19).

Foreign market entry or network entry are therefore considered to be the result of interaction initiatives taken by other firms that are insiders in the network in the specific country. The relationships of a firm are viewd as bridges to other networks that are important in the initial steps abroad and in the subsequent entry into new markets. Although countries and industries are thought to differ in

terms of their relative importance for the firm's relationships, 'it can be expected that the personal influence on relationships is strongest in the early establishment of relationships' (Johanson and Vahlne, 1990, p. 20).

Later on Johanson and Vahlne stated that, 'we have a situation where old models of internationalization processes are still applied quite fruitfully and at the same time a number of studies have suggested that there is a need for new and network-based models of internationalization. We think it might be worthwhile to reconcile and even integrate the two approaches' (2003, p. 84).

2.2.2 The Innovation model

The Innovation model, consistent with the Uppsala School, is an innovation-related learning model, based on a conception of the adoption process. According to this model, internationalization can be viewed as the learning process associated with the adoption of an innovation or a new idea (Table 2.4). The various stages of internationalization are distinguished along the ratio of export sales to total sales, representing the extent to which a firm is involved in export activities.

At a quantitative level, the Innovation model focuses on the export ratio as an indicator of the firm's international involvement. The main difference to the Johanson and Vahlne perspective is that the internationalization of the firm is determined by management

Table 2.4   Stages in the Innovation-related model

Stage	Foreign activities	Export to sales ratio
1 Domestic marketing		
2 Pre-export		
3 Experimental involvement	Growing involvement	Growing ratio
4 Active involvement		
5 Committed involvement		

Source: Adapted from S. Cavusgil, 'On the internationalisation process of firms', *European Research*, 8, 1980.

innovations, and each stage represents an innovation. While in the Uppsala model the firm's behaviour is driven by changes in internal and external conditions, and the focus is on acquiring and using experience and increasing foreign market knowledge, in the Innovation model internationalization is controlled by a development of strategy.

The two models are very similar: they both assume that the process of internationalization is gradual, risk-averse and affected by barriers such as language, cultural differences and scarce information.

2.2.3   The Network model

The Network model is based on the analysis of a firm's changing internationalization situation as a result of its positioning in a network of firms and their relationships. Johanson and Mattsson (1988), the main authors of this approach, instead of considering internationalization as an interaction only between the firm and the market, underlined the existence of networks among independent firms. The basic assumption of the model is that enterprises need an accessible knowledge of one another in order to do business.

According to their model, internationalization depends on network relationships rather than on a firm-specific advantage or the psychic distance of the target market. With these relationships in place, externalization of transactions is more likely to happen than internalization. Due to the resulting informal division of labour among the network's members, each firm will become dependent on these external resources to the extent that exchanges are commenced. Companies can then internationalize with the help of partners who provide contacts and help to develop new partnerships. Thus, internationalization decisions are influenced by the various members of the firm's network.

Having a network orientation and, consequently, identifying the roles and the strengths of the actors within it gives the firm an understanding of possible constraints and opportunities for its operations (Johanson and Vahlne, 1992).

According to Johanson and Mattson the degree of internationalization of the network affects the internationalization process of a particular firm in the network, which means that firms cannot be

analysed separately but must be understood in an interdependency context. In the model, a firm's position before the internationalization process begins, is divided into four categories:

1 The Early Starter;
2 the Late Starter;
3 the Lonely International;
4 the International among Others.

Firms are classified into these four groups according to the degree of internationalization of the market and the degree of internationalization of the firm (Figure 2.3).

The Early Starter firm possesses a low degree of internationalization. The network model describes how the firm's internationalization situation can influence its level of knowledge. As the Early Starter has scarce commitment to the market, a consequence is that it possesses only weak channels of contact with foreign networks, which negatively affect the level of information feedback from the foreign market.

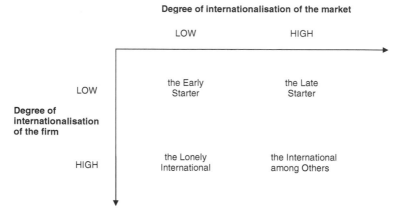

Figure 2.3 Internationalization and the Network model

Source: J. Johanson and L. G. Mattsson, 'Internationalization in industrial systems – a network approach'. In N. Hood and J.-E. Vahlne (eds), *Strategies in Global Competition*, New York: Croom Helm, 1988.

Johanson and Mattsson, differently from Johanson and Vahlne's view of knowledge as only being acquired through interaction with the market, maintain that a firm can increase knowledge with the help of links with other actors in the network. These kinds of relationships might also influence the firm's decision making. The Early Starter's lack of activities involving foreign actors also hinders the acquisition of knowledge because the lowly internationalized position of the network limits the possible spread of resources. Overall, in comparison to the other three firm types, the Early Starter has low levels of internationalization and foreign business knowledge.

Like the Early Starter, the Late Starter has a low degree of internationalization, but is positioned in a highly internationalized market. The Late Starter is characterized by a low level of commitment and activity in international markets, low levels of international experience and few direct international relationships (Johanson and Mattsson, 1988).

However, the Late Starter can exploit a knowledge relative advantage because of its better position: it can enhance its overall experiential knowledge levels through participation in its highly internationalized network. Therefore, a highly internationalized position should provide an inexperienced firm with greater experiential knowledge levels, if compared to an inexperienced firm in an internationally inexperienced network as the Early Starter.

Although the Lonely International firm is based on an internationally inexperienced network, its greater degree of commitment to the internationalization process provides the firm with a greater level of experiential knowledge compared to the Early Starter and the Late Starter.[5] This is attributed to the Lonely International's acquisition of knowledge directly from experience. On the other hand, the less internationalized position of the Lonely International diminishes its advantages concerning its foreign business knowledge because of a non-existent network that the firm might rely on.

---

[5] It is suggested that the Late Starter could benefit from the knowledge of its more experienced peers, but this is not considered enough to offset the experience of the Lonely International.

Johanson and Mattsson describe the International among Others as a firm characterized by a high degree of internationalization, having developed and established resources in foreign markets. However, it can exploit its highly internationalized network position, which provides it with higher levels of business knowledge, thanks to the greater interdependency of the internationalized network. Consequently, the highly internationalized macro-position of the 'International among Others' firm might transpire to provide it with greater experience in integrating and coordinating its network position, thus, improving its level of internationalization knowledge (Johanson and Mattsson, 1988).

2.2.4 The knowledge-based view

The knowledge-based approach builds on the resource-based view (see chapter 4) and considers knowledge as the most important resource of the firm: knowledge-based resources are difficult to imitate, due to their social complexity and heterogeneity (Grant, 1996). The basic assumption of these theoretical frameworks (Conner, 1991; Conner and Prahalad, 1996; Demsetz, 1988; Madhok, 1996; Nahapiet and Ghoshal 1998) is that the growth and competitiveness of firms depends on their capacity to create new knowledge and to replicate it, through markets expansion. Firms compete on the basis of the superiority of their knowledge base, and of their capacity to develop new knowledge by experiential learning.

Knowledge, according to the above mentioned seminal contribution of Penrose (1959), is mainly acquired through experience: consequently, it is subject to gradual formation and accumulation. The firm organization permits an efficient knowledge creation and transfer process. From this point of view, the knowledge-based theory resembles issues of the internalization theory and its developments to knowledge markets (Buckley and Casson, 1976).

Kogut and Zander applied the knowledge-based framework to international business studies and found that firms specialize in the transfer of knowledge that is difficult to understand and codify: firms are able to transfer technologies at lower cost to wholly owned subsidiaries than to third parties. According to this perspective, firms which posses this kind of knowledge, which is difficult to imitate, can leverage on it to penetrate new markets.

Consequently, tacit knowledge, embedded in the organization, is the main platform for competitive advantage in domestic and foreign markets. Entry in new markets is not only a matter of exploiting the current knowledge base, similarly to that of the 'ownership advantage' in the eclectic paradigm. The presence in diverse markets provides new inputs for the firm's knowledge base.

'By recombining knowledge, resting upon what we have called a "combinative capability", a firm exploits its current knowledge for expansion into new markets' (Kogut and Zander, 1993, p. 636). The evolutionary process of the firm's growth abroad often begins with exporting, and then moves to wholly owned entities. The initial entry mode serves as a platform that recombines the firm's knowledge base generated in the domestic market, with the gradual accumulation of learning in the foreign one. In a final stage of this process, the knowledge acquired from the foreign market is transferred internationally and influences the accumulation and recombination of knowledge, including in the domestic market.

In contrast to the classic internalization theory, in the knowledge-based approach 'the multinational corporation arises not out of the failure of markets for the buying and selling of knowledge, but out of its superior efficiency as an organizational vehicle by which to transfer this knowledge across borders' (Kogut, Zander, 1993, p. 516).

2.3   The contribution of international business theories and models to International Entrepreneurship

Researchers have recognized that the internationalization of firms is influenced by multiple factors. Bell and Young (1998), after analysing alternative conceptualizations in detail, argue that neither the Transaction Cost model, the Stage model nor the Network perspective can fully explain the internationalization process of firms. They also maintain that all these theories and models have complementarities that can be used to describe the internationalization process. They present a framework that borrows concepts from the Stage model, Contingency theory, Transaction Cost theory and the Network perspective to explain internationalization both for firms that internationalize from inception and for those that do it after the occurrence of a critical event.

All the International Business threads mentioned in this chapter have linkages with International Entrepreneurship. Indeed, over the years researchers and academics have relied on those International Business approaches to find several theoretical bases for the emergence of this subject. Nevertheless, the basic premises and justifications for the emergence of International Entrepreneurship lie in the criticism of traditional International Business models and concepts.

The distinction made in the International Business field between economics-based theories and behavioural ones is relevant when considering their congruency with an International Entrepreneurship approach. The first group does not seem to be coherent when it tries to explain the emergence of international entrepreneurial firms. The formation process of entrepreneurial firms differs significantly from those firms analysed in the economics-based approaches. According to this approach, firms first develop a strong position within their domestic markets and only later try to exploit this advantage in foreign countries. This is totally contrary, for example, to the development process of Born-Global firms. The Product Life Cycle does not explain why international entrepreneurial firms often engage in international exports, or foreign direct investments avoiding the first phase of product introduction.

On the other hand a closer look at some of these theories reveals important issues, which are at the core of International Entrepreneurship:

- The role of resources and capabilities in collecting information about foreign markets and scouting opportunities is present the seminal work of Hymer, as well as the competitive advantage of multi-location.
- The process view of internationalization is dominant in Vernon's life-cycle.
- Organizational capabilities and assets uniqueness, together with wider opportunities of knowledge arising from multinationality, are treated in Dunning's ownership specific advantages.

The behavioural and evolutionary models provide a fundamental framework for IE studies, since they aim at a deeper understanding of the process of internationalization and decision making. Moreover, a

process view is grounded on learning mechanisms. The latter have been criticized for not being able to explain the Born-Global phenomenon. In particular, the Uppsala model assumption that the commitments of the firms abroad progress in small following increased experiential knowledge has been denied by several studies on international new ventures, especially when applied to knowledge-intensive sectors, which from inception abroad appeared to disregard their domestic markets in favour of the international marketplace.

According to Johanson and Vahlne (1977), experiential knowledge is a critical determinant factor of active involvement in international markets because it provides the framework for perceiving and exploiting opportunities. The born-global and gradual commitment visions can be reconciled through the construct of experiential learning, which can be formed gradually inside an organization during its life or acquired by hiring experienced personnel or consultants. In addition, social and business networks play an important role in determining features and outcomes of the internationalization process and influence the rapidity and intensity of experiential learning. Some firms are born-global because of the entrepreneur/top management team's former experience and/or thanks to their international networks. International experience, learning and knowledge are particularly important since researches in International Entrepreneurship underline the importance of entrepreneur/TMT characteristics such as foreign work experience, foreign education, background and vision as drivers of international entrepreneurial orientation.

Recently, many authors have underlined the importance of the Network perspective, but also the Transaction Cost approach concerning corporate entrepreneurship. The Network approach is particularly useful when considering entrepreneurial firms, which can rely on the diffused knowledge or the accessibility to resources within the network in order to be able to develop an international strategy. Thus the personal and organizational network is a mechanism for reducing cultural distances in international operations, and for supporting the transmission of information and knowledge.

Finally, the Innovation model, focused on the idea that is a learning process associated with the adoption of an innovation, is strictly linked to a stream of research in International Entrepreneurship that, following the Schumpeterian view of entrepreneurship (1934),

assumes the introduction of a product in a new market as an entrepreneurial act. The contribution of different schools of thought is therefore relevant: if directed to a comprehensive approach, it provides interesting insights on the investigation of internationalization of activities in International Entrepreneurship research.

3
Entrepreneurship Studies[1]

The recent growth in international business activities by entrepreneurial firms has been phenomenal, confirming the idea that international activity is a key element of entrepreneurship. Research studies suggest that, as a part of the entrepreneurial process, most entrepreneurs perceive international opportunities from the first day they start their business (Oviatt and McDougall, 1994; Zacharakis, 1997). Even for established firms, the decision to approach foreign markets is one of the possible expressions of entrepreneurship: foreign markets involve a liability of foreignness with a more or less pronounced risk element to cope with and at the same time disclose a wider range of opportunities to the firm. These opportunities are provided by discovery or enactment processes in foreign markets or may be the result of knowledge transfer from different locations and its recombination inside the organization, given the existence of combinative capabilities in the organization (Kogut and Zander, 1993). These issues in International Entrepreneurship (IE) have their foundations in Entrepreneurship theories, which focus on the role of entrepreneurs as actors and on the meaning and outcomes of entrepreneurial action.

Entrepreneurship has become a key issue in modern society, both for academicians and policy makers. The interest of many politicians and public organizations in the issue is connected with the possibilities of job creation, stimulating innovation and economic growth (Audretsch, 2002; *Economist*, 14 March 1998). The last decades have

[1] Sections 3.1, 3.2 and 3.3 have been written by Alfredo D'Angelo.

seen an increasing number of contributions on entrepreneurship. Notwithstanding the relevant literature body on the subject, 'entrepreneurship theory is rather recent and scattered' (Holmquist, 2003, p. 74). The different contributions in this field have their roots in many disciplines, ranging from economics to psychology (Casson, 1982), but generally accepted definitions and theoretical frameworks are still missing. In particular, 'the field of entrepreneurship theory and research is extremely wide but not as deep' (Landstrom, 1999) and more research is needed especially in the organizational side of the matter, even if some authors pointed out the relationship between entrepreneurship and organizational issues as management and strategy (Stevenson and Jarrillo, 1990).

Entrepreneurship and internationalization appear strictly interrelated since they reflect complementary theoretical interests and empirical developments in both fields. Entrepreneurship and internationalization are generally accepted as economic or behavioural processes associated with the creation of value by assembling a unique package of resources to exploit an opportunity (Jones and Coviello, 2005; Johanson and Vahlne 2003; Morris et al., 2001). This process is also implicit in the Oviatt and McDougall definitions (2000 and 2003) of International Entrepreneurship, which, following Covin and Slevin (1991), describe internationalization as a mixture of proactive behaviour, innovation, risk-seeking and value creation. Behaviour can be determined from the decisions and actions in response to certain conditions at a specific point in time.

Covin and Slevin (1991) argue that behaviour is the central and essential element in the entrepreneurial process and that an organization's actions (or behaviour) are what make it entrepreneurial. Moreover they state that 'behaviour is, by definition, overt and demonstrable. Knowing the behavioural manifestations of entrepreneurship, we can reliably, verifiably and objectively measure the entrepreneurial level of the firm' (Covin and Slevin, 1991, p. 8). This implies that a difference exists between an entrepreneurial firm and a non-entrepreneurial one. Managing a firm can mean merely imitating the ideas of competitors in a competitive market that permits a high level of returns. The dimensions of entrepreneurship (innovative, proactive and risk-taking behaviour) can make the difference.

3.1 Entrepreneurship in classical and neoclassical economic literature

An analysis of the most established literature on entrepreneurship can be dated back to the concepts of risk and uncertainty introduced by Knight in 1921, or to Schumpeter's creative destruction in 1934.

Cantillon (1755) was, in the eighteenth century, the first author who paid attention to the figure of the entrepreneur, recognizing the existence of entrepreneurial activity in the economic system. Cantillon – after his observation of French traders – considered an entrepreneur to be an individual who undertakes a business activity in an uncertain situation, which means uncertainty in returns from economic activity. From his point of view, entrepreneurship depends essentially on the willingness and the capacity to take the risk of bankruptcy as a prime mover of market exchange (Binks and Vale, 1990). The entrepreneur was considered as an agent playing an important role in the regulation of supply and demand, acting between capitalists on the one side and workers on the other. The entrepreneur is responsible for all economic transactions by engaging in pure arbitrage, buying at a certain price and selling at an uncertain price (Cantillon, 1755). The most important feature of entrepreneurial activity outlined by Cantillon is its risk-taking nature: according to the author, because the entrepreneur's task is only arbitrage, adjusting existing quantities of supply and demand, he does not need to be innovative.

Another important contribution in the entrepreneurship field comes from the work of Jean-Baptiste Say with the publication of 'A Treatise on Political Economy or the Production, Distribution and Consumption of Wealth' in 1803. Say, extending Cantillon's definition of entrepreneurial function, highlighted the managerial role of the entrepreneur. He challenged the dominant vision at this time that land was the unique source of wealth, addressing the role of commerce and manufacturing as engines of growth, where the essential motivation was an entrepreneur's profit. The three classical factors of production of the micro-economic theory, namely capital, labour and land, needed to be integrated with a fourth one, the entrepreneur, who can organize the other means of production, and accordingly co-ordinate both production and distribution. Moreover, within each industry there are three distinct operations, which

cannot be performed by people: theoretical knowledge, the application of knowledge and execution. According to Say, 'the application of knowledge to the creation of product for human consumption' is the entrepreneur's task. We could conclude that Say was, from this point of view, a forerunner of a knowledge-based approach to entrepreneurship and of firms' management.

In modern economic theory, the advent of a neoclassical economic framework after the Second World War, did not leave much room for understanding the role of entrepreneurship. Samuelson (1947) and Hicks (1939) building on the works of Walras (1874) and Pareto (1909) elaborated a neoclassical general equilibrium model, which was based on three main assumptions: maximizing behaviour, stable preferences and market equilibrium (Becker, 1976; Hodgson, 1993). Individual behaviour is determined by self-interested exogenous preferences and complete and costless contracting (Bowles and Gintis, 2000). The role of the entrepreneur is described through the employment of labour and other factors of production such as capital.

In the neoclassical production function, it is difficult to accommodate innovation and technological change (Solow, 1956). According to Daneke, 'technology and the institutional processes associated with innovation and entrepreneurship have been virtual "black holes" in orthodox (neo-classical) economic theory' (1998, p. 103). Therefore this model disregards vision and strategy that over time allows renewal and growth via competitive advantage and dynamic capabilities (Alverez and Barney, 2000; Teece, 1990; Venkataraman, 1997).

Neoclassical economists have frequently been questioned about whether the model of general equilibrium based on perfect information coincides with reality. Transaction Cost theories (Coase, 1937; Williamson, 1975, 1985) supported this stream. Coase (1937), the founder of the Transaction Cost approach, considering the firm as an island of hierarchical non-market relations surrounded by market relations made the difference between market or inter-firm transactions and internal or intra-firm transactions. The neoclassical theory stresses that price mechanisms allocating resources work within the market only. Instead, the main problem raised by Coase was concerned with the organization of resources within the firm. Coase did not differentiate the entrepreneur from the manager, he referred to the entrepreneur as the person or people who replaces the price

mechanism in allocating the resources in a competitive market system (Coase, 1937, p. 390). The entrepreneur's main function is to replace market transactions with non-market hierarchical relations in order to reduce transaction costs.

The hypothesis of incomplete information led Coase (1937) to modify the standard neoclassical assumption of rationality. He considered market contracts as the outcome of optimization by individuals under a certain set of constraints, including those that give rise to transaction costs. In his work, however, he did not indicate the nature of these transaction costs. The task was consequently taken up by Williamson (1975, 1985), who attributed transaction costs to opportunism and to bounded rationality, which represent the natural behaviour of self-interested individuals coping with incomplete information. Under the state of incomplete information, the entrepreneur acts as an opportunist player who manages to internalize market transactions. Williamson stressed that 'in the beginning there were markets and, only as the market-mediated contracts collapse, the transactions in question were removed from the market and organized internally' (Williamson, 1985, p. 87).

According to Coase, 'the entrepreneur has to carry out his function at less cost, taking into account the fact that he may get factors of production at a lower price than the market transaction which he supersedes, because it is always possible to revert to the open market if he fails to do this' (1937, p. 392).

3.2 The entrepreneur according to the Austrian school

The so called Austrian school is represented by a group of economists, who, during the course of the twentieth century, proposed a view of the economic system alternative to those of the classical and neoclassical. Their role is especially relevant in the field of entrepreneurship, because they considered explicitly entrepreneurship as a driving force of economic development and their works influenced Kirzner's contribution to the subject. In the Austrian school stream, Hayek (1945) and Mises (1949) developed the idea of the market as an entrepreneurially driven process and showed that economic agents are characterized by ignorance – and by perfect information – stressing the importance of knowledge in market interactions.

Mises (1949) in his work emphasized the dynamic and entrepreneurial character of the market process. He saw the market process as generated by the actions of entrepreneurs who operate in uncertain conditions, always looking for profits. The driving force of the market process is provided neither by the consumers nor by the owners of the means of production, but by promoting and speculating entrepreneurs. These are people intent upon profit that take advantage of differences in prices. Profit-seeking speculation is the driving force of the market as it is the driving force of production.

Hayek (1945), analysed the role of other important factors: knowledge and how agents in the market process obtain information. Indeed, Hayek's most important contribution is the concept of discovery procedure. Market competition is seen as a way to discover opportunities which are useful for achieving specific purposes. Hayek's conception of discovery was not related to new technological advances, but rather to minor discoveries of what goods and services consumers wish to buy, including the prices they were willing to pay (Hayek, 1948).

In contrast with the mainstream neoclassical economics theory, Hayek (1945) underlined the role of dispersed knowledge as central in understanding coordination problems that confront social systems. According to Hayek:

> the economic problem of society is thus not merely a problem of how to allocate 'given' resources – if given is taken to mean given to a single mind which deliberately solves the problem set by these 'data'. It is rather a problem of how to secure the best use of resources known to any of the members of society, for ends whose relative importance only these individuals know.
>
> (1945, p. 77)

In the Austrian economics school view, understanding coordination problems seem firmly based on the methodological stance of subjectivism; therefore, what underlines economic progress is the subjective interpretation of the real world that is grounded on perceptions and expectations by economic agents. According to Kirzner (1992), an individual's behaviour is to be understood only by reference to his/her knowledge, beliefs, perception and expectations. This clearly contrasts with positivism and the mathematical model-ling of neo-classical economics (Mises, 1949).

Kirzner (1973, 1997) made his major contribution to the theory of entrepreneurship defining entrepreneurs as 'individuals who grasp opportunities for pure entrepreneurial profit created by temporary absence of full market adjustment' (Kirzner, 1997, p. 690). The role of the entrepreneur is seen as an arbitrageur who drives the process of market exchange by buying low and selling high and maintains constant alertness to equilibrate the market. The neoclassical general equilibrium model where the variables are treated as if they exist simultaneously (Tieben and Keizer, 1997) is undermined here by the dynamic view of the market.

Kirzner in his publication of 1973, 'Competition and Entrepreneurship', tried to overcome the limits of Mises's and Hayek's theories. He has indeed contributed to the Austrian school as well as to entrepreneurship theory giving entrepreneurs a fundamental role in the market process. He stated that entrepreneurs are those who are alert to discover and to exploit profit opportunities. Discovery is not accidental, but it is generated by the possibility of making profit, since entrepreneurs are, according to Kirzner, more alert than others because of their nature, or simply because the profit incentive has more importance to them than to others. The key concept of this theory is therefore alertness, considered as a human capacity to profit from opportunities, which has to be perceived as an entrepreneurial element in the economic decision process.

According to Kirzner, entrepreneurs, both producers and arbitragers, do not require any particular ability or personality to carry out their activities, the only thing they require is a special type of knowledge. Entrepreneurs need to perceive opportunities earlier than others, but do not necessarily have to own resources themselves. As long as entrepreneurs are able to pay the interest, funds are supplied by capitalists. Kirzner takes the concept of uncertainty from Knight: the longer the time before the venture's required outlay can be expected to bring the hoped-for revenues, the less sure of himself the entrepreneur is likely to be. Entrepreneurial activity undoubtedly involves uncertainty and the bearing of risk.

To Kirzner profit opportunity and discovery are the most important elements of the market process, where the entrepreneur plays a predominant role as a discoverer of profit opportunities and so is responsible for movements in prices and quantity production in the short term, but also for progress and growth in the long term. To

understand how some individuals promote their entrepreneurial talents was the main concern of Kirzner's work (1973, 1992, 1997). Mises (1949) stated that the key to the entrepreneurial ability to grasp new opportunities lies in 'human action', that is, in 'all behaviour that cannot be expressed in a model of robots which operate according to maximizing algorithms' (Gunning, 1997, p. 172).

Based on Mises's human action definition, Kirzner tried to examine how entrepreneurs overcome the radical ambiguity in the market in terms of 'sheer ignorance'. As the market is usually at the state of disequilibrium, Kirzner (1973) suggests that the main task for the entrepreneur is to uncover unnoticed profit opportunities. Alertness, which is an unconscious or unplanned learning process undertaken spontaneously by entrepreneurs through their interactions with other individuals in the market-place, was considered the right human act to discover profit opportunities.

The limitations of neoclassical economics with regards to knowledge, market coordination and problems of adjusting are highlighted by Kirzner's definition of the entrepreneur. He stressed the role of arbitrageur as an agent who leads the market towards equilibrium. On the other hand, he did not explicitly consider innovation in his theory. It was Schumpeter who linked the issue of innovation with that of entrepreneurship, defining the concept of innovation in broad terms and describing the entrepreneur as an equilibrium breaker rather than an arbitrageur.

Samuelson reported that: 'At the time of his death, a citation index shows that Joseph Schumpeter was the scholar most often cited in the whole field of economics' (1981, p. 1) and his work on entrepreneurship had been extensively reviewed by many authors. Schumpeter (1934) discussed the role of entrepreneurs in his 1911 book 'The Theory of Economic Development' and in 1934 he defined entrepreneurship as 'new combinations including the doing of new things or the doing of things that are already being done in a new way'.

The introduction of a new good or a new quality of a good, the introduction of a new method of production, the opening of a new market into which the particular branch of manufacture of the country in question has not previously entered, the conquest of a new source of supply of raw materials or half-manufactured goods, the carrying out of new organization in any industry, like the

creation of a monopoly position or the breaking up of a monopoly position, are considered five possible examples of the combination of elements in what Schumpeter intended as innovation, which comprise the expression of entrepreneurship.

Schumpeter opposed Cantillon's view of the entrepreneur as a risk-bearer, who is viewed as leader of the firm and as an innovator in the economic system. Introducing 'new combinations' or innovations, the entrepreneur generates a temporary disequilibrium in the economic system, but the consequence is the creation of a new stable equilibrium, which implies a development of the same system. This concept called 'creative destruction' is to Schumpeter a fundamental element for an efficient system, where the entrepreneur plays a primary role. Moreover, Schumpeter is consistent with previous views concerning the qualities an entrepreneur must have: leadership is required in order to lead existing means of production into new channels, but also a strong personality is important as an entrepreneur will always face opposition from competitors or from society in general.

The Walrasian notion of general equilibrium was more or less accepted by Schumpeter as being the result of a static market system. In this system, where the circular flow reproduces itself endlessly, the figure of the entrepreneur is missing. Focusing his research on the internal forces within the general equilibrium system rather than on the allocation of existing resources in a state of equilibrium, Schumpeter was able to investigate what disrupts the business cycle and leads to innovation and economic development. Finally, he presented a dynamic vision of the processes involved into the market, stating that 'a system – any system, economic or other – that at every given point of time utilizes its possibilities to the best advantage may yet in the long run be inferior to a system that does so at no given point of time, because the latter's failure to do so may be a condition for the level or speed of long run performance' (Schumpeter, 1942, p. 83).

To carry out new combinations, as opposed to reorganizing existing resources and commodities, is considered to be the prime role of the entrepreneur. The entrepreneur generating new combinations leads the discontinuity in the production process in terms of perception and realization (Binks and Vale, 1990). The 'creative

destruction' moment is a result of the entrepreneurs' vision and leadership qualities. The intuition and the capacity of forecasting events or, using Schumpeter's terms, the ability to see things in a way which afterwards proves to be true, even though it cannot be established at the moment (1942, p. 85) is a quality that determines the entrepreneur's success. The entrepreneur can take advantage of being the first to introduce new combinations in production in term of profits, but only temporarily, because competition and new entry erode this profit and a new equilibrium position is reached. Schumpeter states that entrepreneurs:

> have not accumulated any kind of goods, they have created no original means of production, but have employed existing means of production differently, more appropriately, more advantageously. They have been able to carry out new combinations because they are entrepreneurs and their profit, the surplus, to which no liability corresponds, is an entrepreneurial profit.
>
> (Schumpeter 1934, p. 132)

The distinction between the entrepreneur and the capitalist is also present in Schumpeter's work. 'The role of the entrepreneur is to identify arbitrage opportunities, while modern capital markets generally enable him to find a capitalist to bear the risk for him' (Evans and Jovanovic, 1989, p. 809).

The role of the capitalist is reduced here to a mere supplier of capital, even if, under uncertain circumstances, suppliers of capital take a reserve of equity in the business in order to avoid losing their money. In Schumpeter's view innovation is hard to copy and the main challenge for entrepreneurs is to research inimitable assets that might yield a sustainable competitive advantage (Alvarez and Barney, 2000). This field has been treated by the contemporary resource-based, or knowledge-based, approach that considers firms as a network of immobile and inimitable resources, which are combined in order to secure entrepreneurial rents (Alvarez and Barney, 2000; Barney, 1991; Penrose, 1959; Venkataraman, 1997; Wernerfelt, 1984). Managerial and coordinative skills are needed within an innovative organization in order to exploit resources and transform them into high-quality products.

3.3   Uncertainty and creativity

Entrepreneurship involves risk taking in order to bank market opportunities that are untapped or overlooked by competitors. This idea is already present in the first works on entrepreneurship, but the two related issues of risk and creativity need further development. The joint effect of alertness, creativity and risk taking leads to innovation, which involves successful market introduction of new products, services, businesses and organizations.

The risk-taking attitude, in particular, is developed in Knight's contribution. He distinguishes between risk and uncertainty, focusing on the latter as the context of entrepreneurial decisions. On the other hand, the issue of creativity is far more recent in scientific research. With his doctoral dissertation in 1921, 'Risk, Uncertainty, and Profit', Knight declared that the entrepreneur's economic function is that of shouldering uncertainty. Moving from Cantillon's concept of risk, Knight modifies it to the concept of uncertainty, which is a characteristic feature of the society that the entrepreneur has to deal with. Knight differentiates uncertainty from risk. In the case of risk the distribution of outcome in a group of instances is known. This is not true in the case of uncertainty due to the unique nature of the situation. This means that for uncertainty, there is no basis at all for classifying any possible future situation. Nevertheless, a sort of judgement is exercised for the formation of an estimate: this kind of uncertainty is sustained by entrepreneurs. In the light of this, entrepreneurs are considered responsible for economic growth, like improvements in technology and business organization. To Knight, 'it is this true uncertainty ... which gives the characteristic form of "enterprise" to economic organization as a whole and accounts for the peculiar income of the entrepreneur' (Knight, 1921, p. 232).

This distinction between uncertainty and risk is absent in the neoclassical world and in most cases it is either dismissed or simply not accepted, and Knight's concept of uncertainty is often ruled out (Friedman, 1976). In the neoclassical view economic agents are rational, and probabilistic theory, in the form of expectations, is used to evaluate the future. In other words, rational economic agents always demonstrate consistent probability ordering (Choi, 1993).

According to Knight, the capacity to effectively deal with uncertainty requires some characteristics in the entrepreneur, such as a high degree of self-confidence, the capacity to judge your own personal qualities compared to those of other individuals such as competitors, suppliers, buyers and employees. Furthermore, vision expressed as foresighted behaviour, as well as the power of effective control over other people and the intellectual capacity to decide what should be done, is considered essential. Finally, the entrepreneur in Knight's conception is not only remunerated with the profits he/she is able to gain, but also from the prestige of the status and from the satisfaction of being able to succeed. According to Casson (1982; 1990), the responsibility of complex decision making gives the entrepreneur profit returns, ensuring the owners of factors of production a certain level of reward.

Knight's view of profit is a reflection of the distinction between risk and uncertainty. The author states that only uncertainty generates profit and that the neoclassical assumption of zero profit under perfect competition is consistent only with insurable risk. As he puts it: 'Now, since risk does not preclude perfect planning, such risk cannot prevent the complete realization of the tendencies of competitive forces, or give rise to profit' (Knight, 1921, p. 21).

Unlike Schumpeter, Knight did not differentiate between the entrepreneur and the capitalist. It is possible to draw a parallel between Knight's view on uncertainty and the relevance of creativity in entrepreneurial behaviour. In fact, when environmental and market conditions cannot be reasonably foreseen under probabilistic estimates, there is more room for creative interpretation (creativity and proactivity) of business opportunities.

3.4 Entrepreneurship and entrepreneurs

The ability of economics models to understand entrepreneurial behaviour has been questioned by research such as that carried out by Gartner (1990), Teece (1990), Venkataraman (1997) and Alvarez and Barney (2000).

Entrepreneurship as a field of study began to emerge relatively recently. In the last century important concepts and models have been developed and so has empirical research: although recently this field has gained increasing legitimization, a congruent body of study

or a framework that clarifies the nature and the field of entrepreneurship is still lacking. Entrepreneurship has, in fact, meant different things for different authors, because practitioners and researchers have developed their own definitions. This phenomenon has been studied from different perspectives: some authors focus on entrepreneurship in terms of the creation of new firms while others focus on organizational growth, transformation and innovation, others again try to explain and to study the traits and characteristics of entrepreneurs, often linking this economic field with psychology, or they concentrate on the attitude and behaviour of entrepreneurial firms. In defining the characteristics of entrepreneurs and entrepreneurial firms some authors underline attributes such as alertness, while others devote more attention to uncertainty taking or innovativeness.

One of the most significant attempts in defining the domain of entrepreneurship research has been made by Shane and Venkataraman (2000) and Gartner (1989) who focus on entrepreneurship as a creative process. Shane and Venkataraman define the study of entrepreneurship as the, 'examination of how, by whom, and with what effects opportunities to create future goods and services are discovered, evaluated, and exploited' (2000, p. 218). Gartner suggests that focusing on the traits and the personality characteristics of the entrepreneur does not permit the differentiation of entrepreneurs from non-entrepreneurs, because their characteristics do not explain why a person starts a business and another does not.

This means that entrepreneurship is about the creation of new ventures and organizations; the creation of new combinations of goods and services, methods of production, markets and supply chains; the recognition and exploitation of new and existing opportunities, cognitive processes, behaviours and modes of action to exploit new and existing opportunities. Entrepreneurship research examines these creation efforts, the individuals and teams involved, the emergence of new ventures and organizations, and distinctive strategies utilized in the creation process as well as the macroeconomic job and wealth-creation impact of entrepreneurial endeavour. The research field can vary in the context examined; such as new firms and organizations, existing corporations, family businesses, and new international entrepreneurial activities.

In the light of this approach, an effort can be made at better understanding, on an individual-level, of the figure of the entrepreneur,

acknowledged as a key factor within many approaches. Furthermore, it is also important to consider a firm-level approach, distinguishing small-firms and family business entrepreneurship from corporate entrepreneurship. The entrepreneur remains a source of innovation and creativity: this individual differs from a manager who is involved in activities such as ordering, scheduling and administrating, because he/she is able to scout opportunities, address or anticipate market needs, take risks, pool resources for the creation of new products or to shape new ways of providing services.

In general, the entrepreneur can be described as someone able to take the risk of developing and implementing a small new entity, but also as someone able to bring changes and innovation to large already established corporations. From this point of view, companies where intrapreneurship is encouraged provide a fertile ground for the coincidence between management and entrepreneurship, at least on a project basis. Sahlman and Stevenson differentiate entrepreneurs from managers in that 'entrepreneurship is a way of managing that implies pursuing opportunity without regard to the currently con-trolled resources. Entrepreneurs identify opportunities, assemble required resources, implement a practical action plan and harvest the reward in a timely, flexible way' (1991, p. 1).

Hebert and Link (1989) distinguish the supply of financial capital, innovation and allocation of resources among alternative uses and decision making. Thus, an entrepreneur is someone encompassing the entire spectrum of those functions. Innovation or change charac-terize the activity of the entrepreneur and they can be expressed in terms of output of innovative commitment and capacity according to five main categories: introduction of new products or services, introduction of new methods and techniques, the opening of a new market, the conquest of new sources of supply of raw-materials or half-manufactured products, and the creation of new organizations (Burch, 1989; Schumpeter, 1934).

The above-mentioned activities of the entrepreneur are not able in themselves to generate high performance. The performance of entre-preneurial firms comes from the interrelation of several different factors, which also bring the possibility of implementing such activities. The combination of personal characteristics and general management skills, but also a high motivation in success and knowledge of the industry are the most important factors influencing

entrepreneurial performance An entrepreneur's profile makes an unlikely fit into any categorizations or schemes precisely because the entrepreneurial career trajectory does not imply a specific path or previous experiences that everyone has to go through. Nevertheless, from empirical studies some common aspects emerge in the entrepreneur's personality and experiences.

The innovation may be a new product or it may be an idea for a new service and it might be high-tech or could simply rely on traditional technology. This is the case of the inventor, who often bases his invention on a particular expertise gained from previous work experiences. It must be said that this case generally has a poor probability of success: these kinds of entrepreneurs, even if their ideas are good and can potentially bring benefits to customers, may lack managerial qualities and skills which are fundamental to manufacturing and promoting goods. This is why they need to be supported by experienced managers, business angels and venture capitalists. A good chance of success can be brought about by managers. This typology of the entrepreneur can be grouped into two categories: managers in organizations who resign to start their own entrepreneurial career and corporate entrepreneurs.

It frequently happens that even managers with stable incomes, status or a stimulating function in established organizations often leave their jobs in order to start a personal business activity. Working as an employee, in fact, may not offer the chance to reach personal achievements, especially when the entrepreneur feels there is the possibility to succeed in developing new ideas, products or services on their own. Identifying the market potential of new opportunity and developing a business idea drawing on past managerial experience is one of the most common choices for entrepreneurs with a good probability of success.

The second typology is corporate entrepreneurs that work within large companies, which need to renew their strategies and knowledge by means of these individuals able to bring new capabilities and sources of innovation and creativity to the firm from within.

Another typology is the case of young professionals who generally have a high education, often with formal management qualifications, who decide to establish their own business directly instead of working first for an established organization. Even if these kinds of

entrepreneur only have theoretical knowledge and lack of real business experience, as stated by many empirical studies, they are important in particular for high-tech businesses and industries such as computing and information technology. Moreover, young professionals are more attuned to new changes and are more adaptable in exploiting certain possibilities.

Some personal traits help the entrepreneur's business directly such as their education or personal financial position, while others such as creativity and alertness, even if they only indirectly influence the business, are certainly of fundamental importance for the success of the entrepreneur. Here is a list of the most acknowledged successful personal characteristics: perceptive, creative, innovative, hard working, confident, risk taking, receptive to change, well-informed.

Entrepreneurs put a lot physical and mental effort into developing a new firm. They set themselves clear and often demanding goals, always demonstrating that they believe in their personal success and in that of the company. Being always attuned to new opportunities is also a very common and important factor, but alone it is not enough because entrepreneurs, when implementing a new idea, use their creativeness and innovativeness in order to provide the market with products or services that customers will find more valuable and appealing than the existing ones. In order to exploit new opportunities and find out new solutions, entrepreneurs are always well-informed not only about specific matters in their industry: but they are also very interested in scientific discoveries, new trends or cultural, social and political changes.

An adequate educational background, not only in managerial issues, is also fundamental: a good level of general education gives the ability to better understand people, events, economic and historical phenomena, especially in a complex and rapidly changing environment. Indeed, a good general education should help in perceiving and evaluating events or a situation with a critical eye. Moreover, entrepreneurs – and notably international entrepreneurs – travel frequently and know foreign languages.

As the entrepreneur has to turn his/her idea into a good business, he/she also needs a different typology of skills that enhance his/her performance and takes account of theoretical and practical managerial knowledge. Business planning, problem solving, strategic marketing,

financial management and human resource management are some of the most important issues the entrepreneur has to deal with day by day. In order to better understand the topic, it is possible to both divide out the general management skills which are required to organize and to set the physical and financial resources and people management skills needed to obtain support from others. Some important management business skills are:

- *Strategy skills*, considered as an ability to see the business as a whole and understand how it fits into the market in order to implement all the necessary operations to deliver valuable products and services to the customer, preferably doing this better than competitors.
- *Planning skills*, which concern the capacity to foresee and/or to anticipate proactively future market conditions and in the light of this, to adjust and prepare business operations to have a profitable impact on it.
- *Marketing skills*, considered as actions directed to attract and appeal to customers and to satisfy them.
- *Financial skills*, which concern not only the ability to manage money, to control cash-flows and verify expenditures but also the capacity to attract capital and financial resources from investors. As entrepreneurial firms generally have poor financial resources, the ability of the entrepreneur to collect funds and to maintain strong relationships among the investors can be fundamental in the exploitation of contingent market opportunities.
- *Leadership skills*, that is not simply the rigid direction of workers but is also, and more importantly, the ability to inspire people in the tasks they have to undertake, supporting them and helping them to achieve the goals they have been set.
- *Motivation skills*, the entrepreneur gives commitment to people, trying to instil enthusiasm and motivation in doing a task. Being able to motivate, the entrepreneur generally knows what drives people and what they expect from their work.
- *Communication skills*, which the entrepreneur uses in order clearly to express ideas and inform others, but more specifically an

entrepreneur's good communication skills are used in influencing people's actions.

* *Negotiation skills,* when the requests of different parties are not univocal, the entrepreneur understands the motivations and recognizes the possibilities of maximizing the outcomes of all in order to obtain an advantage.

All these different skills are of course interrelated because, for example, leadership requires the ability to motivate, being able to set up a strategy means considering future possibilities and therefore planning. Moreover, it is important to remember that most entrepreneurs learn all these skills through experience, in particular from previous work experience generally in related businesses. The knowledge of the industry is indeed important: as mentioned above, many entrepreneurs set up their own ventures only after having matured and having gained previous work experience as an employee, giving them the opportunity to know mechanisms and make connections that will be of help to them later.

Finally, successful entrepreneurs are aware that these skills need to be constantly learnt through practice, and occasionally renewed according to changes in industry and market conditions, in the business profile or to new entrepreneurial ideas they want to develop. According to Gilad and Levine (1986), an entrepreneur is generally moved by some force which encourages him/her to become an entrepreneur by the means of some attractions (pull factors) and others which make the work as an employee less attractive (push factors). Some important pull factors include the financial rewards, the freedom to work for one's own firm, the sense of achievement, a desire to gain social standing, while on the other hand push factors may be the scarcity of financial income from conventional jobs, job insecurity, career limitation, the impossibility of pursuing personal innovations or ideas or feeling a misfit in an established organization.

Besides strong push and pull factors, there are also factors that block entrepreneurial initiative: the high cost or the impossibility to obtain start-up capital; the presence of risks the entrepreneur considers unbearable; legal restrictions; or lastly, the lack of fundamental resources for the enterprise.

3.5 Entrepreneurial orientation in organizations

As we noted earlier, in literature there has been a gradual focusing away from the entrepreneur level of analysis, which remains anyway important, to a focus on the organizational level.

Some authors studied entrepreneurship, focusing on the traits and the personality characteristics of the entrepreneur without leading to a definition of entrepreneurship or to an understanding of the phenomenon. These studies have shown that entrepreneurs have various innate features, but they were not able to differentiate between entrepreneurs and non-entrepreneurs, because they did not explain why a person starts a business and another does not. Jenk (1950) and Kilby (1971) have criticized research which seeks to develop a personality profile of the entrepreneur; both have encouraged researchers to study the behaviour and activities of entrepreneurs.

As Covin and Slevin (1991) stated 'The adoption of a firm-behaviour model of entrepreneurship has a number of advantages over the more traditional entrepreneurship model and theories that focus on traits of individual entrepreneurs.' A firm-level analysis is consistent with the entrepreneurial effectiveness of the firm. Moreover, as mentioned above, an individual's psychological profile does not make a person an entrepreneur. Behaviour more than any other attributes gives meaning to the entrepreneurial process, and only through actions can we really know the entrepreneur. Similarly, an organization's actions make it entrepreneurial. As, according to Covin and Slevin:

> a behavioural model of entrepreneurship is suggested because behaviours rather than attributes are what give meaning to the entrepreneurial process. An individual's psychological profile does not make a person an entrepreneur. Rather we know entrepreneurs through their actions. Similarly non-behavioural organizational-level attributes, like organizational structure or culture, do not make a firm entrepreneurial. An organization's actions make it entrepreneurial. In short, behaviour is the central and essential element in the entrepreneurial process.
>
> (ibid, p. 8)

Summing up, behaviour is the central and essential element in the entrepreneurial process. Entrepreneurship scholars have also

investigated the firm's entrepreneurial orientation (EO). This refers to a firm's strategic orientation, capturing specific entrepreneurial aspects of decision-making styles, methods, and practices (Lumpkin and Dess, 1996).

Researchers agree that EO is a combination of three dimensions: innovativeness, proactiveness, and risk-taking behaviour (Covin and Slevin, 1991; Wiklund, 1999). Innovativeness reflects a tendency to support new ideas, novelty, experimentation, and creative processes, thereby departing from established practices and technologies (Lumpkin and Dess, 1996). Proactiveness refers to a posture of anticipating and acting on future wants and needs in the marketplace, thereby creating a first-mover advantage *vis-à-vis* competitors (Lumpkin and Dess, 1996). With such a forward-looking perspective, proactive firms capitalize on emerging opportunities. Risk taking is associated with a willingness to commit large amounts of resources to projects where the cost of failure may be high (Miller and Friesen, 1978). It also implies committing resources to projects where the outcome is unknown. This suggests that organizations that have an EO are more able to see opportunities, take risks and exploit these opportunities, committing adequate resources.

According to Miller:

> In general theorists would not call a firm entrepreneurial if it changes its technology or product-line ... simply by direct imitating competitors while refusing to take any risks. Some proactiveness would be essential as well. By the same token, risk-taking firms that are highly leveraged financially are not necessarily entrepreneurial. They must also engage in product-market or technological innovation.
>
> (1983, p. 780)

Entrepreneurial organizations often initiate actions to which competitors then respond, and are frequently first-to-market with new offerings.

EO likely has positive performance implications for the firm. Proactive companies can create first-mover advantages, target premium market segments, and 'skim' the market ahead of

competitors (Zahra and Covin, 1995). They can control the market by dominating distribution channels and establish brand recognition. A firm's EO is typically shaped through the role of its CEO. This is an accepted approach (Covin and Slevin, 1989). CEOs have significant influence over firm behaviour and practices and they provide key evidence to explain why and how firms behave differently.

Hambrick (1981) has argued that the CEO is the most knowledgeable person in the firm about the relevant characteristics of the organization and its industry. The term 'entrepreneurial orientation' (EO) is often used, referring to the CEO's strategic orientation, reflecting the willingness of a firm to engage in entrepreneurial behaviour. In doing this many organizations delegate power and encourage entrepreneurial behaviour at lower hierarchical levels. In large firms CEOs might be separated from 'how a firm operates' by layers of middle managers, but this does not mean that entrepreneurship is solely concentrated at the CEO level. In small and medium-sized businesses the strategic orientation of the CEO is likely to equal the strategic orientation of the firm as a whole, due to its very limited size. In SMEs the predominant role of the CEO influences the general orientation of the firm and influences organizational learning.

These perspectives permit us to reconcile the individual level of analysis with the organizational one and they have in common a view of entrepreneurship in terms of orientation and behaviour.

EO can explain the managerial processes that allow some firms to compete because EO facilitates firm action based upon signals from its internal and external environments (Lumpkin and Dess, 1996).

3.6 The contribution of entrepreneurship theories and models to International Entrepreneurship

The most prevalent and compelling views of entrepreneurship focus on innovation as the key factor in defining an entrepreneur, and in the perception of new economic opportunities and the subsequent introduction of new ideas to the market, without regard to the domestic or the foreign ones.

Researchers agree that entrepreneurship is a combination of three dimensions: innovativeness, proactiveness, and risk-taking (Covin and Slevin, 1991; Wiklund, 1999). The process by which new products and services, new business models are introduced into the market is based on the discovery, enactment, evaluation, and exploitation of opportunities.

A number of scholars with different disciplinary backgrounds have contributed to research in entrepreneurship. These scholars have their roots in different disciplines such as economics, business history/anthropology, psychology and sociology.

For Cantillon (1755), entrepreneurs are a distinctive social class formed of people who are willing to bear the risks shifted onto them by the rest of society. Entrepreneurs exercise business judgment in the face of uncertainty.

For Schumpeter (1934, 1942), an entrepreneur is a leader and contributor to the process of creative destruction. A characteristic of entrepreneurs is that they simply do new things, or do things already being done in a new way (innovation). Entrepreneurial performance involves the ability to perceive new opportunities that cannot be proved at the moment at which action is taken, therefore internationalization as an example of strategic change is defined as an entrepreneurial action.

Hayek's (1948) most important contribution is the concept of *discovery procedure*: market competition is seen as a process whereby to discover opportunities, which are useful for achieving specific purposes. Hayek's conception of discovery was not related to new technological advances, but rather to minor discoveries concerning the wishes and desires of the consumers, including the goods and services which they demanded and the prices they were willing to pay.

For Kirzner (1997), who developed the 'theory of entrepreneurial discovery', which views the market as an entrepreneurially driven process, discovery is not accidental, but it is generated by the possibility of profit, since entrepreneurs are, according to Kirzner, more alert than others because of their nature, or simply because the profit incentive has more importance to them than to others. The key concept of this theory is therefore alertness, considered as a human capacity to profit from opportunities which has to be perceived as an entrepreneurial element in the economic decision process.

Mises (1949) sees the entrepreneur as someone active with regard to the changes occurring in the market. Entrepreneurship is any human action inspired by uncertainty. Following the approaches of Shane and Venkataraman (2000) and Gartner (1989), entrepreneurship research examines these creation endeavours, supporting the creation of new products and services as well as new ventures. This gives the basis to sustain the stream of research in International Entrepreneurship, focusing on International New Ventures or Born-Global firms.

Entrepreneurial behaviour may be manifested by an individual, or a group, that may then give birth to a firm's organization (Gartner, 1985). Established organizations can also behave entrepreneurially (Shane and Venkataraman, 2000). As mentioned above entrepreneurship relies on the discovery, the evaluation and the exploitation of opportunities. Entrepreneurial activities are represented by opportunity scanning and alertness, the evaluation of opportunity, risk-taking behaviour that permits the mobilization of resources and the coordination of resources and capabilities in order to create new products, services or ventures.

Focusing on International Entrepreneurial Organizations, the unit of analysis is represented by firms and not individuals. Entrepreneurial behaviour is investigated at the firm level. CEOs have significant influence over firm behaviour and practices and they are important factors in explaining why and how firms behave differently. It is generally recognized that strategic decisions are influenced by beliefs, value structures, management knowledge, experience and learning (Andrews, 1980; Guth and Taguiri, 1965). This places the entrepreneur or the top management team at the centre of the firm's behavioural model. Accordingly, top management knowledge, experience and learning are important variables in the proposed model of firm-level entrepreneurship, and they can explain, in particular, the path dependence of the firm.

A question remains unanswered: can the entire organization be defined as entrepreneurial and how? Organizations are complex and relatively stable institutions where routines and capabilities are the result of long-lasting learning processes, influenced by managerial decisions over time. In a process view of entrepreneurship, can

organizations be considered more or less entrepreneurial, according to their capacity to change/reconfigure well-established capabilities which inform the entire organization? The next chapter addresses the literature on strategic management to try to find an answer to these questions.

4
Strategic Management Studies

Entrepreneurial firms, as deduced from the description of the entrepreneur, are considered as enterprises led by the entrepreneur-founder or managed by corporate entrepreneurs who have recognized and exploited successfully a business opportunity, assuming risk-taking, innovative and proactive decisions. This strategy is pursued by means of the entrepreneurial process where opportunities, unique resources and organizational assets are combined and converged to support each other.

Entrepreneurial entities may be recognized for their strong knowledge-based essence: the possession of unique capabilities within the firm is considered a source of competitive advantage. Furthermore, knowledge development takes place more easily through close interaction in networks. The latter are an important feature both for small entrepreneurial firms lacking resources and for large established companies which look for innovative projects and renewal of their businesses and competences.

In the following paragraphs some Strategic Management approaches are discussed in the light of entrepreneurship. For this reason, only some streams in this field of studies are considered for their relevance to this book issues. In particular, a general framework (the Resources-Based View) and two related streams of strategic management literature are analysed for their connections with Entrepreneurship studies: Dynamic Capabilities and Networking. A final paragraph on the role of local clusters, as a special case of networking is included. The resource-based view framework also finds many applications in International Business studies and the

same holds for the research stream about networking, which will be reconsidered here from a different but complementary perspective.

In considering the Resource-Based view framework, we also include some considerations about two related fields of research, namely the competence-based and the knowledge-based approach. The latter represents another example of the deep interconnections between recent streams of research in the area of international business and strategic management. Innovation, knowledge and capabilities have been a central theme of research on the strategy and performance of the firm (Knight and Cavusgil, 2004).

4.1   The resource-based view

In 1959, a British economist, Edith Penrose, suggested that the returns earned by firms could largely be attributed to the resources they held. In subsequent years, others, particularly strategic management scholars (e.g., Amit and Schoemaker, 1993; Barney, 1986, 1991; Hitt and Ireland, 1985; Rumelt, 1991; Wernerfelt, 1984), started exploring this field arguing that firms' resources, capabilities, and competencies facilitate the development of sustainable competitive advantages. This approach states that firms hold heterogeneous and idiosyncratic resources (defined broadly here to include capabilities) on which their strategies are based. Competitive advantages are achieved when the strategies are successful in leveraging these resources. Intangible resources are more likely to lead to a competitive advantage than tangible resources because they are socially complex and more difficult to understand and imitate (Barney, 1991; Hitt et al., 2001). One important intangible resource is for example a firm's reputation (Deephouse, 2000). Reputation can be an important strategic resource for many reasons, such as access to resources (e.g., financial capital) and to help a firm take advantage of information asymmetries (Hitt et al., 2001).

Resources to Wernerfelt (1984) are those tangible and intangible resources that are semi-permanently tied to the organization: brand names, technological knowledge developed by enterprise, reputation and qualified personnel. These resources are the basis for the competitive advantages, and comprise three different subgroups: tangible assets, intangible assets and capabilities. Tangible assets refer to the fixed and current assets of an organization, which have fixed

long-run deposits; they are easy to measure and transparent (Grant, 1991), and relatively easy to duplicate (plant, equipment, land, capital, deposits). Intangible assets have relatively unlimited capacity allowing firms to exploit their value (licence, patents, reputation) or sell them like brands.

Knowledge is probably the main firm-specific intangible resource. Grant (1996) suggests that knowledge is a firm's most critical competitive asset. Spender (1996) argues that knowledge and the firm's ability to generate it are at the core of the theory of the firm. Much of a firm's knowledge resides in its human capital. Knowledge is generated through organizational learning (Hitt and Ireland, 2000; Hitt, Ireland and Lee, 2000). Learning new capabilities helps firms to compete effectively, survive and grow (Autio, Sapienza and Almeida, 2000). The traditional view of entrepreneurship focuses on the importance of resources in determining entrepreneurial orientation. The lack of resources limits growth but also constrains all general entrepreneurial activities: resource availability influences the firm's performance positively.

The importance of the entrepreneur is emphasized in the resource base perspective (Penrose, 1995). During the organising process entrepreneurs (including corporate entrepreneurs and top management teams) have to decide which resources are more and which less important, then acquire and use those resources in the firms. The 1998 study by Brush, Green and Hart points out that decisions regarding which resources to acquire are primarily that of the founder/entrepreneur/management team (Vesper, 1990) and the selection depends on their perceptions and expectations on the future of the ventures (Penrose, 1959) and intuition or a systematic assessment of resources (Barney, 1986). This citation shows the importance of the founder/entrepreneur/management team in resource mobilization and the coordination of resources and capabilities for firm performance. At the same time the decisions of managers and entrepreneurs depend on their knowledge, based on the education and experience that determines their capacity to take actions.

The Resource-Based view (PBV) underlines the importance of skills and resources within the firm that allow the development of a sustainable competitive advantage, in particular in international environments. Its foundation rests on the premise that competitive advantage originates at firm (rather than at industry) level (Capron

and Hulland, 1999). Possessing a particular combination of skills and resources provides the firm with the ability to perform more effectively and more efficiently than its competitors, and as firms possess unique sets of skills and resources they differ from one another. The case of an incumbent, which shows certain inimitable assets, could discourage even large competitors from challenging it. Firms might gain a higher performance because of differences in particular resources and capabilities that are difficult to imitate, rather than on their market power. The competition, in fact, is not only based on product markets and a better positioning within it but also on the differentiation in a resource base that can secure a sustainable competitive advantage: resources and capabilities enable firms to deliver new products and solutions and therefore avoid competition with stronger rivals.

The RBV and the knowledge-based perspective of the firm are deeply connected: the former helps to explain how knowledge and resultant capabilities are developed and leveraged by enterprising firms. The integration of specialist knowledge hinges on the nature and quality of the firm's capabilities which evolve a continuous conversion of explicit and tacit knowledge (Polanyi, 1966) into business activities that create value for customers. Tacit knowledge is embedded in individuals and cannot be expressed explicitly or codified in written form (Nonaka, 1994). Ultimately the firm accumulates firm-specific knowledge internally that provides organizational knowledge, a key strategic asset for the firm (Nelson and Winter, 1982). It is reinforced in all the activities of the firm and becomes increasingly embedded in routines (Autio, Sapienza and Almeida, 2000).

Human, organizational and technological resources, which can all be grouped as knowledge-based resources, are some of the most important intangible assets for the firm's performance. Organizational knowledge is an important bundle of intangible resources that can be the source of a sustainable competitive advantage (Hitt, Ireland and Hoskisson, 1999). Researchers argued that knowledge has the highest ability of all the resources to serve as a source of sustainable differentiation, because of its immobility (McEvily and Chakravarthy, 2002) and general applicability (Miller and Shamsie, 1996). Knowledge permits the firm to predict the changes in the environment and the appropriateness of strategic and tactical actions (Cohen and Levinthal, 1990).

Without such knowledge, an organization is less capable of discovering and exploiting new opportunities. Knowledge is difficult to formalize, articulate, and transfer between organizational contexts (Nonaka and Takeuchi, 1995). Knowledge about markets and technology represents two kinds of knowledge that can increase the ability to discover and exploit opportunities. As Wiklund and Shepherd observed:

> market knowledge can increase a firm's ability to discover and exploit opportunities because: (1) awareness of customer problems may have great generality and thus constitute real market opportunities; (2) it is easier to determine the market value of new scientific discoveries, technological change etc.; (3) the locus of innovation often lies with users of new technologies who cannot easily articulate their needs for not-yet-developed solutions to problems, and therefore the organization must share some of the same tacit knowledge as its users.
>
> (2003, p. 2)

Technological knowledge can also enhance the discovery and exploitation of opportunities. Sometimes knowledge can lead to a technological breakthrough that represents an opportunity despite its market applicability not being readily apparent (Abernathy and Utterback, 1978). Technological knowledge can also enhance a firm's ability to exploit an opportunity or to be able to respond quickly when competitors make advancements (Cohen and Levinthal, 1990). It is possible to argue that market and technological knowledge, taken together, represent important knowledge-based resources applicable to a firm's ability to discover and exploit opportunities.

Generally, the human resources referred to are the ability of the entrepreneur, along with his/her experience, market and business knowledge, judgement and intelligence, but they can also be possessed by members of staff who, in entrepreneurial firms, often support and sustain the entrepreneur with their technical knowledge or with their experience. The human capital of an entrepreneur and the internal resources of a firm may influence the competitive strategy pursued by firms as well as their performance (Westhead, Wright and Ucbasaran, 2001).

In general knowledge permits the firm to accurately predict the nature and potential of changes in the environment and the appropriateness of strategic and tactical actions. Without such knowledge, an organization is less capable of discovering and exploiting new opportunities (Cohen and Levinthal, 1990).

It is also possible to include the competence-based framework in a resource-based perspective. According to Penrose and Wernerfeld, as we noted above, capabilities are part of the firm's resources. More recently some authors have further developed a competence- or capabilities-based view of the firm, insisting on the issue that capabilities are at the heart of competitiveness and performance. For researchers, capabilities are often difficult to delineate and thus might be described as invisible assets (Itami, 1987).

Capabilities are understood to encompass the skills of individuals or groups or organizational routines and interactions through which all the firms resources are coordinated (Grant, 1991). Competences are related to capabilities and for some authors they have the same meaning (Prahalad and Hamel, 1990), while for others the are different constructs: the former provide a static while the latter a dynamic view of what the organization is able to do (what and how to do). This term competences is often interchangeable with skills. Competences are also understood as unique skills and activities that a firm can do better than competitors (Lado, Boyd and Wright, 1992).

Core competencies are the collective learning in the organization, especially how to coordinate diverse production skills and integrate multiple streams of technological competencies that empower individual businesses to adapt quickly to changing opportunities (Prahalad and Hamel, 1990). Capabilities are considered by some authors the main source of the firm's competitive advantages since they permit adapting, integrating, reconfiguring capabilities toward the changing environment (Teece and al., 1997). Capabilities are dynamic when they reflect the ability to renew the firm's competence in order to compete in the changing business environment. The issue of dynamic capabilities will be treated in next paragraph.

Intangible assets, distinctive competencies and dynamic capabilities are very important for the market survival of entrepreneurial firms: they are less imitable and therefore are unique, giving entrepreneurial

firms the possibility of coping with their scarce tangible assets and sustaining their activities longer, protecting themselves from larger companies' competition.

The success of a firm does not depend only on the existent resources and capabilities but also on the capacity of the founder/entrepreneur/team management and their ability to adapt to changes in the environment and to develop resources and capabilities. In other words, long-run performance depends not only on the firm's resources and capabilities *per se* but – most importantly – on its capacity to mobilize and dynamically combine external and internal resources, to pursue incremental as well as radical innovations at different units of analysis and to reconfigure and transform capabilities continually in non-imitable configurations.

The firm's competitive advantage is thus a highly dynamic one, and requires continuous innovative reconfiguration as well as resource mobilization, given path dependence and market positions (Leonard-Barton, 1992; Teece, Pisano and Shuen, 1997). The latter argument is the core of the dynamic capabilities perspective, which represents a recent sub-stream of the RBV.

4.2 Dynamic capabilities

According to the Resource-Based approach, a sustainable competitive advantage can be obtained through rare, valuable and inimitable resources, which are heterogeneously distributed across firms, with differences persisting over time. Nevertheless, this does not explain how and why certain firms such as entrepreneurial firms have competitive advantages in situations of rapid and unpredictable change, like for example, in international markets. The explanation is implied in the existence of a certain typology of capabilities: the dynamic capabilities, which have been defined (Teece, Pisano and Shuen, 1997) as the ability to integrate, build, and reconfigure internal and external competencies to address rapidly changing environments. Dynamic capabilities are the firm's processes that use resources to match and even create market change. Dynamic capabilities are thus the organizational and strategic routines by which firms achieve new resources configurations in order to explore and exploit new market opportunities. The connection with the key issues of entrepreneurship literature is clear: dynamic capabilities provide an interpretation

in terms of firms' abilities and routines, of their attitude towards coping with environmental change, but especially in a highly turbulent competitive context where radical and proactive transformations in the organization and its market offer are needed.

The nature of dynamic capabilities lies on the existing resources and knowledge but also in a sort of learning process, addressed to learning how to change the organization and its offer. Furthermore, this learning process is affected by both organizational and environmental factors: dynamic capabilities emphasize two aspects. First, it refers to the shifting character of the environment; second, it emphasizes the key role of strategic management in appropriately adapting, integrating and reconfiguring internal and external organizational skills, resources and functional competencies towards a changing environment (Teece, Pisano and Shuen, 1997).

In this sense, dynamic capabilities are closely related and depend upon market dynamism. More specifically, in the case of moderate market dynamism, where changes are frequent but predictable or linear, dynamic capabilities rely on existing knowledge and the learning process is limited only in organizing and assembling resources as a consequence of market changes. Diversely, when markets are very dynamic, it implies the creation of new knowledge, because dynamism refers to the necessity to be attuned to changing business situations and so to renew competences, to respond innovatively in a market where timing is crucial and the nature of future competition or the composition of markets are uncertain. According to Eisenhardt and Martin (2000), the construct of dynamic capabilities holds and matters only in the latter kind of highly volatile environment.

The understanding of these capabilities is grounded on a view of the firm in terms of business processes, market position and growth paths. Processes refer to an organizational level where routines and current practices are arranged. Position regards a firm's resources such as technological or intellectual assets, knowledge of customers and relations with suppliers. Lastly, paths refer to the growth alternatives available to the firm.

Processes can be divided into three dimensions: coordination/integration, learning and reconfiguration. The first regards managerial coordination of activity from both an internal and an external perspective, and includes routines for gathering and processing information or for coordinating activities in the factory or for

integrating suppliers' work. More important is learning, defined as the repetition and experimentation of processes in order to perform better. It also enables new production opportunities to be identified. In the context of the firm, if not more generally, learning involves organizational as well as individual skills. A new kind of activity and new routines permit the creation of new organizational knowledge, which is useful to generate solutions to diverse future problems. Finally, reconfiguration is strictly connected with changes in the environment.

The second source of competitive advantage lies in the firm's position considered as its specific assets. The authors include: technological assets; financial assets; reputation; structural assets; institutional assets; market assets and organizational boundaries.

Developing dynamic capabilities is also dependent on the path of the firm, and according to the authors, 'the repertoire of routines (its history) constrains its future behaviour' (Teece, Pisano and Shuen, 1997, p. 523). Furthermore, future development in capabilities is directly connected to the technological opportunities in the particular area of industrial activity, which can be either exogenous or coming from an internal innovative activity of the firm. Teece, Pisano and Shuen conclude stating that, although dynamic capabilities are based fundamentally on processes, influenced by positions and paths, they can provide a competitive advantage 'only if (they) are based on a collection of routines, skills, and complementary assets that are difficult to imitate' (1997, p. 525).

Eisenhardt and Martin argue that dynamic capabilities are a set of specific and identifiable processes such as product development, strategic decisions and alliancing. They define dynamic capabilities as 'the firm's processes that use resources – specifically the processes to integrate, reconfigure, gain and release resources – to match and even create market change. Dynamic capabilities thus are the organizational and strategic routines by which firms achieve new resources configurations as market emerge, collide, split, evolve, and die' (2000, p. 1107).

It is interesting to draw a comparison between the issue of dynamic capabilities which refers to a literature stream in strategic management and entrepreneurial capabilities, which belong to the literature stream of entrepreneurship. The latter should be viewed as a broad range of abilities needed to initiate appropriate actions in specific

situations, not purely restricted to improving the existing organizational performance and knowledge base. Entrepreneurial capabilities match up to the entrepreneur's capacity to take initiatives within the organization and to take action in the marketplace. These capabilities go along with the whole entrepreneurial career: from start-up onwards (Obrecht, 2004). This means that the capabilities needed for an entrepreneurial venture result from learning. Personal capabilities are consistent with entrepreneurial capabilities. 'They refer to the abilities that are embedded in the entrepreneur as an individual and whose enactment is dependent on the individual exclusively. Capability meaning the capacity of being used or developed is action oriented' (Obrecht, 2004, p. 250). The recurrence of these initiatives leads to organizational learning and might generate an entrepreneurial orientation of the entire organization.

Results indicate that a firm's higher entrepreneurial orientation, including the propensity to take risks, level of innovation and the ability to recognize opportunities, reaches a wider variety of distinctive competencies and enjoys higher performance (Smart and Conant, 1994). Other findings support the link between the resource-based capabilities of a firm and its competitive advantage: ability to take action is one of the distinctive competencies (McGee and Peterson, 2000). Entrepreneurial capabilities also refer to the ability to initiate and sustain an entrepreneurial dynamism throughout the organization and to stimulate the learning process. In SMEs, and particularly in new ventures, these entrepreneurial capabilities referred to, that is, the action and the learning process of the organization, are not difficult to identify but they are difficult to isolate from particular individuals, notably the entrepreneur/s. In large or established companies, these entrepreneurial capabilities could be referred to as the routines and processes combined and managed by individuals and groups within the firm.

4.3 Networking approaches: a link between strategic management, international business and organizational studies

Networks have become increasingly important to all types of firms as the economic environment continues to be more competitive (Gulati, Nohria and Zaheer, 2000). Such networks involve relationships with

customers, suppliers and competitors among others and often extend across industries and geographic, political and cultural boundaries. A network is a set of actors connected by a set of ties (Granovetter, 1973), and generally the actors' previous experience significantly affects the nature of the network the firm belongs to. Networks have grown in importance because they can provide firms with access to information, resources, markets and even, at times, technologies (Gulati, Nohria and Zaheer, 2000). Networks can also play an important role in providing participants with credibility or legitimacy and serve as sources of information that help entrepreneurial firms to identify potential opportunities (Cooper, 2002). Once they have discovered a new opportunity, entrepreneurs can still rely on networks in order to find the necessary resources to set up the business. Indeed, only a few entrepreneurs already have all the resources that are needed to exploit an opportunity, but they can be acquired more easily by means of networks and at lower than market prices. However, networks can certainly provide the resources and capabilities needed to compete effectively in the marketplace (McEvily and Zaheer, 1999). Moreover they provide the opportunity to acquire new capabilities (Anand and Khanna, 2000; Dussauge, Garrette and Mitchell, 2000; Hitt, Ireland and Lee, 2000). Networks, then, allow firms to compete in markets without already having to own all of the resources necessary to do so. This is particularly important to new venture firms because they often have limited resources (Cooper, 2002; Dubini and Aldrich, 1991; Starr and MacMillan, 1990).

Moreover, in the early phases after the start-up, the firm needs network relationships to obtain a sort of legitimization, because new ventures do not appear as accountable and reliable as existing organizations they need to create the external perception that they are legitimate to garner resources and survive competition with established organizations (Delmar and Shane, 2001).

All these considerations obviously also hold for international networks: entrepreneurs obtain information from their international relationships in order to exploit new opportunities and make the right country market selection as well as the right entry mode selection. They can gain information about: access to cheaper resources or labour conditions, customer habits and needs, legal systems and knowledge in general in order to reduce the risk involved in going abroad. International networks can support International

Entrepreneurship in that they can give access to a broader and more diverse set of opportunities and the resources to exploit them. In spite of the growing consensus on the importance of networks, a debate has arisen over the preference for closed networks with strong ties or open networks with weaker ties. According to several authors, such as Coleman (1988), a cohesive network could help the development of 'social capital', because it generates expectations and obligations and actors are prompted to behave in a trustworthy way. Moreover, in such networks information is reliable and collective interests are put first.

Strong ties are also emphasized by Uzzi (1997) who highlighted three main components that regulate the behaviour of partners: trust, fine-grained information and joint problem-solving arrangements. The relationships are coordinated by trust and so access to better resources is ensured; information is more reliable and widespread and finally the joint-problem solving arrangements deepening relationships lead to a continuous flow of knowledge and innovation. On the other hand Granovetter (1973) maintains that weak ties are of greater importance in the distribution of new information, because people then have the possibility of moving from one circle to another without constraints, and also because being in strong networks leads firms to become too dependent on the specific network tie and thus, unable to act alone to exploit potential opportunities. Uzzi (1997) recognized that an 'optimal' network should also be open to arm's length ties in order to avoid lock-in.

The composition of the network and the degree of information, skills and resources it has are significantly important for the success of the firm. Since each actor has a position within networks, they can be analysed along different dimensions: inter-organizational links among nodes of physically close networks and distant international markets or social relationships among entrepreneurs and in general individuals. To our research social and local networks seem to be core concepts in explaining entrepreneurial competitive advantage.

Social networks focus their attention on the relationships between entrepreneurs and all the other individuals that provide useful resources in order to run a business. Even if entrepreneurs have talent and the right capabilities, they need support, complementary resources, knowledge and access to distribution channels through their social networks. The latter are generally composed of personal

contacts the entrepreneurs may have with friends, business people and even family members. Social networks are also largely invisible and mostly unknown to others outside the network, which gives the firms involved a competitive advantage. Differently from formal inter-organizational ties, they can be activated whenever it is necessary. Indeed, depending on the phase the firm is going through, entrepreneurs turn to certain of their personal connections.

In the first phases, when the entrepreneur is trying to explore the possibilities of setting up the business, it has emerged that they first explore the possibilities of starting their own business within a small circle of close contacts, and only later in the phase of planning and establishing the business put considerable time to both developing and maintaining their social relations and so to mobilize a larger social network to get information and resources. Time spent developing social relationships can be considered a source of competitive advantage, since most successful entrepreneurs seem to regard developing new contacts with individuals, and re-establishing or maintaining relations with people with whom they have not been recently in contact, as high on their list of priorities. Therefore, in order to build a network of reliable and useful relationships, entrepreneurs are willing to spend time with people to learn who will be good contacts for their business. Entrepreneurs may be classified according to the number and the strength of their social relationships into four categories: atomistic, collective, safe and hub entrepreneurs (Hinttu, Forsman and Kock, 2002).

The 'atomistic' entrepreneur has only a few and weak social relationships and is considered lonely and often cut off, especially in international environments. The 'collective' entrepreneur tries to obtain information from different sources in order to take less risky decisions. Nevertheless, since the information comes from weak ties its reliability cannot be guaranteed. The 'safe' entrepreneur deals with long-lasting social relationships, being a reliable source. The disadvantage, as mentioned above, is becoming too dependent on the network, and there is also the risk of strategic lock-in. The last typology, the 'hub' entrepreneur relies on many strong relationships, and has gained a very strong and central position. He/she is connected to many networks and can consequently obtain a lot of new information, which can be used for connecting different activities and parts of the business in order to create new opportunities.

The same authors have also proposed a complete model that delineates the main factors that have impact on social relationships, in particular when deciding to internationalize. The authors suggest that different types of relationship are important. Indeed, in order to get information for example about foreign buyers, the entrepreneur may consider it useful to rely on both strong and weak social ties. The former may provide trustworthy information, while from the latter the entrepreneur gets information faster and without constraints. This is particularly true in internationalization processes, even if it is argued that strong ties might be essential in a context of problem solving and, furthermore, adapt better to fostering innovation. Other important issues concern how central and valuable entrepreneurs are in their social network: a central one can see new opportunities sooner and get better information, thus being able to coordinate actions among different partners later, when needed. Moreover, it is also suggested that a central actor in a social network is considered as attractive to others, with the consequence that for the entrepreneur it will be easier to expand his/her contacts.

The content of a relationship deals with the functioning of social networks. All the activities within the network are regulated by information transfer, joint problem-solving agreements and trust, all of which together strengthen the social relationships and promote mutual learning. Regarding accessibility, the three authors consider different typology: continuing, sleeping/terminated and future relationships. These kinds of relationships obviously indicate a variety of links the entrepreneur considers more or less important: a continuing relationship can be either a strong or a weak tie, but most importantly is considered fundamental to business and therefore highly intensive. On the other hand, terminated relationships are no longer based on mutual help and so are difficult to reactivate. Sleeping relationships may be very useful because they are old relationships, not already terminated, that are put on hold. Their significance comes from the fact that the entrepreneur can activate them when needed. Future relationships represent a potential for future opportunities. Entrepreneurs are always attuned to developing and discovering new useful social ties.

Studies in entrepreneurship associate the operations of entrepreneurial firms with networking activities. Social networks significantly facilitate the operation of entrepreneurs (Aldrich and Zimmer, 1986;

Aldrich and Martinez, 2001; Johannisson, 2000), while networking is one of the major strategies pursued by entrepreneurial firms in order to gain access to resources, and cope with environmental uncertainty and impediments in their operations (Alvarez and Barney, 2001; Floyd and Wooldridge, 1999).

The extent of the network can be national or international. Particular attention has been given to the latter because nowadays customers, suppliers and partners are increasingly spread over wider geographical areas. Entrepreneurs often have work or study experiences abroad so they have cultivated international ties and knowledge. International social connections are an advantage for international entrepreneurial businesses.

The networking dimension appears important in International Entrepreneurship, especially for the born-global firms, which rely on inter-firm alliances and interpersonal social networks in order to overcome resource constraints and lack of knowledge when they internationalize (Brush, 1995; Madsen and Servais, 1997; Oviatt and McDougall, 1995).

Research in International Entrepreneurship supports the idea that International New Ventures are embedded in social networks (often informal), which help them in going international, by supplying information about foreign markets, helping to identify customers abroad and by pointing to cross-border opportunities. Social network ties supply information about prospective customers, find co-operative partners and offer new business opportunities abroad.

The 'international among others' case in the Johanson and Mattson (1988) model seems to be a convincing representation of successful international entrepreneurial firms, which have developed and exploited a highly internationalized network, with the consequence of benefiting on an international scale the spread of knowledge and resources within social ties.

4.4 Networking in local clusters and entrepreneurship

Networking is not necessarily set up in wide geographical areas. In most cases enterprises engage close business relationships in small, notably local, contexts. Entrepreneurial firms, as already mentioned, require a set of initial resources and capabilities that can be found in

specific locations, and which provide new entrants with a competitive environment, but also a set of opportunities and threats. In this sense, location choices are often a critical factor for entrepreneurial firms and are driven by the opportunity to obtain the most profitable and feasible match of firm and location-specific characteristics. Entrepreneurs have to compare the cluster where they benefit from agglomeration economies but face a competition with similar firms, with an isolated entry where they are temporarily shielded from intense competition but need to develop some crucial resources by themselves instead of relying on the cluster to get them. Entrepreneurs will enter the cluster only if they expect that all the benefits and the value of entering will be higher than the cost of entry.

Firms in the same industry, tend to agglomerate in given geographical areas, in order to exploit 'location externalities', which help production, facilitate the access to financial resources and heighten demand. In more detail, firms may experience strategic enhancement which originate from:

- easy access to information by means of enterprises' associations, service centres or consortia, reducing search costs;
- technological and knowledge spill-overs thanks to the high number of imitative processes and a high rate of spin-offs;
- easy access to the labour market, and in particular to highly specialized workers;
- advantages of backward and forward linkages associated with large local markets (i.e., improving the quality of matching crucial inputs and intermediate goods between suppliers and demanders);
- the possibility to share infrastructure, logistics and also inputs with other firms located close to each other.

(Almazan, de Motta and Titman, 2003; Baum and Haveman, 1997; Zucchella, 2006)

Firms within clusters gather information through learning from the experience of other actors in the industry. Being located in clusters gives firms the possibility of getting information about intentions or actions of competitors; furthermore, local spill-overs are passed through industrial alliances, mobility of specialized workers or the same input supplier. Nevertheless, clusters foster entrepreneurial

entry because firms see their entry costs reduced, as existing infrastructures and inputs can be shared or obtained at lower costs than developing new ones alone. Moreover, enterprises may increase their efficiency by outsourcing, leasing or renting marginal activities and focusing on core competencies.

Local clusters may also improve the demand in industries where it is necessary for the customers to know the producer. Clustering may reduce consumers' search costs, thus increasing the likelihood of visitation and purchase, compared to firms in a separate location. Since access to financial resources is fundamental, entrepreneurial firms with weak financial resources may benefit from a cluster location where access to capital is easier thanks to the local financial system and closer proximity of their partner firms and banks.

Finally, local clusters have influences also from an internationalization strategy point of view. According to Zucchella (2002), the expected consequences on district firms' internationalization are threefold:

- a higher export intensity in relation to comparable non-district firms;
- international orientation from the outset of entrepreneurial activity;
- a higher propensity to experience forms of internationalization other than export like alliances, joint ventures (JVs) and foreign direct investments (FDIs).

These international characteristics of clusters seem to recall the concept of 'international among others' with regards to the network model. These typologies of firms find their natural location within clusters where all firms can exploit their accumulated and widespread knowledge about foreign markets. New ventures might find it easier to develop internationally when locating within such a cluster which can be considered as a locus of International Entrepreneurship.

4.5   The contribution of strategic management studies to International Entrepreneurship

According to strategic management studies, and in particular adopting the Resource-Based view perspective, it emerges that at the heart

of long run performance and competitiveness there are unique, valuable, inimitable resources and capabilities. Among the key resources of an organization we considered the entrepreneur and top management team and the knowledge base of the firm.

The importance of the entrepreneur is emphasized in the Resource-Based perspective (Penrose, 1995). Cooper, Gimeno-Gascon and Woo (1994) suggest that entrepreneurs can provide a firm with human capital and resources, in the form of the entrepreneur's life experience, education, skills, problem-solving ability, discipline, motivation and self-confidence. These individual entrepreneurial capabilities may turn into organizational ones and give rise to an entrepreneurial orientation for the firm when organizational learning processes take place. Organizational learning is a process through which the members of an organization have to interpret knowledge in order to share it and to distribute it within the organization.

Knowledge is a fundamental resource for any firm. It supports, in particular, the entrepreneurial orientation of the firms because it increases the ability to discover and exploit opportunities; it permits the firm to anticipate the changes in the environment and to assume appropriate strategic and tactical actions. Knowledge is the critical firm-specific intangible resource. It resides in human capital and it is generated through organizational learning. From an organizational learning perspective, it has to be emphasized that entrepreneurial capabilities match the entrepreneur's capacity to take the initiative within the organization and take action in the market. These capabilities also refer to the ability to initiate and to sustain entrepreneurial dynamism throughout the organization and to stimulate the process of learning.

The success of a firm does not depend, in fact, only on the existing resources and capabilities but also on the capacity to mobilize and dynamically combine external and internal resources, adapting them to the changes in the environment, and developing new routines and capabilities. In large or established companies, these dynamic capabilities could be referred to as routines and processes combined and managed by individuals and groups within the firm, while in SMEs personal capabilities are involved in the processes and it is not possible to divide the personal from the organizational capabilities or learning, processes and paths. Since dynamic capabilities are systematic methods for modifying operating routines and emerge from

experience accumulation, articulation and codification, it is more likely that they will be outlined in a large, established, international organization, while in new or small international organizations dynamic capabilities are more likely to be embedded in a few individuals, notably the entrepreneur/s.

Entrepreneurship at both the individual and organizational level requires access to opportunities and the capacity to exploit them: these two activities are strongly supported by the networking attitude. Discovery and learning take place to a significant extent in networks, both local and international. The international business literature, the dynamic capabilities framework and the entrepreneurship studies all converge on the role of social and inter-organizational networks in supporting competitiveness and growth.

Another dimension of the literature about networks along which different disciplines converge, including economic geography, is the local versus the global one. An influential element considered to be important for International Entrepreneurship is geographical location within specific local clusters, where the presence of an international background and sticky knowledge enhances the possibility for each new venture to start its entrepreneurial activity on an international scale, benefiting from localized knowledge, and the availability of partners and of business opportunities.

5
A Theoretical Model for International Entrepreneurship

Entrepreneurship calls for two perspectives, which have been frequently evoked in the previous chapters: the individual (Entrepreneur) and the organizational (Entrepreneurial organization) one. The perspectives of resources and capabilities and the more recent related view of dynamic capabilities permit to reconcile the two dimensions. The entrepreneur/s and the top management team are a key resource, and can develop routines and capabilities in the entire organization by supporting organizational learning. The entrepreneurial organization is capable of coping with highly turbulent environments and of exploring and exploiting opportunities over time, by renewing not only their products, processes and markets, but by radically reconfiguring capabilities, when needed. This perspective is coherent with a behavioural and process view of entrepreneurship.

In developing an international entrepreneurial activity the objective is the creation of new wealth, which the entrepreneur is generally driven to by a desire for change. The success or failure of the venture is based on an entrepreneurial process, which leads the entrepreneur to exploit new opportunities, find unique resources and set up an organization. Trying to combine these three decisive factors in an innovative and dynamic way is the main goal for the entrepreneur in developing the venture.

Exploiting innovative ideas in order to create value must first be preceded by the identification of the potential of change, which means the entrepreneur has to fill the gap between the actual and the possible (Wickham, 1998). The motivation, which brings the entrepreneur to bridge this gap, is twofold: the potential to

99

create value, as already mentioned, and the possibility of achieving personal goals.[1]

Building a stable and profitable business which survives in a competitive environment and thrives more efficiently than competitors is of course important for any economic activity. Entrepreneurs are often motivated by factors other than making money: the creation of something new which becomes successful in a challenging competitive environment, might give a sense of achievement which could prove more significant. Entrepreneurs may also be motivated by the opportunity to design their own venture and therefore their own working environment giving them a sense of control. Every entrepreneurial venture is different with its own history of successes or failures; nevertheless it is useful to consider the entrepreneurial venture process using a common framework valid for all enterprises. According to Wickham (1998) there are three factors which the entrepreneur is responsible for bringing together: market opportunity, a business organization, and the resources to be found and invested.

International Entrepreneurship (Figure 5.1) can be viewed as an international creation process, that involves both the generation of new ventures and organizations and the proposal from established firms of new combinations of goods and services, methods of production, markets and supply chains (Gartner, 1989; Shane and Venkataraman, 2000). This is based on the recognition and exploitation of new and existing opportunities, cognitive processes, and behaviours and modes of action to exploit new and existing opportunities in foreign markets. Opportunities are examined and exploited by individuals and organizations leveraging on their knowledge, experience and learning.

An opportunity represents the potential to serve customers, creating value both for them and for the firm: it can be either an opportunity left available in the market by already established firms or a new market space shaped by the entrepreneurial creativity. The entrepreneur has the task of scanning the market for this type of

---

[1] A third motivation could be a social or structural change: an entrepreneur's aim could be to provide society with new products or services, changing the market structure or turning it into a more competitive one.

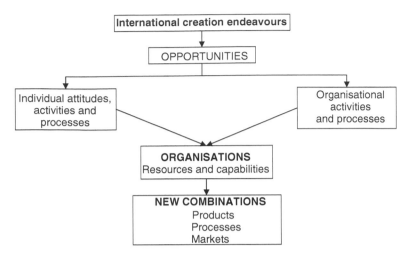

Figure 5.1   The process of International Entrepreneurship

Source: Personal elaboration.

opening and, on the basis of his/her new idea, subsequently implementing the business better than the competitors. An improved/new way of doing business is embodied in the innovation that the entrepreneur presents to the market, but any ensuing success will be obtained only if the customers themselves accept it as an effective improvement on what already exists. Entrepreneurship scholars agree that entrepreneurial opportunities exist primarily because different actors have different opinions and beliefs about the value of resources and about the potential value of these resources when converted into outputs. When the horizon of opportunities is the global market, the potential to create value enlarges. Firm internationalization can be conceived from this perspective as a process that enlarges its creative endeavour and opens new paths of growth in terms of new markets. On the other hand, selling and sourcing abroad enlarges and diversifies the knowledge base of the firm, with feed-back effects in terms of knowledge recombinations and the development of novel combinations, according to the above mentioned knowledge approach to international business.

An organization must be created by the entrepreneur in order to supply the market with the innovative product or service, which

means that a number of people or members of the team have to be coordinated, as well as other resources. Organizations can vary in terms of size, rate of growth, the industry the firm operates in, the kind of products or services commercialized, and finally the culture, attitudes and beliefs that affect the way people behave within the organization.

An International Entrepreneurial Organization (IEO) often tends to be a network of relationships between collaborators and the entrepreneur who leads them. In this sense the network includes people who formally work in the firm but also considers the individuals and organizations which are actually external to it, such as customers, suppliers and investors. These relationships may be formal or informal, driven by long-term or short-term interest or even regulated by contracts. The network provides a receptive structure open to new ideas or the need for change.

In general, International Entrepreneurial Organizations are characterized by the strong leadership of the entrepreneur and at the same time, the organization, as it is perceived through the network view, might be less bureaucratic, hierarchical and generally less formal than established counterparts, in order better to support organizational learning processes.

The bundle of resources on which the organization is built, includes, first of all, the capital which is invested in the venture, the people who contribute with their knowledge, skills and efforts, and finally physical assets such as productive machinery and equipment.

Intangible assets are particularly important for IEOs: they characterize the entrepreneurial firm as an entity able to develop a sustainable competitive advantage. Dynamic capabilities are also fundamental since the entrepreneurial firm operating in an ongoing and unpredictable economic environment develops new abilities/reconfigures existing ones, enabling it to exploit opportunities rapidly.

All these three factors are reciprocally interdependent: with the entrepreneur, organization, resources/capabilities and opportunities converging and supporting each other. These interactions are fundamental elements of the entrepreneurial process, because together they constitute the strategy adopted by the firm over time. It means that entrepreneurship has to be viewed in its dynamics.

Resources have to be configured and integrated to form the organization structure and its processes and to develop distinctive capabilities.

Capabilities are constantly adjusted to changing environments and when turbulence imposes more radical changes, they need deeper reconfigurations. In this way, entrepreneurial organizations maintain this innovative, opportunity exploring and exploiting attitude over time.

The International Entrepreneurial Organization must be proactive, and aimed at dynamically responding to future opportunities and threats in the light of experience. The use of this kind of feedback makes the International Entrepreneurial Organization a learning organization. International entrepreneurs are motivated by the search for new opportunities. A business opportunity is the chance to do something differently and better. An innovation is a way of doing something differently and better, so innovation can be seen as a means of exploiting an opportunity. All goods are regarded as being made up of three factors: natural raw materials, physical and mental labour, and capital. An innovation is a new combination of these three things (Hitt et al., 2002). As expressed by Hitt and colleagues (2002) innovative ideas are fundamental for the success of an entrepreneurial business and even if opportunities are different there are common patterns in the way opportunities can develop. Foreign market entry is an expression of innovation on the one side – as Schumpeter wrote more than 70 years ago – but on the other – according to the most recent stream of IB studies on the knowledge based perspective – it is an enlargement of the opportunities basket and it supports the recombination of the firm's knowledge base, thus feeding back new combinations.

5.1 International Entrepreneurship: the firm's capabilities and learning processes

The capabilities, which are needed for an entrepreneurial venture, result from learning. As mentioned above, IEOs are characterized by the peculiar role of learning processes: even though any firm can be considered a learning organization, IEOs are distinguished by intense, rapid learning from multiple sources. This means that, in order to be entrepreneurial and grow intensively in foreign market, they need to develop unique assets and continually to reconfigure their capabilities according to a rapidly changing and challenging environment. These processes of learning on the one hand need to be

supported by the absorptive capacity of the organization (Cohen and Levinthal, 1990) and, on the other hand, the variety of learning sources and creative endeavours approached continually originates new combinations of knowledge. The sources of learning for IEOs vary according to the experience of founders/managers, experience gained in international operations, imitation of successful strategies of similar firms (very common in local clusters where observation of other firms' moves is easier). Knowledge acquired from different sources needs to be shared and reconfigured in firm-specific resources and capabilities, characterized by uniqueness, scarce imitability and high value perceivable by global customers.

The first step in the organizational learning process is the development of new knowledge. There is no unique process to generate knowledge, however. Learning from experience is usually described as the most common way for organizations to acquire knowledge; for instance, learning from experience is often considered crucial for internationalizing firms (Johanson and Vahlne, 1977). This form of learning can involve learning from the experience of founders or congenital learning (Huber, 1991; Sinkula, 1994); learning through the individual or organization's own experience or experiential learning/experience accumulation (Huber, 1991; Zollo and Winter, 2002); and learning by bringing experienced individuals or another organization's experience into the organization through selective recruitment (grafting) (Huber, 1991). Learning from experience entails acquiring mostly tacit knowledge. That is knowledge that cannot be easily articulated since we do not know that we know it (Polanyi, 1966). Intuiting, which is defined as the preconscious recognition of a pattern and/or possibilities intrinsic to personal experience, is closely related to experiential learning, but its origins through expert intuition or entrepreneurial intuition are different to those of common experiential learning (Crossan, Lane and White, 1999).

In the Uppsala/stage model, the learning which comes about through a firm's own experience is considered critical to the internationalization process (Johanson and Vahlne, 1977). Only the acquisition of international market knowledge through experience reduces a firm's uncertainty about the internationalization process, thus allowing it to expand internationally (Johanson and Vahlne, 1977).

Internationalizing firms may use networks to support their internationalization. A firm's knowledge of business networks also seems to determine the acquisition of international market knowledge, and thus influences internationalization. For instance, the perceived usefulness of the experiential knowledge of the network was found to be another determinant of international market knowledge (Blomstermo et al., 2004; Chetty and Eriksson, 2002; Ling-yee, 2004).

Learning in the Uppsala model is said to be reactive, as opposed to proactive in international entrepreneurial firms, due to being focused on acquiring more knowledge about already identified solutions to solving internationalization problem (Forsgren, 2002; Yli-Renko, Autio and Tontti, 2002). With regard to learning by international new ventures, the main thrust of research has also been directed toward identifying antecedents of learning in this type of firms (Autio, Sapienza and Almeida 2000; Sapienza, Clercq and Sandberg, 2005; Yeoh, 2004; Yli-Renko, Autio and Tontti, 2002; Zahra, Ireland and Hitt, 2000b). International market diversity, mode of market entry, top management previous experience, entrepreneurial orientation and social capital all have a positive influence on different forms of learning in these firms. More specifically, international market diversity and a high-control mode of market entry have a positive effect on technological learning, with the relationship being stronger when firms implement knowledge integration activities (Zahra, Ireland and Hitt, 2000b). Top management's prior experience moderates the effect of international diversity on learning (Yeoh, 2004). In contrast, age at first international entry has a negative relationship with a firm's international learning effort (Sapienza, Clercq and Sandberg, 2005). Thus, the younger the firm is when it internationalizes, the more learning about internationalization occurs. Finally, a firm's entrepreneurial orientation and social capital also have a positive impact on learning about international markets (Sapienza, Clercq and Sandberg, 2005; Yli-Renko, Autio and Tontti, 2002).

The advantage is related to the fact that because of their youth when they start internationalizing, they may not yet have developed organizational routines that could hinder both this process and their learning about international market knowledge and internationalization knowledge, while older, more established firms might have (Knight and Cavusgil, 2004).

Table 5.1 Learning in traditional firms and in International Entrepreneurial organizations

	Traditional firms	International Entrepreneurial organizations
Nature of learning about international markets and internationalization	Firm's own experience, thus slow and sequential. Learning from networks but not often. Reactive	Congenital learning, learning from top management previous experience, vicarious learning, grafting, and searching, learning advantage of new firms. Learning from networks Proactive.
Antecedents of learning	Learning about the internationalization process. Psychic distance. Variation in scope of internationalization or international market diversity. Experience of domestic markets. Network relationships and mutual commitment. Social capital	International market diversity. Mode of market entry. Top management previous experience. Entrepreneurial orientation. Social capital.

Source: Personal elaboration.

Other forms of learning relevant to the internationalization process of these firms are the acquisition of experiential knowledge through hiring knowledgeable staff (grafting) (Bengtsson, 2004; Saarenketo et al., 2004), imitation of other firms that have internationalized successfully (vicarious learning), searching for international market knowledge, and congenital learning, that is, learning brought into the organization by founders (Bengtsson, 2004; Saarenketo et al., 2004) (Table 5.1).

From a comparison between learning processes outlined in organizational learning literature, it can be concluded that, in general, organizational learning involves four general processes, or steps, that have to be followed for an organization to learn (Crossan, Lane and

White, 1999; Huber, 1991, Zollo and Winter, 2002). First, organizations generate or acquire knowledge through distinct knowledge-creation processes (learning from experience, from imitation, searching, congenitally and grafting). Second, in order for the learning process to continue, the members of an organization have to interpret and understand newly acquired knowledge. Third, the already interpreted knowledge has to be shared or distributed and integrated through the organization. Finally, once the new knowledge is distributed, it has to be stored in the organization's memory, or institutionalized, so that others can use it when they require it (Crossan, Lane and White, 1999, Huber, 1991, Zollo and Winter, 2002). In this way, routines are changed and new routines are created, capabilities are improved and renewed.

5.2 Typologies of International Entrepreneurial organizations

Two main streams have emerged in International Entrepreneurship literature (McDougall and Oviatt, 2000), as mentioned in the first chapter. One stream focuses on international new ventures: start-ups that are international from inception. The other stream looks at the internationalization of established firms.

5.2.1 International New Ventures and Born-Globals

The object of this paragraph is to describe the dynamic and newly established small firm, which becomes international at inception or a very short time after foundation. The growing importance of this new phenomenon seems to challenge most of the already established theories on internationalization, and in particular the process stages theories of the Uppsala School and the Innovation-related export-developing models. These theories that consider internationalization as a process of gradual commitment, including a progressive number of stages in a relatively long period of time, have been challenged. Some advocates of accelerated International Entrepreneurship, have in fact identified an increasing number of firms that were rapidly present abroad after their birth, instead of following the traditional path which presupposes domestic expansion before foreign export activities in psychically and geographically close markets. The existence of this typology of firms has been verified by empirical studies, in both low- and high-tech industries and the geographical localization has also been heterogeneous.

Although many researchers have shown great interest in the matter and despite the relatively long period of analysis, the types of small firms that become international at their inception have been labelled in very different ways in articles published over the years, with the consequence that any approach to the field is generally confusing. Labels such as 'Global start-ups', 'High Technology Start-ups' or 'Instant Internationals' have been used to identify these firms, but the two most popular names have been 'Born-Globals' and 'International New Ventures'.

In 1993, McKinsey and Rennie introduced the concept 'Born-Global'. On the basis of studies about Australian exporters, they described a Born-Global as a firm that, from its inception, views the world as its market. Knight (1994) also stated that these firms are typically young and reach an export sales level of at least 25 per cent within three years. Knight then suggested that the international activities are the result of the proactive behaviour of the company and not merely the result of an unsolicited order from abroad.

The second most acknowledged label was introduced in 1994 by Oviatt and McDougall, and defined the International New Venture as 'a firm that from its inception seeks to derive a significant competitive advantage from the combination of resources and sale of outputs in multiple countries. The distinguishing feature of these start-ups is that their origins are international, as demonstrated by observable and significant commitments of resources in more than one nation'. According to Oviatt and McDougall (1994), to determine whether a new venture will be an International New Venture, researchers should determine if there is a demonstrated resource commitment to sell the output in multiple countries during the start-up phase. Furthermore, they distinguished between different types of International New Venture based on two dimensions: the number of countries in which the firm is active and the number of activities along the value chain that are coordinated internationally (Figure 5.2).

The 'international market makers' are firms that are mainly involved in export or import activities either focusing on few countries ('export/import start-up') or serving a large number of countries ('multinational traders'), while the 'geographically focused start-ups' are firms that serve the specialized needs of a region by using foreign resources and by combining multiple value chain activities. The

		New international market makers	
COORDINATION OF VALUE CHAIN ACTIVITIES ACROSS COUNTRIES	FEW	Export/Import start-up	Multinational trader
	MANY	Geographically focused start-up	Global start-up
		NUMBER OF COUNTRIES INVOLVED	

Figure 5.2   Types of International New Venture

Source: B. M. Oviatt and P. P. McDougall, 'Toward a theory of international new ventures', *Journal of International Business Studies*, 25(1), 1994.

'global start-up', finally, is the best example of the International New Venture because it gains a competitive advantage by controlling a large number of organizational activities in an unlimited number of geographical locations. These firms behave proactively: in fact they do not only respond to the globalization of the market, but they acquire resources and sell outputs wherever in the world they have the greatest value.

Besides the concepts discussed above, a large number of studies were published in which similar or related phenomena were discussed. In all cases, attention has been obviously directed to the analysis of small entrepreneurial firms that are internationally oriented from their first years of establishment, and which generally accepted theories of international business are unable to explain regarding either their existence and behaviour.

All of this, however, seems to lack congruency in literature as to what concerns the object of the study when empirical studies are carried out. Indeed the temporal gap between the foundation and the moment of first international sales is a general and largely adopted principle through which International New Ventures or Born-Globals are identified, but it is, at the same time, a source of controversy. While some researchers such as Oviatt and McDougall refer to a period of six years as a standard gap in initiating international operations from the start-up of a business, other authors have adopted different criteria. Knight and Cavusgil (1995) but also Servais and

Rasmussen (2000) define Born-Globals as 'firms that were established after 1976 and have reached a share of foreign sales of at least 25per-cent after having started export activities within three years after their birth', while Rennie (1993) considered Born-Globals to be firms that begin to export only after two years' foundation and reach 75 per cent of their revenues from exports.

The same variety exists relative to the criteria applied to identify an international new venture or Born-Global when trying to recognize their sources of competitive advantage. Though the general objective of most of the studies has been to understand the reasons of the emergence of this phenomenon and the distinctive characteristics of these kinds of firms acting abroad, some authors differentiated their analysis, choosing more specific research objectives. For example, Madsen and Servais (1997) developed a model where the characteristics of the environment, of the organization and of the founder are considered fundamental, while Coviello and Munro in 1995 adopted a network theory perspective to examine the role played by network relationships, together with the role played by the founder for international market development and marketing-related activities among entrepreneurial firms. Furthermore, Knight and Cavusgil (1995) highlighted the crucial role of knowledge-based resources such as innovativeness and organizational capabilities for the international business performance of entrepreneurial firms.

Lastly, it is worthwhile to remember that a significant part of the International New Venture and Born-Global literature, especially in the first years of establishment, has been assumed to apply largely to high-tech business, since the effects of globalization were easily detected in these sectors. Nonetheless, some researchers have shown that it is not limited to such sectors. Indeed, they have shown that the phenomenon also occurs in sectors such as the wine or footwear industries. Consistent with this view, Zucchella (2001) maintains that 'the "high-tech bias" may lead research to indicate the industry/product as a qualifying feature of born-global firms, while it is only one of their possible attributes'.

Summing up, International New Ventures or Born-Globals are start-up companies or newly established companies that start to internationalize in their first years of existence. According to this view, they are juxtaposed with the international stages theory that views the internationalization process as a gradual and sequential

one: the firm first gains experience and knowledge in the domestic market and only later, by means of exportation, reaches culturally and geographically closer countries. This experiential learning, which is at the base of the stages model, is criticized by advocates of the born-global, international new ventures phenomenon. Such firms, because of their size and age have generally few, but unique resources or capabilities, and in order to exploit them, they adopt a global strategy that enables them to reach a profitable number of customers by a horizontal segmentation of the market. Among these key resources, it is possible to identify founders with either a strong international vision and/or previous international experience and social network. In this way it is possible to reconcile the born-global phenomenon with the experiential learning construct as the foundations of the sequential model of internationalization.

Madsen and Servais (1997), attribute the rise of Born-Globals to three factors: new market conditions (the emerging of niche markets), technological developments in the areas of production, transportation and communication, and international experience through work and education. Moen and Servais (2002) argue that Born-Global firms are characterized by a management with international orientation. They also see differences in the environmental situation, where Born-Globals have a more attractive export market but a less attractive home market than traditional firms have.

Born-Globals often have better competitive advantages in the area of technology. McDougall, Oviatt and Shrader (2003) came to the conclusion that managers in Born-Globals have comprehensive international and industry experience, and that Born-Globals place more emphasis on innovative differentiation, quality and service than traditional firms do. Rialp-Criado et al. (2005) made a literature review on the most common characteristics of Born-Globals. A global vision, international experience, management commitment, personal and business network and market knowledge, unique asset base, value creation through product differentiation, niche markets, narrowly defined customers groups and flexibility are important characteristics of Born-Globals.

They seem to be pushed into globalization by global customers and tiny national/regional market segments. They can sustain their immediate global scope thanks to their entrepreneurial vision and competencies, and the deep awareness that their competitive

advantage in foreign markets and the uniqueness of their assets also rest upon the knowledge-augmenting opportunities inherent in foreign markets and customers. Development drivers of born global firms in the last decade are far from being completely explored: together with 'environmental' factors, such as world market globalization, industry- and business-specific factors, according to the taxonomy presented in the first chapter are also important.

The theory of Born-Globals has its origin in Entrepreneurship theory, where the internationalization process of born global firms is considered to be initiated by the entrepreneur (Autio, Sapienza and Almeida, 2000) with an innovative, proactive and risk-taking approach (McDougall and Oviatt, 2000). This process can also be the result of mental models possessed by the Top Management Team, especially in corporate ventures. Harverston, Kedia and Davis (2000) have focused on the founders and the managers showing that managers in Born-Globals have, to a great extent, experience of international settings, international contacts and a more positive attitude toward internationalization, which influences the firm's possibilities of success in the international market. Coviello and Munro (1995) have shown the importance of networks as drivers of small-firm internationalization and as an important factor during foreign market selection, selection of mode of entry, product development and market diversification activities. Moreover, the firm's local environment and its geographical location influence the internationalization process of Born-Globals. Studies conducted in Italy (Maccarini, Scabini and Zucchella, 2003), in Portugal (Sopas, 2001) and New Zealand (Brown and Bell, 2001) show that a growing interest is increased in local clusters, where firms within a specific industry are situated in a geographic region or an industrial district. More recently some authors have posed the question of the persistence of an entrepreneurial orientation of born-global firms over time, suggesting the study of the different stages these firms go through in their life (Gabrielsson et al., 2006).

5.2.2 Corporate entrepreneurship and subsidiaries' international activities

International entrepreneurial activities are certainly not the exclusive domain of small–medium sized companies and of the entrepreneurs who founded them. In response to competitive and performance

problems many corporations have implemented changes in order to restructure and become more entrepreneurial. Corporate entrepreneurship has been defined as a 'process whereby an individual or a group of individuals, in association with an existing organization, create a new organization or instigate renewal or innovation within that organization' (Sharma and Chrisman, 1999). On this basis the literature suggests two different approaches: focused corporate entrepreneurship and dispersed corporate entrepreneurship, also called 'intrapreneurship'.

The first typology identifies a new division whose task is to identify and develop new business opportunities for the company. The characteristics of this division are autonomy, a small structure and strong internal integration together with high availability of financial resources and permanent support from the management.

Dispersed corporate entrepreneurship is based on the idea that every employee in the enterprise has the potential for entrepreneurial activities. In order to reach this objective, entrepreneurial groups are formed leaving others to normal managerial tasks. The development of widespread entrepreneurial culture within the company, as the basis for any initiative, is pursued. The challenge for corporate management is to instil the personal involvement and commitment in its employees that drives entrepreneurship (Bartlett and Ghoshal, 1994).

The pursuit of entrepreneurial activities in large multinational corporations (MNE) can take place inside the firm, involving the organizational structure, developing certain capabilities or social characteristics; or outside it, shaping new organizational boundaries and involving activities such as international cooperation, strategic alliances or acquisitions. Large firms are increasingly seeking the benefits of entrepreneurial activities, in particular concerning international markets by means of subsidiary initiatives. According to Birkinshaw (1997), the latter are proactive operations, carried out by operational units controlled by the MNE, and situated outside the home country, that advance a new way for the company to better use or find new resources and opportunities. From the perspective of a MNE subsidiary, market opportunities and resources are conceived within its national market.

In MNEs the proactive role of subsidiaries has been progressively subject to attention, from the seminal work of Hedlund (1980, 1986)

on heterarchical international organizations as opposed to the traditional hierarchical ones. The traditional role of the subsidiary refers to the adaptation of the product to local markets and becomes a sort of centre able to recognize changes in demand and to signal this information to head office. Recent research recognized that subsidiaries also have unique capabilities of their own and, most importantly, they develop critical relationships with local customers and suppliers. The local context with its environmental dynamism and complexity, political conditions, economic rules, laws, and sociocultural influences reaches managers sensitive to the opportunities that exist in their environment, influencing an entrepreneurial culture within subsidiaries. The subsidiaries' capabilities concern the ability to pursue local opportunities and the possibility to exploit them, not only in cooperation with the parent company, but autonomously. Entrepreneurial subsidiaries expand their operations, set goals and strategic positions diversely from their parent companies, and develop their own organizational culture. The development of entrepreneurial capabilities at the MNE's subsidiaries level can be connected to the need of international firms to respond to local customers.

International management literature has extensively considered the issue of eventual trade offs between local needs orientation and global management of activities. Levitt (1983) argued that companies that compete on a national basis are highly vulnerable to companies that compete on a global basis. This assumption is grounded on the idea that customer preferences tend to standardize globally, due to growing interconnection and interdependence among local systems. In such a framework, global players serving standardized global needs have a competitive advantage thanks to economies of scale exploitation (Levitt, 1983) and to a number of other beneficial effects, such as economies of replication, economies from international production and economies of learning (Baden Fuller and Stopford, 1991; Yip, 2003). The evolution that has occurred in the last two decades reveals that Levitt's assumption has no general validity: national and local differences in customer needs continue to exert a strong influence in a number of markets and contemporarily, the costs of local customer adaptation can be low, when basic design and key components remain common on a world or regional basis.

The growing flexibility in manufacturing technologies and productive organization coupled with parallel flexibility in designing organizational boundaries and developing networks of alliances with complementary firms, enabled businesses to exploit the benefits of global sourcing and of the integration of some activities while pursuing local responsiveness. The strong need of local responsiveness could be one of the drivers of MNEs subsidiaries' entrepreneurial behaviour and enables them to proactively influence local industry conditions. This local responsiveness pursued by local subsidiaries can be addressed either by adopting/adapting the parental strategy or implementing an entrepreneurial action.

A body of research has progressively emerged which consider the subsidiary as the unit of analysis (Birkinshaw and Morrison, 1995; Delany and Molloy, 1998; Griffin, 2003; Young, 2004). This literature addresses research on subsidiary initiatives and mandate expansion (Birkinshaw and Morrison, 1995; Delany and Molloy, 1998; Taggart, 1996; White and Poynter, 1984), appropriate parenting styles (Campbell and Goold, 1987) and corporate entrepreneurship (Birkinshaw and Morrison, 1995). Consistent with this issue, the role of subsidiary management as actors developing and implementing strategies to expand and sustain their subsidiary in the environment has been emphasized (Birkinshaw, 1997; Griffin, 2003; Molloy, 1992; Taggart, 1996).

A number of contributions suggest that leveraging on entrepreneurial subsidiaries' activities can have a positive effect in determining the parental success of multinational corporations (Zahra, Dharwadkar R. and George, 2000a). The question about how the subsidiary evolves and implements its strategy has been the subject of a significant amount of theoretical and empirical work (Birkinshaw and Morrison, 1995; Delany and Molloy, 1998; White and Poynter, 1984; Young, Hood and Hamill, 1988).

Consequent to these studies, some researchers have started to examine the responses of subsidiaries when subject to strategic challenges (Anagnostaki and Louri, 1995; Benito, 1997; Griffin, 2003). When threatened, subsidiaries have the capability to respond entrepreneurially, by pursuing proactive actions and introducing innovation in the markets: these are two of the dimensions commonly used to identify entrepreneurial behaviour.

Proactiveness denotes the commitment of individuals to initiate changes in the industry, rather than to react to competition (Lumpkin and Dess, 1996; Miller, 1983). Innovativeness concerns the creation, development and introduction of new ideas, products, systems, processes and organizational forms (Guth and Ginsberg, 1990; Schumpeter, 1950). Birkinshaw (2000) in his consideration of subsidiary entrepreneurship, draws on the works of Schumpeter (1934) and Kirzner (1973) and focuses on the entrepreneur as an agent of market change and applies that concept to the internal market of the MNE.

Despite this potential concerning entrepreneurial intensity among MNE subsidiaries, few studies have examined the sources of these peculiarities from the international perspective, considering the implications of the corporate context and the local market environment for a subsidiary's entrepreneurship. Zahra, Dharwadkar and George (2000a) analysed the main variables influencing subsidiary entrepreneurship dividing the corporate context and the local environment context as shown in Figure 5.3.

As for the corporate context of a subsidiary, it is considered to be influenced by its 'mandate' and by the controls the parent company has over the subsidiary's activity.

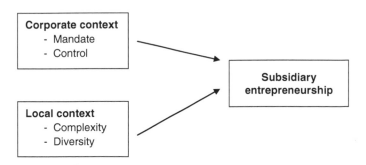

Figure 5.3 Factors affecting subsidiary entrepreneurship

Source: Adapted from S. Zahra, R. Dharwadkar and G. George, *Entrepreneurship in Multinational Subsidiaries: The Effects of Corporate and Local Environment Contexts*, 2000). Available at: http:www.gatech.eduworkingpaper199999_00-27.pdf 2000.

Global subsidiary mandate. The mandate, which influences a subsidiary's sphere of action, determines roles and objectives but also the scope of a subsidiary's operation. It generally reflects the parent goals, but also the subsidiary's resources and skills and the interactions between them. A global mandate means that the subsidiary plays a dominant role in making decisions about the products to be manufactured and the markets to be covered (Roth and Morrison, 1997). Although the MNE seems to reduce its importance, it is still present, checking and evaluating the subsidiary's performance and ensuring that the activities are consistent with the MNE's overall objectives. The subsidiary remains an integral part of the MNE's network while the Headquarter (HQ) continues to provide the resources that the subsidiary needs (Bartlett and Ghoshal, 1986). This typology of mandate enhances the subsidiary's entrepreneurship: the localization of the most relevant value-chain activities in different geographic places in the world facilitates exposition of multiple resources, basically concerning local knowledge, which allows reduction of costs and the generation of innovativeness. Moreover, the continuous contacts that the Global Subsidiary Mandate allows with customers, suppliers and counterparts permit the development of different, and more suitable, solutions and more effective systems of management. Finally, a Global Subsidiary Mandate increases entrepreneurship because the subsidiary produces and sells its own products, with the result that planning, design and manufacturing experimentation increases.

Autonomy. The necessity of giving more autonomy to the subsidiaries has increasingly gained importance. The role subsidiaries play in today's MNEs has undergone several changes in recent years and the most relevant is the fact that from a passive role with the parent, subsidiaries now develop and implement strategic initiatives that are viewed as equally important by local managers. They are, in fact, closer to their local markets and are frequently better informed about market needs. The freedom to act independently from HQ has enabled subsidiary managers to pursue innovative activities they consider important for the international success of the MNEs. It has been suggested that this autonomy is relevant because of its motivating role: managers can feel a sense of empowerment that translates into a greater willingness to explore, support and pursue

innovative and risky projects (Birkinshaw, 1999) and in general permits them to behave as real entrepreneurs; allocating resources to new business opportunities without involving the parent company.

Strategic and financial controls.   MNEs' headquarters cannot give complete freedom to the subsidiary, because it has to balance this autonomy with the corporate need for integration and coordination. Indeed duplication of activities and a need for better coordination are the main problems with autonomy. For these reasons, MNEs need to control, monitor and evaluate the performance of their subsidiaries. The control systems can influence a subsidiary's future entrepreneurship. Control systems can be either strategic or financial. Strategic controls involve qualitative assessments of the subsidiary's performance based on its objectives and competitive environment, while on the other hand, financial controls usually focus on documentable and quantifiable outcomes and evaluate the progress the subsidiary makes in reaching previous established goals. When strategic controls prevail, managers are more inclined to support risky ventures whose outcomes are uncertain; while when financial controls compel managers to achieve short-term goals, they are less likely to take risks or support projects whose outcomes cannot be guaranteed of success. In this sense, the authors suggest that the use of financial controls is negatively associated with a subsidiary's improvement of entrepreneurial activities.

The second group of variables influencing a subsidiary's strategic choice deals with the local environmental context. The characteristics of host countries and local market conditions are considered to significantly influence the level of subsidiary entrepreneurship. According to the three researchers, firms that compete in turbulent environments are more likely to be entrepreneurial than firms in stable environments. As shown in Figure 5.3 environmental turbulence is characterized by the dynamism, hostility, and complexity of the subsidiary's local environment.

Environmental dynamism.   This considers the technological or market shifts that change the subsidiary's environment. Competing in a dynamic environment generates a sort of pressure which causes the subsidiaries to improve their technological assets, to revise product characteristics and to build new capabilities. Proactiveness and

innovative attitude are entrepreneurial skills that the subsidiary has to develop in order to have success abroad. As managers perceive higher levels of dynamism in their environment, the subsidiary's entrepreneurship will intensify.

Environmental hostility. Dynamic competition also means the presence of rivals and when they make unfavourable market changes, the subsidiary has to react, trying to search ways to reduce the overall negative effect of these new conditions. This typology of hostility is considered positive in association with a subsidiary's entrepreneurship, because it is forced to experiment with new forms of management, to set up new projects and to discover new solutions in order to satisfy eventual new customer needs. In general they have to turn to their unique resources and capabilities, but also to their quickness and creativity.

Environmental complexity. 'If the local environment is viewed as complex, then the subsidiary is expected to become more proactive in its operations and supportive of entrepreneurial risk taking' (Morris, 1998). Furthermore, the complexity of today's global business environment, as a catalyst for innovation and risk taking, has been a major reason for the growing emphasis on entrepreneurship among MNEs. Increased environmental complexity is associated with higher levels of entrepreneurial activity.

5.2.3   The pursuit of an integrated model of IE for different IEOs

Although International Entrepreneurship researchers have mainly focused on two categories of firms (Born-Globals and MNE subsidiaries), there are also other entities, which have received less attention, but might also be considered as relevant expressions of the phenomenon.

Important proof of the existence of other international entrepreneurial entities is given by some companies, especially small-medium firms that show typical entrepreneurial characteristics, but they are neither Born-Globals because they do not develop international activities from their foundation, nor subsidiaries because they are not linked to any Multinational enterprise. In 2001, Jim Bell and his colleagues defined a group of firms that might be a subject of International Entrepreneurship: the 'Born-Again Global' firms: 'These

are firms that have been well established in their domestic markets, with apparently no great motivation to internationalize, but which have suddenly embraced rapid and dedicated internationalization'. These firms seem not to have a precise collocation within International Entrepreneurial models, but nevertheless they demonstrate a proactive behaviour, they own knowledge-based resources and show a receptive attitude to international opportunities, which are all common characteristics of the two other typologies of international entrepreneurial firms. In order to overcome the obstacles related to the existence of many subjects of study, Jones and Coviello (2005) developed a recent model where entrepreneurial internationalization behaviour is described as it might be experienced by any firm, in any industry, in different situations.

This general model considers many variables affecting internationalization concerning the dimensions of time and behaviour. The most relevant variables regard entrepreneurial and firm factors, but also environmental and performance factors. The model depicts a 'process of cyclical behaviour' where the entrepreneur and the firm are the main actors, but where environmental changes may affect international behaviour as well as performance factors which operate as feedback. According to the authors, internationalization of any entrepreneurial typology of firm occurs as 'value-creating events', consisting of cross-border business activities between the firm and organizations or individuals in foreign countries.

Despite INVs studies having been at the centre of International Entrepreneurship, recent studies point to the need of expanding its boundaries to previously established firms. The motivations for, and effects of, internationalization for these companies have been explored from economic and organizational perspectives, but they have been less frequently viewed from the point of view of entrepreneurship. This perspective is essential considering the turbulence of the current international business environment that emphasizes the importance of entrepreneurship in both established and large firms.

Thus the study of internationalization of established firms (both large and small and medium-sized) from an entrepreneurial perspective is now an important issue that defines the research agenda in entrepreneurship, international business and strategic management studies (Meyer, Neck, H. N. and Meeks, 2003). Zahra and Garvis (2000)

show empirical evidence, from a sample of large and established internationalized companies, about the positive influence of entrepreneurial orientation on higher profits and growth (including export growth) in international environments with higher levels of hostility. In established organizations key entrepreneurial capabilities, that is, proactiveness, risk-taking and innovativeness, can be found equally at both the personal (entrepreneur, management team) and at the organizational level.

5.3 Alternative models of International Entrepreneurship

Past research shows a need to develop an integrative framework that can serve as a foundation for future theory building and empirical analysis about International Entrepreneurship. In this paragraph two distinct models are presented: that of Zahra and George (2002) and Jones and Coviello (2005). These models, representative of status in the field of International Entrepreneurship, can be considered as also representative of the recent debate on the subject. Here we want to present two different alternative models that approach International Entrepreneurship without exhaustive reviewing of modelling literature in this area. Zahra and George (2002) present a model in which three factors influence International Entrepreneurship: organizational, environmental and strategic (Figure 5.4).

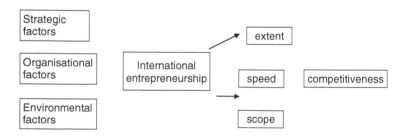

Figure 5.4 An integrated model of International Entrepreneurship
Source: Adaptation based on S. A. Zahra and G. George (2002).

The authors consider organizational factors referring to the TMT, firm resources, and firm-related variables (such as age, size, financial strength, location, and origin). Strategic and environmental factors are considered potential moderators of the relationship between organizational factors and International Entrepreneurship dimensions. As they indicate, the strategic management literature suggests that a firm's general and task environments significantly influence the motivation or the rate of internationalization (Hitt, Hoskisson and Kim, 1997). Companies with specific competences, that is, in production, can transfer these capabilities to international markets, gaining advantages from their international expansion. The difference between the domestic market and the emerging opportunities are considered 'differentials' or 'proximity'. They consider differentials also in national culture, customer profiles and habits among others.

Environmental factors are referred to competitive forces (number of competitors, bargaining power, etc.), growth opportunities (rate of market growth, countries with open markets, etc.), regulatory environment, industry profitability, institutional environment, and economies of scale. In their model these factors operate as moderators determining the strength of the relationship between organizational variables and International Entrepreneurship dimensions. International Entrepreneurship is studied in three dimensions: extent, speed and scope. Extent is considered as the dependence of the firm on international revenues or the number of new markets that a firm enters. Speed measures the rate at which the firm enters new markets. Scope evaluates the breadth of the internationalization process. It regards geographic scope if regions are the unit of analysis, or economic or product scope, if breadth of the product mix are considered. Outcomes from International Entrepreneurship are represented by financial and non-financial performance indicators.

In Jones and Coviello's model (2005), as stated earlier, entrepreneurial internationalization behaviour is depicted in a highly variable context, as it might be experienced by any firm, in any industry, in any situation. This general model considers many variables affecting internationalization concerning the dimensions of time and behaviour. The most relevant variables regard entrepreneurial and firm factors, but also environmental and performance factors. The model [see Figure 5.5] depicts a 'process of cyclical behaviour', where the entrepreneur and the firm are the main actors, but environmental

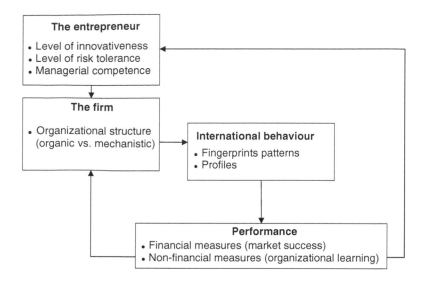

Figure 5.5 Model for empirical examination

Source: M. Jones and N. E. Coviello, 'Internationalization: Conceptualising an entrepreneurial process of behaviour in time', *Journal of International Business Studies*, 36, 2005.

changes may affect international behaviour as well as performance factors which operate as feedback.

According to Jones and Coviello, internationalization of any entrepreneurial typology of firm occurs as 'value-creating events', consisting of cross-border business activities between the firm and organizations or individuals in foreign countries. Jones and Coviello's model refers to 'fingerprint patterns' and to 'profiles' defined as a 'composite of the number and range of cross-border business modes established by the firm, and the number and distance of countries with which those modes were established, at a specific point in time. Changes in the composition are described as dynamic profiles' (2005, p. 293). Different 'fingerprints' together with the entrepreneur's particularity and especially the firm's non-financial measures may be seen as elements to indicate differences between firms. Finally, according to this model, entrepreneurial international behaviour, seen as a form of innovation, may occur or cease at any time, leading to several international decisions, processes and activities and

allowing the possibility of every company that shows typical entrepreneurial aspects in an international environment to be considered
as a suitable firm for International Entrepreneurship models.

5.4   A resources and capabilities-based model

Innovation is considered by many scholars and managers to be
critical for firms to compete effectively in domestic and global markets (Hitt, Keats and DeMarie, 1998; Ireland and Hitt, 2000). There is
a strong inter-relationship between innovation, internationalization
and entrepreneurship. Drucker (1985), for example, suggests that
innovation is the primary activity of entrepreneurship. Lumpkin
and Dess (1996) argue that a key dimension of entrepreneurial
orientation is an emphasis on innovation. Thus, an entrepreneurial
mindset is required for the founding of new businesses as well as the
rejuvenation of existing ones (McGrath and Macmillan, 2000). From
the pioneering work of Schumpeter (1934) up to the recent surge of
studies on entrepreneurship, one of the expressions of entrepreneurship has been recognized as the decision of foreign market entry.
Therefore, we may conclude that an important value-creating
entrepreneurial strategy is to search for new market (internationalization) and to invent new goods and services and commercialize them
(innovation) (Ireland et al., 2001). This contribution aims in
particular at highlighting the relevance of a dynamic capabilities
approach for a better understanding of entrepreneurial activities and
their international growth. The reason for this choice is rooted in the
research question underlying this work: what are the resources and
capabilities at the individual and organizational level that support
International Entrepreneurship?

In applying the dynamic capabilities framework to International
Entrepreneurship, the level of analysis should be represented by entrepreneurial international businesses. This means that the level of analysis is the international venture as it is shaped, organized and managed
by the entrepreneurial effort, vision and competences. The dynamic
capability approach could prove useful in the perspective on
International Entrepreneurship, in order to explain the creation and
improvement of entrepreneurial activities, competencies and capabilities. Entrepreneurship and Dynamic capabilities are strictly interrelated
since reconfiguring capabilities is a core entrepreneurial-intrapreneurial

activity. Dynamic capabilities are defined as higher order competences and this means that they have an entrepreneurial nature.

Innovation, reconfiguration/transformation, learning and path dependence in order to better perform in the marketplace are common issues of the two theoretical frameworks. In order to capture the entrepreneurial behaviour of the firm and to analyse which are the resources and capabilities in entrepreneurial international ventures, some assumptions are needed.

Entrepreneurial behaviour is studied through the attributes described by Covin and Slevin (1991). Proactiveness, innovativeness and risk-seeking behaviour are analysed to individuate entrepreneurial firms. Following the Jones and Coviello approach (2005), like entrepreneurial behaviour, internationalization behaviour is also overt and demonstrable and manifest in a recognizable way. The most widely used measures include entry-modes, the countries of involvement and time-related dimensions.

As mentioned above, entrepreneurial capabilities match the entrepreneur's capacity to take initiative within the organization and to take action in the environment, as well as depending on prior personal knowledge with the firm's learning and path dependence. This is particularly true in individual enterprises and SMEs where entrepreneurs and top management coincide and it is difficult to separate the personal and individual competences from the organizational ones.

As Figure 5.6 shows the International Entrepreneurship process first involves International Opportunity Scanning and Evaluation. Central to this process is the entrepreneur and/or the TMT. Once opportunities in the overall market-place are identified and evaluated, the entrepreneur/TMT mobilize resources in order to develop new combinations for the market. The resources mobilization could be realized by external acquisition or by internal development. The latter refers both to the internal development of non-existent or latent resources, and to the combination of resources used for different purposes. The ability to integrate and to reconfigure internal and external resources and competencies leads firms to develop dynamic capabilities. The ability to reconfigure activities to the changing environments is a topical issue in the Entrepreneurship agenda. International Entrepreneurship is the combination of entrepreneurial, opportunity-seeking and strategic

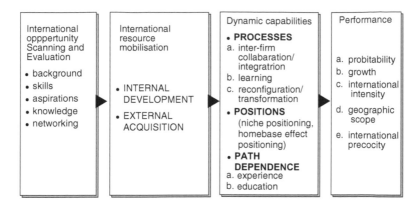

Figure 5.6 An interpretative model for International Entrepreneurial organizations

Source: Personal elaboration.

advantage-seeking actions towards business concepts that gives superior value creation and at the same time reduction of competitive threats (Hitt et al., 2001).

Focusing on entrepreneurship permits consideration of the process and the behaviour by which firms gain competitive advantages on the market. Entrepreneurial firms continue to perform due to the inability of other firms to imitate the advantages of these firms. The ability to sustain this entrepreneurial behaviour, through innovation, risk-taking and proactiveness, permits firms to compete in the market. Finally, dynamic capabilities enable the firm to perform in terms of profitability, growth, export intensity, geographic scope and international precocity.

5.5   International opportunity scanning and evaluation

This process involves the entrepreneur or the TMT, who are – according to literature on Entrepreneurship – the individuals that identify new opportunities and convert them into marketable products and services. This involves the process of discovery, evaluation and exploitation of opportunities as well as the set of individuals who

take place in this process (Venkataraman, 1997). Covin and Slevin in their behavioural model of entrepreneurship, focusing on the firm level rather than on the individual entrepreneur, note that 'individual level behaviour on the part of the entrepreneur may affect organization's actions, and in many cases, the two will be synonymous' (1991, p. 8). Moreover Madsen and Servais (1997) argue that the entrepreneur is the key antecedent in Born-Global firms. Similar conclusions have been drawn by Ibeh (2003).

The process of discovery and evaluation of opportunities involves background, skills, aspirations and knowledge in terms of learning experience, as well as personal networking. The ability of the individual to receive and interpret information, in the face of environmental turbulence and uncertainty, is central to entrepreneurial behaviour that is described as being active, proactive and aggressive in pursuing opportunities in overseas markets (Obrecht, 2004). According to Johanson and Vahlne (1977), experiential knowledge is a critical determinant factor of active involvement in international markets because it provides the framework for perceiving and formulating opportunities. Moreover networks and social networks can provide firms with access to information (Granovetter, 1985; Gulati, Nohria and Zaheer 2000). In Figure 5.1 we identified as starting point the existence of international creative endeavours: an international vision and the pursue of international operations expose the firm to multiple and diverse sets of opportunities across different countries. The absorption capacity at the individual and organizational level on the one side and the ability to evaluate and select these opportunities on the other constitute the first step in the entrepreneurial process.

5.6 International resource mobilization

Firms build resource positions either acquiring kinds and combinations of external resources, or developing firm specific resources internally or partnering with other firms for joint development and sharing.

External acquisition involves the sourcing of resources and capabilities in order to introduce new products, services and ideas in the market. Provision from suppliers, from networks and joint ventures are the main external acquisitions considered. The relevance of the issue of international sourcing as an expression of entrepreneurship

has been recently outlined in the work of Servais, Zucchella, Maccarini and Palamara (2005).

Internal Development may refer, for example, to investments in R&D and the consequent patenting of innovation, but also the provision of training courses for managers, employees and workers. The latter enables firms to develop new skills and capabilities. For the entrepreneur/TMT, training courses or meetings are particularly important because they allow them to expand their vision and entrepreneurial orientation, in terms of alertness, discovering, scanning and evaluating new opportunities as well as reconfiguring and coordinating resources and competences.

5.7 Dynamic capabilities

As mentioned in Chapter 4, dynamic capabilities are considered as the ability to integrate, build, and reconfigure internal and external competencies to address rapidly changing environments (Teece, Pisano and Shuen, 1997). Accordingly, the competitive advantage of the firm depends on its managerial processes, its position and its path dependence. In this entrepreneurial approach to the dynamic capabilities model, entrepreneurial behaviour is crucial, because: (a) it permits coordination and integration of internal and external activities, resources and technologies; (b) it permits the shaping of learning processes within the firm; and (c) it permits the reconfiguration of the firm's asset structure in terms of market, product portfolio, and/or internal processes.

5.7.1 Processes

International Entrepreneurship focuses on risk taking, proactiveness and innovativeness in the global marketplace. The theoretical framework presented establishes a connection between entrepreneurial behaviour and dynamic capabilities, especially in terms of managerial processes. Risk taking, proactiveness and innovativeness are drivers capable of explaining (a) reconfiguration, especially in the case of innovation (Christensen, 1999; Schumpeter, 1934); (b) networking because each business network necessarily involves risks and an intense engagement of each node (Brown and Duguid, 2002); and (c) learning because it is often a synonym of inclination to rethink competences and skills.

The coordination/integration process is here referred to both from the external (inter-firm network) and the internal perspective. The former refers to the need to coordinate and to integrate external processes with other firms in the network or group (in the case of subsidiaries) while the latter refers to the ability to coordinate, develop and integrate internal processes in order to perform more efficiently/effectively or to realize new products, services and offers in the markets.

In SMEs these entrepreneurial capabilities referring to the action and learning of the organization are not difficult to individuate but they are difficult to isolate from individuals, especially if referred to the entrepreneur. In large or established companies, these dynamic entrepreneurial capabilities could be referring to routines and processes combined and managed by individuals and groups within the firm. Since dynamic capabilities refer to the organizational and strategic routines by which firms achieve new resource configurations as markets emerge, collide, split, evolve, and die (Eisenhardt and Martin, 2000, p. 1107), they can be seen to derive from organizational learning.

5.7.2   Position: location factors

According to Teece, Pisano, Shuen (1997), positions are considered as specific assets that determine the firm's competitive advantage at any point of time. In this work, business-specific factors such as niche orientation and location-specific factors are considered as two leading measures of position for international firms. Traditional measures of positioning (i.e., reputational and financial ones) do not fit well with IEOs, which are frequently new firms or subsidiaries of larger units.

Niche orientation expresses an entrepreneurial attitude in terms of creative global market micro-segmentation deriving from opportunity scanning and evaluation at a global scale, carried out by small and also infant firms to quickly gain a significant international market share. A deep niche positioning drives high levels of export intensity and early and fast international growth. Location-specific issues, notably location in a densely knit cluster of similar/complementary businesses, are the second driver of early and fast international growth. In this case, IEOs benefit from location advantages and part of their international entrepreneurial effort is the result of a collective learning and strategizing at the cluster level.

Traditionally, International Business literature, and in particular the theories explaining the internationalization of firms, have focused their attention on a set of issues, amongst which location-specific factors can be found. The eclectic paradigm (Dunning, 1981) includes location advantages in a general theoretical framework, together with ownership and internalization ones. With Porter's (1990) contribution, the home country location advantage gained further evidence in firm Internationalization studies. Such a perspective suggests that the home location has an effect on international competitive positioning and performance, and on internationalization processes and their outcome accordingly. Later on, a growing number of studies focused their attention on the role of smaller sub-national territories on the competitiveness and internationalization of firms.

Focus on the local-regional scale has two drivers: on the one side it reflects the idea that the competitive advantage of the firm does not depend solely on internal assets but also on positive externalities, a subject already long explored by regional and geographic economy studies. The second one refers to a progressive geographical clustering of economic activities, in particular starting in the 1980s, that is, almost in correspondence with the intensification of globalization forces, thus giving rise to the paradox of 'sticky places in a slippery space' (Markusen, 1996). Also from this point of view the research interests of geographic economy and business studies converged.

The local environment is supposed to be a vital component for firms' competitiveness in the global arena. This argument is further developed in a model for firm internationalization, by Lindmark (1994). The localization of a business affects the internal resources of the firm as well as the opportunities of the firm to access external resources. The assessment of internal resources and the use of them also affect export performance.

A very strong link exists between the clustering of economic activities and the international performance of firms belonging to such clusters, as we commented in Chapter 4. The phenomenon has undergone recent development in literature, demonstrating the growing interest of diverse authors on the subject (Brown and Bell 2001; Enright, 1998; Porter, 1990; Storper, 1992). Cluster SMEs have traditionally taken advantage either of local competitors' former employees' experience, or more generally of the overall knowledge capital available in the local cluster, selecting foreign markets with

high growth potential for their products from the beginning of the business activity. Later on positive performances encourage entrepreneurs to increase their international commitment, in terms of export intensity and geographic scope. More recently also, large firms and MNEs subsidiaries have frequently decided to enter into local clusters in order to benefit from these positive externalities. In other cases, large companies have been the originators of local clusters, thanks to frequent corporate spin-offs and local outsourcing practices.

The cluster provides access to positive externalities (skilled and specialized labour, specialized services, access to a kind of 'collective international knowledge' and easy access to information on the internationalization strategies of the main local competitors). Easy and immediate access to information – vital for international expansion – is due to a complex blend of imitative behaviour, high frequency of spin-offs, organization of international trade fairs based in the district territory or lower cost participation in foreign events, and other actions carried out by institutions that mediate and intermediate between the firms and the markets, like enterprises' associations, shared service centres and export consortia (Becattini, 2000; Pyke, Becattini, Sengenberger, 1991).

The international commitment of cluster-based firms could lead to growing emphasis also on non-export internationalization modes, like alliances, JVs and FDIs. Also in this case, belonging to a cluster may provide an advantage to small firms in terms of access both to information and to services provided by district meta-organizers.

5.7.3 Position: niche orientation

The concept of niche strategy has assumed different meanings in literature. Born as a sort of 'defensive' concept, in which a niche is considered as a protected space (Caves and Pugel, 1980; Newman, 1978), it has developed into a 'strategic' concept, in which the niche is the result of a creative segmentation of the market, in order to anticipate customers' value functions. Moving from a reactive strategy to compensate SME size disadvantage (Acs and Audresch, 1990), to a strategic answer (entrepreneurial action) to the complexity of the global competitive arena.

Penrose (1959) states that in every economy market, niches exist which are not appropriate for mass production and thus cannot be supplied by bigger firms. Consequently, in order to act in market

niches, SMEs have to specialize in certain demands and customer types and have to build up specific resources. Smaller firms can be important players in niche markets while other SMEs cannot compete with their larger rivals which occupy dominant market positions. On the other hand, not adopting a defensive vision *à la* Penrose, but a proactive one, entrepreneurs can horizontally segment – in a creative way – the world market, seen as a single entity, aiming to identify/shape a restricted group of clients, wherever they may be located (Takeuchi and Porter, 1986), with a supply of homogeneous products/services.

Operating within a narrowly defined market niche leads to an international market horizon in order to break even, since the domestic one – at a small niche level – does not permit adequate sales volumes to be reached. All over the world, niche firms share some fundamental similarities: they possess unique assets, focus on narrow global market segments and are strongly customer-orientated, the entrepreneur's vision and competencies being of a crucial importance.

Niche strategy is a key competitive strategy for firms, especially for SMEs, allowing them to maintain a long-term competitive advantage also with reference to bigger firms (Kotler and Scott, 1993). Niche strategy is a mix of unique resources, competences and abilities that create a favourable competitive environment. This strategy reduces the degree of complexity of the international market in terms of knowledge and control of the segment created; it reduces complexity in the competitive environment, thanks to the non price competition and the paucity of direct competitors; it reduces the degree of organizational complexity, thanks to the centralized organizational structure, typical of SMES. Also large firms have gradually adopted a niche – or better, multi-niche – approach and positioning, because it fits better with the actual structure and functioning of international markets and permits a better customer focus and response.

The niche approach implies a non-generic vision of the market turned to interpreting its complexity and variety, and to orienting the entrepreneurial action to the proactive client's service (Maccarini et al., 2004). These are fundamental characteristics both of a 'demand-based' niche strategy – where the niche is born from a specific and explicit need of the market – and of a 'supply-based' niche strategy – determined by the research of a potential market of implicit needs.

Competition in a global niche market requires proactive, innovative and risk-seeking strategies: such attributes identify an entrepreneurial approach to international strategy. The entrepreneurial capacity to identify opportunities regardless of where they are located, and to observe the competitive arena in terms of potential customers, rather than potential markets, is a key feature in determining a niche strategy, and outlines the role of International Entrepreneurship in terms of shaping a market niche according to a creative market micro-segmentation (Zucchella, 2001).

5.7.4 Paths

As far as path dependence is concerned, the evolutionary perspective on economic behaviour, or any perspective that allows a meaningful role for entrepreneurship, is a natural home for the concept of path dependence. Minniti and Bygrave (2001) posit that entrepreneurs make decisions relying on two types of knowledge. The first is specific knowledge that refers to the particular product or industry, and may be acquired by all firms regardless to their entrepreneurial orientation. The second is general knowledge and refers to how an individual or organization can be entrepreneurial. This type of knowledge refers to alertness to new opportunities and the subsequent exploitation of them, leading the organization to pursue innovation (Kirzner, 1973, 1979). Thus, entrepreneurial learning, which is built upon the second type of knowledge, is path dependent and includes learning from successes and failures in the activities of the firm (Gaglio, 1997; Minniti and Bygrave, 2001). Other studies argue that the entrepreneurial process is based on a trial and error procedure since entrepreneurs learn from their discoveries and mistakes (Butos and Koppl, 1999; Cope and Watts, 2000; Deakins and Freel, 1998; Harper, 1996, 1998). Many studies associate learning with International Entrepreneurship.

Theories of International Entrepreneurship argue that some firms became international because of entrepreneur-specific capabilities (Bloodgood, Sapienza and Almeida, 1996; Knight and Cavusgil, 1995; McDougall and Oviatt, 1996). McDougall, Shane and Oviatt (1994) find that founders of these firms are alert to new international market opportunities because of their knowledge and learning acquired from earlier activities.

Intangible resources and capabilities are mainly attributable to the knowledge possessed and accumulated by the entrepreneur and the top management team, which frequently coincide in small firms. Capabilities, indeed, can be considered as strategic assets that are accumulated through a pattern of investment over time (Ward, Bickford D and Keong Leong, 1996). Entrepreneurial firms rely on intangible knowledge and different studies focus on the motivation of the entrepreneur, and his/her ability, as fundamental elements that develop the organization (Morris and Lewis, 1995). The findings reveal a positive relationship between an entrepreneur's international attitude, orientation, experience and network and positive international development (Andersson, 2003; Ibeh and Young, 2001; Kuemmerle, 2002; Preece, Miles and Baetz, 1998; Westhead, Wright and Ucbasaran, 2001).

The resources and capabilities of the firm have thus a cumulative nature and are the key resource. This is particularly true for knowledge, and for subsequent capabilities developed over time. This originates path dependence and limits the spectrum of alternative paths available when a deep strategic change is needed.

On the other hand, the entrepreneurial orientation and capability of a firm requires the ability to identify and stretch new growth paths and this lies with the presence of a management team, characterized by broad vision, alertness and commitment, of high organizational absorptive capacity, of proper organizational learning processes which permit the reconfiguration of capabilities.

5.8 International performance

Measuring performance is complex because its operationalization may refer to different aspects of the organizational effectiveness of firms (Dess and Robinson, 1984; Shoham 1988; Sullivan, 1994; Venkataraman and Ramanujam, 1986). In international firms, performance may be measured in terms of profitability, growth, export intensity, geographic scope and international precocity.

It is generally affirmed that entrepreneurship can have a positive influence on the performance of the firm (Covin and Slevin, 1991). If entrepreneurship is the key factor in innovation, to exploit new economic opportunities and to introduce new ideas in the market, this means that entrepreneurship is a driver in value creation, operating both in the domestic and in foreign markets. This evidence is

supported by a number of studies linking entrepreneurship with international performance (Balabanis and Katsikea, 2003; Dimitratos, Liouhas and Carter, 2004; Ibeh, 2003; Knight, 2001; Zahra, Neubaum and Huse, 1997).

From the pioneering work of Schumpeter (1934) up to the recent surge of studies on entrepreneurship, one of the expressions of entrepreneurship has been recognized in the decision *per se* of foreign market entry. Nowadays most firms recognize that this decision is a necessity more than an option (Zucchella and Maccarini, 1999), due to the saturation of domestic markets, the need to react to global competition, the need to reach an adequate market size in niche productions, and the necessity of following customers or suppliers. In addition to this, phenomena to do with regional integration have rendered the concept of the foreign market less clear-cut than before. This means that the frontier of entrepreneurship in International Business is now more complex and multi-dimensional to define and leads to multi-scaled international performance in terms of intensity, scope and precocity.

As far as intensity is concerned, exporting seems to be the predominant international activity of small firms (Audretsch, 2002; Kundu and Katz, 2003; Tesar and Moini, 1998; Westhead, Wright and Ucbasarab, 2001). Wolff and Pett (2000) argue that export strategy is the primary foreign-market entry mode used by small firms in their internationalization path (Leonidou and Katsikeas, 1996), because it offers a greater degree of flexibility and it permits the achievement of an international position without overextending their capabilities or resources (Young et al., 1989). Literature on the effect of exports on firms' profitability is quite large and most of it concludes that, because of the scale and scope of economies gained through larger volumes of sales and increased international experience (Cooper and Kleinschmidt, 1985; Grant, Jammine and Thomas, 1988), high export intensity leads firms to better performance. More generally, both for small and large companies, the ratio of foreign sales to total sales is one of the most commonly adopted measures of international presence and expresses the commitment and results of foreign operations in terms of selling capacity.

According to the fourth dimension of export performance, that is, geographic scope, some authors, in transferring a common approach generally used for FDI to exports (Tallman and Li, 1996), split firms

between regional and global players, depending on the choice of operating on a macro-regional area or on the global market (Maccarini, Scabini and Zucchella, 2003). The former are firms competing on a macro-regional market – in this case the UE – where natural and artificial barriers have weakened. New supranational and integrated spaces can be considered the new domestic market. Another criterion in order to measure scope could be represented by the number of foreign countries involved as well as their diversity. Scope is relevant for International Entrepreneurship because it supports diversity in international learning and opens a wide and diverse set of business opportunities.

Precocity refers to how close the first international operations are to the initial foundation of the firm: the highest precocity is found in international new ventures. Precocity and scope influence intensity because they are both connected with experiential learning (Johanson and Vahlne, 1977; Kolb, 1984), which proves vital for export performance. The sooner a firm goes international and the more wide reaching its action, the higher its export intensity is likely to be. Moreover, firms that are global from inception very frequently rely on the experiential learning and personal network previously accumulated by the entrepreneur and/or its export managers (Maccarini et al., 2004). This issue allows precocity to be considered as a measure of international performance from an International Entrepreneurship point of view.

6
Empirical Analysis

6.1 Research questions and methodology

According to Marshall and Rossman (1999), for social researchers in applied fields, research is a process of trying to gain a better understanding of the complexities of human experience and, in some kinds of research, to take action based on this understanding.

Since International Entrepreneurship is intertwined with a set of different issues such as the management of change, innovation, uncertainty, new product development and environmental changes, it has been investigated from different discipline perspectives such as marketing, industrial economics, economics, sociology, psychology, history and anthropology. Each of these disciplines has its own paradigm, units of analysis, assumptions and research biases. Due to the lack of a comprehensive theory in the field of International Entrepreneurship, the research problems and questions are focused on the description of the entrepreneurial impact on international organizations. Therefore, the purpose of this study can be described as mainly exploratory and, to some extent, descriptive, as our aim is 'to build a rich description of complex circumstances that are unexplored in the literature' (Marshall and Rossman, 1999, p. 33). Meanwhile, since we are interested in identifying the driving forces that influence entrepreneurs' perceptions, decisions and actions towards involvement in international operations, this research could be explanatory where the findings are sufficient to show relationships between events and the meaning of these relationships (Table 6.1).

Table 6.1 Different types of research purpose

Types of research purpose	Description	General research questions
Exploratory	• To investigate little- understood phenomena • To identify or discover important categories of meaning • To generate hypotheses for further research	• What is happening in this social program? • What are the salient themes, patterns, or categories of meaning for participants? • How are these patterns linked with one another?
Explanatory	• To explain the patterns related to the phenomenon in question • To identify plausible relationships sharing the phenomenon	• What events, beliefs, attitudes, or policies shape this phenomenon? • How do these forces interact to result in the phenomenon?
Descriptive	• To document and describe the phenomenon of interest	• What are the salient actions, events, beliefs, attitudes, social structures and processes occurring in this phenomenon?
Emancipatory	• To create opportunities and the will to engage in social action	• How do participants problematize their circumstances and take positive social action?

Source: Adapted from C. Marshall and G. B. Rossman, *Designing Qualitative Research*, 3rd edn, London: Sage, 1999.

As an organizational science, international entrepreneurship research has certain tools available which include field methods (such as surveys, case studies and action research), computer databases, simulations and combinations of various approaches (Snow and Thomas, 1994). Field studies involve real entrepreneurs and ventures as opposed to *ad hoc* groups or events that are created and studied in a laboratory. Field research can realistically examine entrepreneurial processes and outcomes more deeply than other methods. They provide mechanisms for observing individuals and organizations in their entrepreneurial processes and behaviours. In entrepreneurship, field studies have many forms, including single and multiple case studies, questionnaire surveys, action research and field experiments. Sample sizes have ranged from the single case to several thousand observations and the unit of analysis has spanned the entrepreneur as an individual, the traits and personality of entrepreneurs, and the behaviour of the entrepreneur, as well as the behaviour and structure of an entrepreneurial organization.

In Table 6.2 a list of data collection techniques is proposed, according to the research methodology involved.

Before a theory can be tested it must be constructed. The process of theory construction includes steps such as delimitation of the phenomenon studied, the identification of the relevant construct and the development of hypotheses (Eisenhardt, 1989; Yin, 1989). Theory building draws on inductive logic, and emphasizes qualitative methods such as in-depth interviews, interpretative data analysis and intuitive inferences. After a theory has been assembled it can be tested. Researchers within this perspective aim at creating generalizations that are empirically testable, using a quantitative perspective as opposed to theory building.

Research in International Entrepreneurship is still in its infancy, when compared with other social science fields (Hitt et al., 2002). This study wants to respond to this request, building on a theoretical framework. In order to develop the latter, previous literature has been analysed, in order to capture the main streams of research. Case study analysis has been applied in order to create a connection between the proposed model and the empirical reality that would permit the development of a testable, relevant and valid framework. According to Guba and Lincoln (1994), two approaches or methods – quantitative and qualitative – are available to researchers. The qualitative approach

140

Table 6.2 Types of organizational research methods and techniques

Features	Methods	Data collection techniques or principles
Natural environment, uncontrolled	Field methods (e.g. surveys, case surveys, case studies, action research, grounded and ethnographic research)	Structured observation Unstructured or semi-structured interviews Questionnaires Archival analysis
	Computer data bases	Researcher access to information collected by others
	Experimental simulations	Researcher tries to create a realistic facsimile of a situation, sets it in motion ad observes its behaviour
	Laboratory experiments	Researcher examines organizational processes under tightly controlled conditions
Artificial environment, controlled	Computer simulation	Researcher uses mathematical modelling to construct a complete and closed model

Source: T. Volery, 'On field research methods for theory building and testing'. In L.-P. Dana, (ed.), *Handbook of Research on International Entrepreneurship*, Cheltenham and Northampton, MA: Edward Elgar, 2004.

implies an emphasis on processes and meanings that are not measured in terms of quantity, amount, intensity or frequency. This approach provides a deeper understanding of the phenomenon within its context. Moreover, qualitative researchers stress the socially constructed nature of reality that states the relationship between the researcher and the phenomenon under investigation. On the other hand, quantitative researchers emphasize the measurement and analysis of the causal relationships between variables, not processes.

Cochran and Dolan (1984) have also related differences between qualitative and quantitative research to the distinction between exploratory (qualitative) and confirmatory (quantitative) analysis. Or, as stated by Sullivan (2001), the distinction between qualitative and quantitative approaches depends primarily on two factors: (1) the state of our knowledge on a particular research topic, and (2) the researcher's assessment regarding the nature of the phenomenon being studied. According to Sullivan (2001), when there is little theoretical support for a phenomenon, it may be impossible to develop precise hypotheses, research questions, or operational definitions. In such cases, qualitative research is appropriate because it can be more exploratory in nature.

According to Marshall and Rossman (1999), qualitative research is appropriate for understanding human phenomena (entrepreneur's orientation, action and behaviour), and is useful in investigations of the interpretations and meanings that people give to events that they have experienced (entrepreneur's perception).

According to Yin (1989), a case study is an inquiry that investigates a contemporary phenomenon within its real-life context, especially when the boundaries between phenomenon and context are not clearly evident. He has also explained that a 'case' may be an individual, or some event or entity that is less well defined than a single individual, for example, a process or an organization. He also highlights that the unit of analysis can be the case itself and relates the unit of analysis (and therefore the case) to the way the initial research questions have been defined. Miles and Huberman (1994) also see the case as the study's unit of analysis and picture it as the 'heart' of the study. Therefore, according to Yin (1989), the case study can assume not only a single or a multiple-case design, but both types of design may have either a single unit or embedded multiple units of analysis.

Qualitative rather than quantitative methodologies may be appropriate to explore this area of interest. In this respect, we found that the qualitative approach suits the purpose of this study. We analyse three cases (Eisenhardt, 1989, 1991; Yin, 1989) concerning different international firms (an international new venture, a multinational subsidiary and an established international medium-sized firm) which possess attributes of proactiveness, innovativeness, and the capacity to identify and exploit opportunities and to assume risks on an international scale. This work aims in particular at identifying which resources and capabilities that support international entrepreneurship are at both the individual and the organizational level.

Cases were extracted from a sample of 66 firms. The sample is represented by respondents to a survey which involved 244 firms (return rate 27 per cent, i.e., 178 questionnaires were filled). The sample was extracted from a list of manufacturing firms headquartered in northwestern Italy reported by the Chambers of Commerce information systems for having some form of international activity (export, import, FDIs, JVs). The selection was made according to the criteria of representativeness of the population of Italian international firms, according to ICE surveys (Italian Trade Commission).

All the firms were first informed about the research by mail, and successively contacted by phone to obtain their support in the research. Firms were selected according to the International Entrepreneurship literature, that shows Born-Globals, MNEs and established firms as the main subjects of study. We further contacted 18 firms by phone, and based on the criteria of 'accessibility' and 'acceptance', three firms were selected whose managers or decision-makers accepted the invitation to undertake interviews after one or two phone calls.

The interviews were conducted between July and December 2005. The interviews conducted in this study were focused on a pre-determined set of discussion topics. However, opportunity was left open for any type of response. In fact, we used the interview guide approach in this study, because it provides topics or subject areas within which the interviewer is free to explore, probe and ask questions that elucidate and illuminate the subject under investigation. The interview guide enabled us to build a conversation within a particular subject area, to ask questions spontaneously, and to establish a conversational style, but with the focus on a particular subject that had been predetermined (Marshall and Rossman, 1999).

The type of interview conducted was face-to-face and in-depth, enabling the interviewer to explore a few general topics through discovering the participant's view (Marshall and Rossman, 1999). Though much more like conversations than formal interviews with predetermined and structured questions, interviews were focused on certain topics (research problems and research questions). Each interview lasted around two hours, and two–three interviews per firm were necessary to have a complete picture of the problems under investigation.

6.2 General information

In this section the characteristics of the firms analysed are described. In this respect, the entrepreneurs' responses during the interview and to the questionnaire are taken into consideration. A summary of these data is presented in Table 6.3.

6.3 Case study 1: Barrera SRL

Barrera Srl is a small firm with two workers, specializing in designing, assembling, testing and selling highly innovative machinery for the footwear industry. The company was started in March 2004 by two promoting partners: Mr Giuseppe Barrera and Mrs Stefania Agazzone. It is based in Italy, in the footwear industrial district of Vigevano (Lombardia). All the firm's products are used in a specific phase of the production chain of shoe manufacturing which concerns the thermo-treatment of shoes. Barrera's machines are constructed for humidification, ironing, stabilization, shoe cooling, glue drying and reactivation.

The organization of Barrera Srl is not particularly structured and formalized, which is explained by the small size of the firm. The company is composed of two partners: Mr Barrera and Mrs Agazzone. The latter is responsible for the administration of the company, while Mr Barrera is assisted by a designer and two workers specialized in assembling and testing footwear machinery. Internal relationships among individuals working within the firm are generally informal and, at the same time, the company is not based on a high level of hierarchy.

6.3.1 International opportunity scanning and evaluation

The reason inducing the entrepreneur to set up the firm in this case was related to the high demand made by Mr Barrera's previous clients

Table 6.3 General information on the case studies

Name of the firm	Typology of IEO	Products	Year of foundation	Turnover in 2004 (in millions of euros)	Number of employees	Year of internationalization	International activities	Export sales on total sales	Countries involved
BARRERA S.r.l.	Born Global	Footwear Machines	2004	0.168	2	2004	Export	50%	Spain, Turkey, Mexico
Fresenius Medical Care Italy S.p.A.	Multinational subsidiary	Equipment and disposables for dialysis treatments	1989 through acquisition	Not declared	About 150	–	–	–	Italy
RC Group S.p.A	Born Again Global	Air conditioning and refrigeration systems for high tech centres and buildings	1963	47.606	205	1983	Export, FDI, Joint Ventures	48%	Saudi Arabia, Argentina, Australia, Austria, Bahrain, Belgium, Bosnia-Herzegovina, Chile, Cyprus, Croatia, Denmark, Egypt, Arab Emirates, Estonia, Russia, Finland, France, Germany, Japan, Jordan, Great Britain, Greece, Indonesia, Iran, Iraq, Ireland, Israel, Italy, Kuwait, Latvia, Libya, Luxemburg, Morocco, Norway, Holland, Oman, Pakistan, Poland, Portugal, Qatar, Czech Republic, South Africa, China, Serbia/Montenegro, Singapore, Syria, Slovenia, Spain, Sweden, Switzerland, Thailand, Tunisia, Turkey, Hungary, Yemen, Zimbabwe

for innovative, reliable and fast machinery. Mr Barrera designs and creates machinery, focusing both on his innovative ideas and following definite client needs.

Thanks to his past working experiences and the previous personal, social relationships with clients and distributors, Mr Barrera recognized the opportunity to supply only high-tech, high-quality innovative machines predominantly to Western countries, where he firmly believes that an unexploited market niche exists concerning high-quality footwear production. He evaluated that this market niche might enable his firm to avoid competition with Asian or Latin-American enterprises. From this point of view, Mr Barrera pioneered a creative micro-segmentation of the international market (alertness to opportunities, capacity to imagine creative endeavours), took a relevant risk in a declining industry (risk propensity) and set up a new business from scratch in an area where most entrepreneurs were withdrawing (proactivity).

6.3.2 International resource mobilization

Barrera SrL designs, tests and sells shoe-making machines, relying on external firms for the supply of goods such as rolled steel sections, or for electronic products such as electronic boards for control panels. Despite the fact that Barrera is a newly established company, it is developing close and non-formalized relationships in Italy. These relations often change from commercial to cooperative ones concerning the selection of materials or the joint solution to problems specific to the Barrera case. Raw materials and components are from firms located in the same area because of the competitive advantages and positive externalities of the district: high competences, lower costs and informal relationships and past social networking.

While the production organization rests on local networking and outsourcing, the sales organization rests upon consolidated social networks of the entrepreneurs and on newly developed agreements. As far as internal development is concerned, products are designed, tested and developed directly by Mr Barrera.

6.3.3 Dynamic capabilities: processes

The entrepreneurial vision of Mr Barrera permits the coordination of internal and external activities, since materials, semi-processed goods

and different technologies are bought from other firms and they need to be assembled for selling.

Learning processes are developed thanks to the competences Mr Barrera has acquired from previous experience and now shares within the firm. In the 1960s he worked in a shoe factory in South Africa for two years and when he came back to Italy, he worked as an apprentice in a small footwear machinery company in Vigevano, developing competences in mechanics and electronics, and since he was able to design, he started to promote his first machinery in the same enterprise. Later, in 1975, he was offered a partnership in the company.

In rapidly changing industries like the shoe-making machinery sector, due to saturation of the market and competition from the emergent economies (predominantly Asian), the ability to reconfigure the firm's asset structure and product portfolio is an entrepreneurial skill. Barrera Srl chose to enter a high-quality footwear machinery market niche, geographically extended worldwide. Aiming to supply only high-tech, high-quality innovative machines predominantly to Western countries where there is still a niche for high-quality footwear production, Barrera Srl can be considered to stand outside the low-quality competition, and so it was able to cope with the recent crisis. The goal is to avoid competition with Asian or Latin-American enterprises and at the same time to concentrate on a market where the competitive variable is not based on low-prices, but on the quality of materials used, on technological innovation and on a qualified post-sales service to the client.

Barrera's machines are innovative, with respect to those on the market, for their use of high quality materials such as the stainless steel employed in the machinery servicing the carpentry processes. They also save energy and limit water consumption (energy saving: 40 per cent electrical energy; 30 per cent water), since heat production is not continuous as in competitors' machinery. The firm was founded in 2004 and the goal is to renew the product every five years to avoid imitation by competitors, because Mr Barrera considers product reconfiguration as a strategic objective for competition, development and growth.

Learning in the firm seems to be congenital, due to the previous experience of the entrepreneur. The path through which this individual

market and technological learning is progressively accumulated, distributed, stored and institutionalized could represent a critical feature for the firm.

The possibility to dynamically develop capabilities is strictly linked to the personal skills of Mr Barrera. Processes and information are not collected and shared by any information system, reducing the possibility of standardizing routines and organizational capabilities. This is a limit for this particular firm because activities such as ordering, selling, designing, as well as strategic and technological decisions, are managed directly by the entrepreneur, leveraging on his personal previous knowledge and his entrepreneurial orientation. Moreover, the entrepreneur's social network is also crucial to new venture start-up and fast growth.

6.3.4   Dynamic capabilities: positions

Prior personal market and industry knowledge, accumulated by Mr Barrera through past working experiences, represent two other types of position in the market. In fact, this knowledge and the firm's acquired reputation permits access to the international market, in which Mr Barrera decided to operate since he recognized an opportunity to service a niche in the footwear industry based on quality competition and using the social network to access the market.

Moreover, location in a district and the niche positioning are precisely due to knowledge the entrepreneur has accumulated during 40 years of working in this industrial and regional context. Past working experience is an important asset for the enterprise, since it has allowed Mr Barrera to develop a high competence in designing and selling machinery, and to widen his contacts with both Italian and foreign footwear companies. Reputational assets are relevant in this case even if the firm is a new venture because the Mr Barrera transmits his own personal reputation into the new venture.

Being located in a district benefits both this cooperation and the other neighbouring companies, which together all have access to the collective knowledge of the district to find specialized workers and suppliers. Commercial cooperation among firms is the main form. Firms in the Vigevano district cooperate by sharing information about customers and agents. With regards to formal ties in the organizational network, an important role is played by the Assomac

institution, an enterprises' association that carries out functions such as market research on behalf of firms and advertising campaigns in the specialized press or through international fairs, which cannot be internalized by small firms.

In summary, reputational assets, innovative niche positioning and location in a cluster are the main positioning strengths of the firm. Their combination through the entrepreneurial efforts of Mr Barrera represents the basis for the new business. For a long-run sustainable advantage in highly turbulent markets, the entrepreneurial effort needs to be perpetuated through capabilities reconfiguration over time.

6.3.5 Dynamic capabilities: paths

The entrepreneur is particularly important within Barrera Srl. Mr Barrera decided, after 38 years, to develop a new activity in the same industry in order to exploit all his capabilities and knowledge. These are crucial factors which explain a great deal about the entrepreneurial firm's success. He is able to understand the problems related to the working activity, and therefore through his creative endowments to constantly conceive innovative solutions in order to facilitate the duties of the employees in the production of shoes.

He is an open-minded man: Mr Barrera likes to travel abroad, thanks also to his working activity. His conception about the facility to move and to know new cultures and of the necessity to develop and to weave relationships with foreigners is particularly important.

Mr Barrera also has a high-risk propensity. This is confirmed by the fact that he decided to invest in this new activity, in spite of the fact that its creation occurred during a crisis which was affecting both the Italian machinery sector as well as the correlated footwear production. He states that today, many firms in the district should invest in new technologies and markets instead of focusing on competition with Asian firms.

He has fundamental skills thanks to his experience, while others have been self-taught. His strong personal curiosity, together with the necessity to assume new technical competences, has led him to improve his knowledge on subjects such as physics, electronics, hydraulics and mechanics.

He is able to speak five languages: English, Spanish, French, Portuguese and German. Most of them (Spanish, Portuguese and

German) are self-taught and generally improved during business trips abroad. This wide knowledge of foreign languages has helped Mr Barrera in his personal career since it has been fundamental for him, both in the past and nowadays in this new company, to come into contact with clients abroad.

He worked as an apprentice in a firm in South Africa, and later in Vigevano. He became an expert in the fields of mechanics and electronics, and he started to promote his first machines in the same enterprise. Later, in 1975, as the company where he started as an apprentice grew in size and importance, he was offered a partnership in the firm. He started to travel around the world in order to promote the company's name and products. Having the chance to meet customers and to see different production lines allowed him to develop the ability to judge the needs of customers and to conceive innovative answers and solutions to aggregate varied customer's necessities.

In addition, Mr Barrera also developed relationships with other entrepreneurs, managers and agents. Nowadays this worldwide social network represents the market portfolio of Barrera Srl, because clients recognize the quality of products and trust in the reliable service of Mr Barrera.

Finally, Mr Barrera trusts in visibility as a success factor in the business environment. For this reason, he has been actively participating in associative group activities since 1980. He has been elected Assomac President for two mandates; he is a committee member of Confindustria in Rome and he has recently been nominated President of the agency for local territory development.

His ability to dynamically reconfigure capabilities is path dependent because it is rooted in previous experiences and knowledge accumulated by the entrepreneur. For this reason he reconfigures capabilities within his field of experience (technologies for shoes production).

6.3.6 Performance

Although Barrera Srl can rely on the long experience of its founder, it is a newly established enterprise and, like every young company, needs a minimum span of time in order to evaluate returns and performances. Nevertheless, the company in its first year of life had good returns considering the large amount of expenses due to initial investments. Furthermore, the company has not completely

launched all products, which is further evidence of the youth of the enterprise and brings the conclusion that Barrera is still settling its activities and so should be judged from a long-term perspective.

For these reasons, Barrera showed an active balance for the first six months, followed by a four-month drop in profits, which led the company to overall negative profitability for the first year of activity. Barrera's turnover in the first year was very low (about 168,000 euros), but as Mr Barrera stated, the business goal is to quadruple it in coming years.

As far as international performance is concerned, the worldwide market, with special focus on EU markets, has been chosen as the natural one for several reasons. The crisis of the internal productive system with the failure of many Italian firms together with the natural propensity of the entrepreneur to deal with foreign clients, are the most important reasons. Furthermore, the specificity of the product positioned in the high quality segment presupposes a limited number of clients who are spread in a global context, and to reach them obviously means to operate beyond domestic boundaries.

Since Barrera is a newly established company and of small dimensions, the international expansion modality exclusively regards their exports. 50 per cent of Barrera's revenues come from Italy, where the products are sold to 31 clients, who are generally final footwear manufacturers, while the remaining 50 per cent is sold through export to both Europe and extra-UE countries. Spain in 2004 was the only country in Europe to which Barrera sold its products and counts for 10 per cent of the revenues. Turkey and Mexico are the most important markets and account respectively for 35 per cent and 5 per cent of extra-UE revenues. All exports to each country rely on one re-seller, since the company does not directly contact final customers for foreign sales. Recently, Barrera Srl has been considering the possibility of going beyond the export modality through agreements involving the assembling of products with a potential partner located in India, a low-cost labour country. Before starting this partnership, Mr Barrera is planning how to control the production to avoid know-how leakage risks.

The third international performance measure refers to precocity, which the firm shows in reaching foreign countries after its foundation. Barrera shows an international propensity from its inception, and it can be defined as a Born-Global.

6.3.7 Discussion

According to International Entrepreneurship literature, Barrera Srl is considered a Born-Global firm, having started international activities soon after foundation. The entrepreneur plays a central role in this firm, leveraging on his past work experiences, market and industry knowledge, education and social network. These characteristics are consistent with the literature on Born-Global firms that consider networks, intangible assets and entrepreneurs/management teams as key drivers of fast internationalization process. On the other hand, the importance of the entrepreneur's former experience and background – including his social network – permits us to highlight the fact that international ventures might also rely on experiential learning and show path-dependent strategic choices. The previous experience of founders and management teams are recombined into the new venture so that path dependency can give rise to novel combinations, arising from opportunities discovery and exploitation. In the case of Barrera, this is represented by innovative market positioning (discovery of unexploited market niches) and the highly specialized design and production of technologies and components for advanced footwear machinery.

From an analysis of the organizational learning processes for generating knowledge in the context of traditional and Born-Global firms, it can be inferred that learning through the organization's own experience fits the way that traditional firms learn through internationalizing, while this form of learning does not fit the internationalization from inception process followed by Born-Global firms. In fact, Born-Global firms may display congenital learning and grafting to begin their internationalization from inception. The pace of expansion for these types of firms is too rapid to allow learning from the firms' own experience. The gap between individual experience and knowledge base (founders, management team) and organizational learning and knowledge base is one of the less explored issues in Born-Global literature, even though bridging this gap represents the main challenge to the survival and success of these organizations.

Intuiting, on the other hand, is expected to occur in both types of organizations, although entrepreneurial intuiting may occur more often in Born-Global than in traditional firms. Moreover, sharing

and integrating learning occurs through dialogue, shared experiences, and joint action within the firm, it is expected that the smaller size of an internationalizing firm will mean that the dissemination and integration tasks will require less resources and will happen faster. Thus, it can be concluded that Born-Global organizations will integrate new learning more completely and rapidly across the firm.

Finally, the institutionalization and codification of learning requires a high amount of resources, it is expected that traditional firms would be in a better position to develop and implement these processes. Moreover, often, Born-Global firms, due to their size and age, may not develop systems, structures and procedures through which they could embed their learning. This is particularly true for Barrera Srl, in which strategic decisions, technical configuration and operative production are managed directly by the entrepreneur, reducing the possibility for the organization to accumulate routines and to learn. The path the firm followed is strictly linked to the entrepreneur since his education, work experiences, personal network and vision represent the basic source of competitiveness for the enterprise. These features could impede the enterprise in developing organizational learning, narrowing the options along the dependence path and limiting future performance.

Since dynamic capabilities are systematic methods for modifying operating routines, and emerge from experience accumulation, knowledge articulation and knowledge codification, we can wonder about how and why a new venture should develop them. At first glance it is not likely that Born-Global firms would develop dynamic capabilities until they are established. On the other hand, Born-Global firms have learning advantages and lower organizational barriers to cross. This could enable them to render their initial entrepreneurial effort more systematic over time, establishing organizational conditions for capabilities reconfiguration.

6.4   Case study 2: Fresenius Medical Care Italy

Fresenius is a global health-care company with products and services for dialysis, both in hospitals and for the medical care of patients at

home. The Fresenius Group consists of three business segments, each of which is responsible for its own business operations worldwide: Fresenius Medical Care, Fresenius Kabi and Fresenius ProServe.

Fresenius Kabi is the European leader in the field of nutrition and infusion therapy, with subsidiaries and distributors worldwide; while Fresenius ProServe specializes in international health-care services and facilities management within the Fresenius Group. The comprehensive scope of services offered by the Fresenius ProServe companies ranges from consultancy, planning, constructing and equipping of hospitals, to the technical and general management and operation of health facilities all over the world. It also provides planning, construction, service and technical operation of medical-technical and pharmaceutical production plants.

The Fresenius Medical Care worldwide company is the world's largest, integrated provider of products and services for individuals with chronic kidney failure and the world's largest provider of dialysis products, such as haemodialysis machines, dialysers and related disposable products.

Fresenius Medical Care Italy, with about 150 employees, is the local subsidiary of Fresenius Medical Care. Fresenius entered the Italian market through the acquisition of Italian dialysis firms: in 1989 Sis-ter SpA and in 1991 Biofil Srl. Later on, in 1996 Fresenius Medical Care Italy was founded. Nowadays, the main functions of the subsidiary are represented by operative marketing, selling and post-sales assistance to customers, and the market is represented by the Italian one. Operative marketing concerns the adaptation of the group strategy to the local market, and because of the type of product realized and clients served, this function is strictly linked to post-sales services.

Production in Italy does not refer to Fresenius Medical Care Italy, but directly to the production manager in Germany. This could entail an apparently limited mandate for the subsidiary, thus involving no room for developing entrepreneurial behaviour. The case study will demonstrate that even when local activities are apparently limited, the subsidiary can behave autonomously and take strategic action. From the subsidiary's point of view, what matters more than the extension of the activities performed in the local market, is the possibility of pursuing local strategies,.

The Italian market is highly concentrated (i.e., the four main competitors share over the 80 per cent of the market). This happens because of the strong influence of NHS regulation on local customer needs (mainly hospitals) and behaviour. This oligopolistic structure of the industry has been consolidated by vertical and horizontal integration processes, leading the main firms to compete both in the haemodialysis and in the peritoneal segments, even though the relative market shares are widely different. As far as the Italian market is concerned, at the end of 2002 the Italian Registry of Dialysis and Transplants reported 39,000 patients. Each firm is typically a subsidiary of a multinational company performing in the local market, and only a few local competitors exist.

6.4.1 International opportunity scanning and evaluation

Operating in a highly concentrated market based on price competition leads firms to need to invent some different forms of provision in order to take the advantage over competitors. In 1998, Fresenius introduced the 'service dialysis provision', followed over the years by their competitors. In this form of supply the provision consists of each component used for the dialysis treatment (machine, fluid and disposable items), receiving a payment proportionate to the number of treatments provided. In this case, medical centres do not have to address their requests for different products to different suppliers, but can just deal with one supplier who provides all the products for the dialysis treatment.

Later on in 2002, Fresenius, thanks to the competence in managing and building dialysis centres developed within the group, proposed to hospitals with constraints on health-care expenditure an 'integrated service provision', represented by the building of new centres for dialysis treatment with the supply of machine, fluid, disposables and even personnel.

This opportunity was recognized by the CEO due to the growing constraints to health-care expenditure and the emergent organizational problem for customers (mainly hospitals) represented by the need to reduce buying process complexity, through reducing the number of suppliers dealt with directly. These ideas arose through networking with other subsidiary CEOs. In fact, the headquarter periodically organizes international meetings for the subsidiary CEOs in order to share results and goals within the firm. These summits

permit networking between colleagues and the sharing of experience among subsidiaries. Thanks to similar ideas in other countries, Fresenius Medical Care Italy decided to introduce these new forms of provision, showing proactiveness and innovativeness.

6.4.2 International resource mobilization

Research is primarily managed in Germany, the United States and in Italy where the main factories are located.

Suppliers of haemodialysis machines, dialysers and related disposable products are represented by other companies of the same group, and suppliers of fluids are represented by local independent firms, because the costs of transportation from Germany is more expensive. Production is realized in a few factories spread in macro-regions, in order to serve many different countries and to reach high economies of scale. The top production manager is located at the macro-region level (i.e., in Italy production of filters is realized for the European countries and the top manager is in Germany).

6.4.3 Dynamic capabilities: processes, positions and paths

The health-care industry market is highly dynamic and its evolution depends to a great extent on technological, medical, policy and regulatory developments. Significant importance is due to the regulatory environment, which in many countries – like in Italy – is managed by the National/Regional Health Service. Changes in regulation and/or in financial reimbursement lead to corresponding changes in the demand for health services, and in the industry structure. The ability to respond to these transformations has led many firms to adapt their strategy to the market, and in some cases to proact, reconfiguring their offers to reach customers and to solve their increasingly complex problems.

As mentioned above Fresenius in 1998 introduced the 'service dialysis provision' to the market, and later in 2002, the 'integrated service provision'. Resources are available within the group and capabilities have been developed during the time. The Fresenius Chief Executive Officer said that 'In this industry because of the highly standardized products, competition is price-based and firms need to invent other forms of provision. It is not a problem of process management, because our firm possesses both resources and capabilities, but an opportunity to compete.'

It thus provides a good example of national responsiveness to customer needs and global integration of other activities (R&D, manufacturing, partially sourcing, etc.). At the local-firm level, the strategy is based on the adaptation to the changes in the market, on the environment – adaptive strategy – on proaction, innovative interpretation of market opportunities and customer problem solving.

The provision of the integrated dialysis service is a proactive response to the environment. The approach is customer-oriented. While the group strategy is defined at the worldwide level, the local subsidiary is the one to adapt to local economic and normative environment, and sometimes to proact in developing innovative value propositions. Managerial competences are required for the first case, while the latter calls for entrepreneurial ones: opportunity scanning and innovative value propositions development through international and global/local networking. This leads to the assumption that the former, compared to the latter, offers greater leverage on the global value system and sourcing opportunities as well as on the same local sourcing opportunities (for example sticky manufacturing competences in the Italian biomedical district) and local customer knowledge. The latter is dominated by regulatory issues, so it is more explicit and accessible than other kinds of local customer knowledge.

Moreover, being part of a MNE with a strong presence in highly diverse markets like that of the United States, enabled Italian subsidiaries to transform an apparent disadvantage (i.e., the impossibility of having economies of learning in relation to other countries' customer knowledge) into a competitive advantage when local market conditions change radically, resembling another country's experience. 'Every six months the group organizes a meeting among the subsidiary CEOs to show the results and the goals of the firm. It is a great opportunity to meet other colleagues. Experiences are shared among subsidiaries because now I need a suggestion, and tomorrow the CEO subsidiary in Spain will need a suggestion from me' (Fresenius's CEO).

While the HQ possesses competencies and capabilities in R&D, in production and in marketing, subsidiaries are local customer-oriented and develop capabilities in addressing rapid responses to their needs. For this reason, subsidiaries have a great degree of freedom in

suggesting new investment ideas or competitive actions to the HQs that increase competitive advantage in the global market, presenting HQ with the business plan for their projects. Questioned on subsidiary entrepreneurial vision and vocation, the Fresenius' CEO affirmed 'This is the pleasure of my work: you need to renew the offer to the market and the integrated dialysis service provision is a good example. If there was not this freedom I would simply be an employee'.

The introduction of the 'integrated service provision' is a tendency and it does not mean that all dialysis treatments are provided to patients directly by firms, but this offer is increasing in Italy as direct alternative to traditional hospitalization.

Developing competences and capabilities, Fresenius is playing the role of integrated service provider, moving from technological competences to the service sector, having improved customer problem solving and value-chain management capabilities. The proactive strategy approach to customers' needs and to the changing environment is a measure of the capabilities the firm has developed, reconfiguring their offer. Learning in this firm is organization-based through personal relationships with other subsidiaries of the group and collective, and shared problem solving about new forms of provision.

6.4.4 Performance

Because of the reluctance to disclose financial and business information, considered by the Fresenius CEO as strictly confidential, it is impossible to describe and measure the performance of Fresenius Medical Care Italy. Moreover, examining a subsidiary does not permit a successful measurement of international performance in terms of intensity, geographic scope and precocity, but some financial and market information could still prove useful to demonstrate the performance of this firm.

In 2004 the market shares of Fresenius Medical Care Italy were the following: 32 per cent in the haemodialysis segment and 18 per cent in the peritoneal sector, increasing market share by 2 per cent in haemodialysis with respect to 2002. The revenues in 2004 increased 10 per cent with respect to 2003 while the employees augmented from 136 in 2002 to 150 in 2004.

The Fresenius group performed in the Italian market acquiring an Italian manufacturer of dialysis equipment (Sis-ter SpA) in 1989 and founded the subsidiary in 1996. The Italian subsidiary is locally oriented since the Italian market is the only one in which the firm competes.

6.4.5 Discussion

International Entrepreneurship literature suggests that local subsidiaries, showing entrepreneurial orientation in terms of innovativeness and proactiveness can be considered in the same field of research. Fresenius Medical Care Italy seems to behave entrepreneurially, according to the measures of Covin and Slevin (1991) who, in particular, refer to proactiveness in terms of attitude to change industry patterns while interpreting customer needs innovatively.

The Fresenius Italian dialysis subsidiary, followed by other competitors, introduced new forms of service provision to the market. Because of the highly standardized product and price competition, it reinvented the value chain, realizing a new way of providing dialysis treatments; and moving from the individual sale of each component for the treatment to the provision of an integrated service to local customers where single activities are carried out by different actors. It took risks (although calculated ones) in managing the process of provision and responding to customer demand.

In this case, both opportunity scanning and capabilities are acquired by the social network in which the CEO is involved. As mentioned, being a part of a group gives the opportunity to share information and experiences, leveraging on the periodic meetings organized by headquarters. They enable subsidiaries to have access to the information, ideas, models and patterns used by other managers in the group. This fact allows managers to enrich their competences and capabilities through consultation with managers from other regions facing similar market challenges.

Strategic objectives concern the survival of the firm and the sales volume needed in order to gain (or to maintain) market share. The pace followed is gradual and customer-oriented in order to adapt to the local market offerings.

Since the institutionalization and codification of learning requires a high amount of resources, it is to be expected that MNEs would be in a better position to develop and implement these

processes. Moreover, these firms, due to their size and age, develop systems, structures and procedures where they embed their learning. Learning leverages on the network and it is developed mainly within the organization: in MNEs knowledge is expected to be accumulated, articulated and codified in order to be used by each of the local organizations of the group. As Fresenius Italy showed, patterns from other subsidiaries are applied to the Italian market, using and developing local capabilities in response to Italian market needs.

6.5   Case study 3:   RC Group SpA

RC Group is an Italian company with more than 200 employees, producing air-conditioning and refrigeration systems for high-tech centres and buildings. The company was founded in 1963 by the father of Mr Roberto Caciolli (at the time of the interview CEO of the company). The headquarters are in Valle Salimbene (Pavia) where one of the three factories is based. The other two factories are located in Rome and in Zeccone (Pavia), where the production was moved in 2003 when the factory in Florence was closed.

The firm produces air-conditioning systems for Information and Communication Technology buildings, operating in different industries. The most important is represented by Information Technology, Telecommunication, Banking and hi-tech offices and Hospitals, while less important are Shopping Centres and applications for small offices and private houses. The three factories are specialized in assembling products, while R&D, administration, finance, sales and marketing are managed from headquarter; 50 per cent of the production is outsourced to small firms in Italy, located close to the main factories.

Nowadays the main worldwide competitor is represented by Emerson Electric, a US multinational with a 95 per cent market share, while RC Group is considered the second player. Since 1963, the firm has used a customer-oriented approach, responding to specific requests for high-specification air-conditioning systems for electronic equipment. It has always operated in a market niche. The market space was identified and exploited because large foreign multinationals provided standard machines.

Although the dimension of the firm requires a formal organizational structure, the working environment is informal, as are the relationships between individuals. Within the firm each individual is responsible for his/her own work, every activity and function takes place in open-plan offices, and the CEO operates in the same room as the administrative and financial staff. Since its foundation, the firm has imported 50 per cent of raw materials from United States and Japan because the main producers of electronic equipment were localized in those countries, although they operated in Italy through distributors. RC Group started international activities, that is, exporting, at the beginning of 1983. The founder gave the responsibility of managing international activities to his son Roberto Caciolli and after 16 years he became CEO of the firm.

6.5.1   International opportunity scanning and evaluation

In order to discuss the international opportunity scanning and evaluation process of RC Group, a short summary of the history of the company is needed. In 1963, the firm was set up when the founder, as consultant of Honeywell, was asked to manage a project to produce electronic equipment for air-conditioning systems. A commercial agreement permitted RC Condizionatori to be founded and to grow.

It started exporting at the beginning of 1983, due to an unexpected factor. The founder was informed by the managers of Honeywell that an important American multinational, operating in the same industry in Europe, had decided to leave the European market, in order to avoid restrictive industrial and economic regulation. Having evaluated the market potential, RC Group decided to contact each European distributor of the American multinational, proposing informal commercial agreements for the sale of the air-conditioning machines.

The decision to internationalize was based on the opportunity to operate through an already established network and draw on the experience of distributors with an in-depth knowledge of each country involved. In 1983, export was 15 per cent of the sales, 37 per cent in 1985 and 39 per cent in 1990, while the turnover increased from 4 million Euros in 1983, to 8 million Euros in 1985 and to 27 million Euros in 1990.

The RC brand gained international recognition within a few years and in 1987 RC Group was invited by the Import Chinese Agency to the first air-conditioning exhibition. The same year an agreement with a government company (nowadays Le Novo) was signed for the distribution of the products. In 1992, RC Group was the main player in China for the air conditioning of communication centres. Exploiting competitive advantages based on low labour costs, in 1992 RC Group signed a commercial agreement, based on knowledge transfer, with a Chinese firm (Tiianjin Computer Room Equipment Factory), while in 1997 a new factory in China was founded through a joint venture. In 2000, RC Group's Chinese firm produced 30 million Euros with 900 workers, but the following year the partnership failed and the factory was closed.

In 2003, after a period of reconsideration regarding the Chinese entry and subsequent failure, RC Group set up a Representative Office in Beijing. The firm established a support network for sales and service of RC Group products all over China. Nowadays the RC Group network includes 4 offices, managing more than 50 local sales partners and 20 after-sales partners covering an important share of the Chinese market. RC Group's CEO considers China a very important market, with an increasing level of growth but due to the previous experience, knowledge transfer is not involved. Chinese products will be based on mature technologies for European and American countries, thus avoiding the risk of imitation by Chinese competitors. Moreover, local production will be provided only in that region.

In this respect the network, partners and the market knowledge of the distributors of the foreign markets are considered the main factors explaining the international opportunity scanning and evaluation process. The opportunity scanning process in international markets begins casually (serendipity) but the firm shows a very high propensity to exploit opportunities, building on external networks to access foreign market knowledge. It also shows risk propensity in committing important resources to fast foreign market development, without previous experience, and in venturing later on into China. The role of the export manager, the son of the entrepreneur, corresponds to this new era of the firm's international growth. Contrary to Mr Barrera, he has no

experience but a good cultural background, international vision, curiosity, risk propensity, willingness to commit and capacity to build internal and external networks. In particular, the training courses and masters followed by the export manager are symptomatic of high absorptive capacity when faced by learning opportunities. This also permits transformation of the Chinese initial failure into a second opportunity to access a difficult market with a new strategy.

6.5.2 International resource mobilization

As far as resource mobilization is concerned, sourcing involves construction goods such as rolled steel sections and electronic boards for control panels. A strong network with suppliers represents for Mr Caciolli a competitive advantage, because 'assembling without stores give us the possibility to reduce costs and space, but in order to respond efficiently to our requests, suppliers have to know the stock level of their provision in time. For this reason, last year we implemented an integrated information system with some of them.'

Since its foundation, the firm has imported 50 per cent of raw materials from the United States and Japan because the main producers of electronic equipment were localized in those countries. Nowadays, import represents 50 per cent of sources: 98 per cent from Europe, mainly from Germany and France, and 2 per cent from Canada and Australia for a few special innovative products.

As far as internal development is concerned, RC Group invests more than 5 per cent of its turnover in research and development and three engineers are in charge. Moreover the firm has deposited 20 European patents and it is developing other 15.

In order to develop competences and capabilities RC Group plans training courses for managers, employees, engineers and workers. This means that the continuous learning philosophy of the export manager is also transmitted to the organization, to build up absorptive capacity at the organizational level. This is one of the foundations of dynamic capabilities.

6.5.3 Dynamic capabilities: processes

For Mr Caciolli, innovation is an important part of RC Group's philosophy: 'We were first in employing plastic pipes in production, in

applying microprocessor electronic controls when electro-mechanisms were still used and first in building packaged units with direct and indirect Free-Cooling and bringing extra-silent models to the market.' Products are innovative and customized because of the nature of the machines, which are designed in order to solve specific clients' problems and requests.

The main clients belong to industries such as IT, banking, health care. Offices managing information data such as internet-protocol centres, gateways, telecommunication companies and bank offices need air conditioning for data storage and data-processing areas. Electronic equipment produces high and concentrated heat loads, requiring a precisely controlled environment for the continuous and safe working of the equipment.

On the other hand installation for shopping centres, banks and hospitals need air conditioning to cool open spaces and to keep customers, visitors and patients comfortable, as do management and administrative computer centres, operating theatres and high-tech scanning machines.

Since products normally operate 24 hours a day, 7 days a week, 12 months a year, the priority of RC Group is the continuous development of the quality of its products. Energy efficiency, reliability and control systems represent the main characteristics required. RC Group achieves energy efficiency thanks to energy-index maximization design of all the units, by innovative technologies, the use of Free-Cooling systems and the use of microprocessors at the forefront of technology with proprietary regulation logic able to optimize unit performance.

The reliability of a piece of equipment is internationally defined by the MTBF Index (Mean Time Between Failures), that is, the period of time elapsed between one failure and the next one, given that routine maintenance procedures for the equipment are conducted within the set-down procedures. The RC Group Service Organization guarantees an after-sales service with reaction times corresponding to the importance of the intervention demanded. RC Group has always been at the leading edge of applied research and new technologies to improve its production capabilities.

Following the new technology evolution in different industries, in 2004 RC Group presented the SILVER BULLET system, based on two innovative elements: 'Oil-Free' technology and cooling power

through inversion. It works with a compressor produced in Australia, which does not require oil lubrication, while the latter uses a Canadian component in which shafts and impellers levitate during rotation and float on a magnetic field, produced by bearings. Compared to traditional systems, this one increases average efficiency by 35 per cent. Rather obviously but worth emphasizing, Oil-Free systems work without oil, avoiding all the problems linked to chemical reactions between ester oil, used with green refrigerants, and humidity in the circuit, which can lead to the creation of dangerous acids. The absence of oil requires a global redesign of the cooling circuit, in particular of the condensing coils and the evaporator. This study requires time and, moreover, many training hours on site and year-long research. This is the reason why RC Group decided to invest in this particular technology, in order to gain the necessary know-how and to be ready for action as soon as the Oil-Free compressors come on stream.

Core competences are based on R&D and in the designing of an electronic control system that is completely managed within firm. A team of 4 engineers design with 3D software. CAD technology also permits control of the outsourced production.

Innovation also involves the organizational structure and information system. Due to the growing complexity of the firm, Mr Caciolli reorganized the firm, leveraging on the flow of information:

> Activities are managed by teams and information is fundamental to increase efficiency: each team needs information from the others and for this reason an integrated information system is available for the economic and productive cycles. There are also three Product Development Teams responsible for the incremental development of products. Within every team each function is represented: administration, marketing, production, mechanical engineer, electronic engineer, electric engineer and post-sales service.

Moreover information is shared in open space offices and without secretaries, where each employee is responsible for their own work.

There is no turnover in workers in areas such as R&D, designing or engineering: the CEO considers this to be a distinctive competency that permits education through routines and individuals. Moreover the decentralization of responsibilities and the sharing of information through intranet system permit RC Group to develop organizational learning.

Another form of learning concerns international activity. Since 1983, it has focused on relationships with distributors and partners. Mr Caciolli was supported in efficiently organizing and maintaining relations with foreign clients by two employees, who acquired competencies in this area. Nowadays, this activity is managed by three employees in the administrative area, while the strategic positioning and planning is directly carried out by the CEO.

Networking is an important feature for RC Group. External networking involves relations with suppliers on the one hand and partners and distributors on the other hand. The former is based on the time-to-time market and the integrated information system that permits reduction of costs and storage space. The latter has allowed the firm to internationalize in Europe and in China, leveraging on the experience of partners and distributors with an in-depth knowledge of each country involved. Nowadays they represent market knowledge for RC Group.

6.5.4 Dynamic capabilities: positions

The firm does not draw any advantages from positioning in Italy, while being localized in China permits leverage on low labour costs in producing air-conditioning systems for that region. As mentioned above, operating in a narrow niche of the air-conditioning industry enables the firm to avoid the price competition imposed by big competitors, and allows it to concentrate on a market where the competitive variable is not based on low prices but on customer satisfaction, on technological innovativeness and on a qualified after-sales service to the client.

6.5.5 Dynamic capabilities: paths

Mr Caciolli is 45 and his educational background is based on electronic engineering studies at the University of Pavia. He started

work as a computer programmer at the Technical Service Office of the University of Pavia in order to develop and to plan an integrated information system for the university. At the same time, he worked as an apprentice in RC Group, as a business administration programmer. In 1983, he became responsible for international sales at RC Group and later became the Sales Manager. Since 1997 he has been the CEO, in this role he plans the organizational structure and designs the internal information system. The training career of this entrepreneur has drawn on his managerial abilities and on technical competences. He has fundamental skills, thanks to his experience. His curiosity and his affability with the workers and engineers of the firm led him to improve his knowledge on subjects such as administration, electronics and mechanics. He speaks English. He has followed different courses in Marketing at the University Bocconi in Milan, the Master in International Finance at the University of Pavia, and he is currently attending courses in the Faculty of Economics at the University of Pavia.

He appears to be a highly perceptive individual, able to understand the problems related to the organization and its efficient management. Mr Caciolli also has a high-risk propensity: in 1983 he decided to manage the international relationships with foreign distributors, while in 1992 he was convinced of the growth potential of the Chinese market.

The experience gained from the failed business in China in 2000 has permitted reinvestment in the same market, adopting a different strategy. Nowadays, knowledge transfer is not involved and Chinese products will be based on mature European and American technologies, thus avoiding imitation by Chinese competitors. Moreover, local production will provide only for that region.

6.5.6   Performance

RC Group is an established firm with long-term experience in the market of air-conditioning systems for Information and Communication technology buildings, operating in different industries.

From its foundation in 1963, the firm has increased turnover from 2 million Euros to 47 million Euros in 2005. In 2000, partnership in China and increasing Internet applications, with the consequent need for air-conditioning systems, took the turnover to 89 million Euros in 2001, in 2003 the turnover decreased to 44 million Euros, and nowadays is still growing. In the last ten years, the number of employees has not changed, because RC Group decided to outsource the production to small firms close to the main factories.

As far as international performance is concerned, the firm has imported components since its foundation because the main component suppliers were located in the United States and Japan, although they operated in Italy through distributors. Nowadays, import represents 50 per cent of sources: 98 per cent from Europe, mainly from Germany and France, and 2 per cent from Canada and Australia. Export started in 1983 with Mr Caciolli, due to an unexpected and exogenous event. In 1983 export was 15 per cent, in 1985 it was 37 per cent, while nowadays it is 48 per cent.

In China, international activities involved commercial agreements in 1987 and 1992 and Joint Ventures in 1997. The Chinese subsidiary is actually composed of four offices, managing more than 50 sales partners and 20 after sales partners.

The RC Group sales network covers the whole world. This network is supported by a widespread and qualified Service Organization that guarantees after-sales service.

In 1982, 12 European Union countries were provided for by distributors (mainly Switzerland, Germany, Holland and Sweden), while in 2005 RC Group served 56 different countries: Saudi Arabia, Argentina, Australia, Austria, Bahrain, Belgium, Bosnia-Herzegovina, Chile, Cyprus, Croatia, Denmark, Egypt, Arabic Emirates, Estonia, Russia, Finland, France, Germany, Japan, Jordan, Great Britain, Greece, Indonesia, Iran, Iraq, Ireland, Israel, Italy, Kuwait, Latvia, Libya, Luxemburg, Morocco, Norway, Holland, Oman, Pakistan, Poland, Portugal, Qatar, Czech Republic, South Africa, China, Serbia/Montenegro,Singapore, Syria, Slovenia, Spain, Sweden, Switzerland, Thailand, Tunisia, Turkey, Hungary, Yemen, Zimbabwe.

6.5.7 Discussion

The RC Group represents an established firm, showing innovativeness in terms of product, organizational structure and information systems. It also shows risk-seeking behaviour, especially in setting up international activities in China after a negative experience during the 1990s.

According to Bell, McNaughton and Young (2001) RC Group can be considered a Born-Again Global, since the international activity started from a specific factor some years after inception, but after this event the firm has been able to grow very fast in international markets. In the case of RC, the event is not only the occasion *per se* but also the fact that the son of the entrepreneur had just joined the organization with no experience but strong commitment, good cultural background, high absorptive capacity, risk propensity and international vision.

Networking and organizational learning are the two main factors influencing the performance and the international entrepreneurial orientation of RC Group. In particular, networking influenced the opportunity scanning and evaluation process, through which the founder decided to export in Europe, leveraging on a consolidated network of distributors. On the other hand, learning allows the dynamic reconfiguring of capabilities in order to perform better in terms of products and markets.

Nowadays networking involves suppliers that are connected through an integrated information system in order to reduce costs and space in storage, and distributors that allowed internationalization in Europe and in China. Leveraging on their experience and strong market knowledge, they represent a competitive advantage for RC Group.

Organizational learning is built on the individual competences and routines developed over the years and collected and distributed through an informal organizational structure and an information system.

RC Group demonstrates a knowledge accumulation and distribution process that permits the sharing and the dissemination of learning to relevant parties within the organization. In addition, this phase relates to the integration process in that the new practice is enacted by the organization to disseminate the new learning.

Members take coordinated action in order to diffuse the new activities, changes or routines. Finally, these processes, linked to the absence of turnover in workers and employees, allow the new learning to become embedded in the organization's systems, procedures, routines, practices and structures. That is, learning becomes part of the organizational memory.

Conclusion

The subject of this work has been to understand the entrepreneurial phenomenon from an international perspective. This recent area of study, although rich with ideas in many dimensions, is still lacking a solid and accepted theoretical basis. Different areas influence International Entrepreneurship: Entrepreneurship, International Business, Strategic Management.

Many researchers have called for a unique and comprehensive approach, taking into account the various methodological and theoretical models in order to develop a coherent theory that might capture the dynamic processes characterizing International Entrepreneurship.

This work proposes a theoretical frame in order to respond to this call, based on a resources-based perspective of the firm, where knowledge and learning are the fundamental issues. In addition to this, entrepreneurship is considered at the cross-road of individual and organizational perspectives, in their reciprocal interrelations. The third issue of this book is that entrepreneurship is a process and not an event. From this point of view, an organization is entrepreneurial not just because it is newly born, but because it can demonstrate its possession of entrepreneurial capabilities over time.

In particular, the field of observation is defined by International Entrepreneurial Organizations (IEOs). Literature typically addresses two special cases of international entrepreneurship, that is, International New Ventures and MNE subsidiaries. The former are represented by new firms that engage in international markets, the latter are represented by established subsidiaries that compete

entrepreneurially in the market. In a resource-based and dynamic view of entrepreneurship, the attention shifts from the firm's age and/or governance to its entrepreneurial orientation and capabilities and to entrepreneurial behaviour as a process in time.

Based on three cases, this work analysed an international new venture, an established multinational subsidiary and an established medium-sized firm that demonstrate entrepreneurial behaviour, to answer the following question: which resources and capabilities at the individual and organizational level support international entrepreneurship?

The research model proposed was constructed from a review of International Business, Strategic Management and Entrepreneurship studies. With respect to the growing number of studies using entrepreneurship and social network in the investigation of internationalization and to provide a theoretical perspective in explaining the economic role of the entrepreneur, we applied Schumpeter's view of the entrepreneur and Kirzner's 'Theory of Entrepreneurial Discovery' (1997), which explains how entrepreneurs drive the market through discovery and exploitation of the opportunities overlooked by others. Similarly, Hayek (1948) sees market competition as a process through which to discover opportunities, while according to Shane and Venkataraman (2000), Gartner (1989) and Schumpeter (1934) the core issues are innovation and creation. This involves new ventures and organizations, new combinations of goods and services, methods of production, markets and supply chains, recognition and exploitation of new and existing opportunities, cognitive processes, behaviours and modes of action to exploit new and existing opportunities. Opportunity exploitation involves risk and uncertainty (Cantillon, 1775; Knight, 1921). Innovativeness, risk-taking and proactiveness are measures of Entrepreneurial Orientation (Covin and Slevin, 1991; Wiklund, 1999).

In searching for entrepreneurs' sources of information about international market opportunities, we integrated the part of social network analysis that embraces Granovetter's (1985) view of economic action.

The importance of the entrepreneur is emphasized in the resource-based perspective (Penrose, 1995). On the one hand, during the organization process entrepreneurs have to decide which resources

are more important, then acquire and use them in the firms and, on the other hand, decisions of managers and entrepreneurs depend on their knowledge, education and experience, which determine their capacity to take actions.

The success of a firm does not depend only on existing resources and capabilities but also on the capacity of the founder/entrepreneur/team management and on their ability to mobilize and dynamically combine external and internal resources, adapting them to changes in the environment. According to the perspective of this work, dynamic capabilities represent an expression of entrepreneurship at the organizational level. The present research has been developed building on a dynamic capabilities framework because it can provide an answer to the above-mentioned question regarding the move from individual to organizational entrepreneurial features.

In doing this it has been necessary to define the main characteristics of international entrepreneurial firms, that is, a two-level approach: the analysis of the entrepreneur and firm's resources and capabilities.

The entrepreneur is particularly important for this research area, especially in small and medium enterprises because it has been noticed that specific behaviour, such as proactivity or a high risk-propensity, business capability or other unique qualities that might help generate innovative ideas, may be the cornerstones on which an International Entrepreneurship theory can be built.

In analysing both literature and case studies, the role of individuals in entrepreneurial organizations is crucial, but individuals – as well as organizations – must be analysed in conjunction with their networks. A social and organizational perspective of international entrepreneurship is found in the three case studies to be a fundamental determinant and interpretative key for international commitment and performance. Networking and experience (from multiple sources) feed intense and rapid learning processes in IEOs. A better look at the processes underlying international entrepreneurship confirms that learning plays a central role. In particular, the dynamic capabilities approach applied to International Entrepreneurship studies seems to best explain international firms' entrepreneurial behaviour. Ability to coordinate and to integrate internal and external resources, to

reconfigure the firm's asset structure in terms of product portfolio and/or internal processes and personal or organizational experience, coupled with a personal or organizational network, seem to be the most important resources and capabilities able to explain and to identify international entrepreneurial firms.

In the Barrera case study, although the firm has been recently set up, the international entrepreneurial behaviour seems to be based on its unique resources, innovative outputs and the entrepreneur's experience and personal relationships with clients and suppliers. Furthermore, Barrera's location within an industrial district underlines the importance of the geographical choice of companies that need to benefit from the positive externalities of these locations.

On the other hand, in the Fresenius case study, entrepreneurial behaviour at the subsidiary level derives from the ability to assemble and exploit an appropriate combination of internal and external resources and capabilities in order to introduce new forms of service provision to better perform in the market. Fresenius took risks in managing the process of the 'integrated dialysis provision' and responding to customer demand and showed proactive behaviour in introducing a change in the offer that directly affected the industry (Miller and Friesen, 1982). Moreover, being part of an MNE, with social and formal linkages among the subsidiaries, enabled the Italian subsidiary to have economies of learning from other countries' customer knowledge, recombining knowledge pockets from other countries' experience. This is consistent with the knowledge-based perspective of international business.

In RC Group the decision to internationalize involved the opportunity to operate through an already established network with an in-depth knowledge of each country involved. In this firm organizational learning, based on the internal information system in the organizational structure, and networking are the foundations for the development of capabilities. RC entered into a fast internationalization process some years after foundations, almost casually but immediately showing an entrepreneurial orientation, where the lack of previous experience in the founders and managers is replaced by networking attitude, capacity to learn from mistakes and to take risks.

This book on the one hand proposes taking stock about international entrepreneurship, reviewing its rich and diverse theoretical foundations and, on the other hand, to look ahead, proposing a step forward in the study of international entrepreneurship, starting from the definition of international entrepreneurial organizations (IOE) and then moving to the identification of their common traits in terms of processes, positions and paths.

References

Abernathy, W. J. and Utterback, J. M. (1978), 'Patterns of industrial innovation', *Technology Review*, 80, 40–47.

Acs, Z. J., Audretsch, D. B. (1990), *Innovation and Small Firms*, Cambridge, MA: MIT Press.

Aharoni, Y. (1966), *The Foreign Investment Decision Process*, Boston, MA: Division of Research, Graduate School of Business Administration, Harvard University.

Aharoni Y. (1971), 'On the definition of a multinational corporation', *Quarterly Review of Economics and Business*, V.II, Autumn, 27–37.

Aldrich, H. E., and Martinez, M. A. (2001), 'Many are called, but few are chosen: An evolutionary perspective for the study of Entrepreneurship', *Entrepreneurship Theory and Practice*, 25(4), 41–56.

Aldrich, H. E., and Zimmer, C. (1986), 'Entrepreneurship through social networks'. In D. L. Sexton and R. W. Smilor (eds), *The Art and Science of Entrepreneurship*, Cambridge, MA: Ballinger, 3–23.

Almazan, A., de Motta, A., and Titman, S. (2003), 'Firm Location and the Creation and Utilization of Human Capital', *NBER working paper* 10106.

Almeida, P. (1996), 'Knowledge sourcing by foreign multinationals: Patent citation analysis in the US semiconductor industry', *Strategic Management Journal*, 17, 155–165.

Alvarez, S., and Barney, J. (2000), 'Entrepreneurial capabilities: A resource-based view'. In Meyer, G. D., and Heppard, K. A. (eds), *Entrepreneurship as Strategy: Competing on the Entrepreneurial Edge*, California: Sage Publications.

Alvarez, S. A., and Barney, J. B. (2001), 'How entrepreneurial firms can benefit from alliances with large partners', *Academy of Management Executive*, 15(1), 139–148.

Amit, R., and Schoemaker, P. J. (1993), 'Strategic assets and organisational rent', *Strategic Management Journal*, 14 (January), 33–46.

Anagnostaki, V., and Louri, H. (1995), 'Entry and exit from Greek Manufacturing industry: A test of the symmetric hypothesis', *International Review of Applied Economics*, 9, 85–95.

Anand, B. N., and Khanna, T. (2000), 'Do firms learn to create value? The case of alliances', *Strategic Management Journal*, 21(3), 295–315.

Andersen O. (1993), 'On the internationalisation process of firms: A critical analysis', *Journal of International Business Studies*, 24(2), 33–46.

Andersen, O. (1997), 'Internationalization and market entry mode: A review of theories and conceptual frameworks', *Management International Review*, 37(2).

Andersson S., (2003), 'The entrepreneur and the internationalisation of the firm', *Proceeding of the 7th Vaasa International Business Conference*, Vaasa, Finland.

Andrews, K. R. (1980), *The Concept of Corporate Strategy*, 2nd edn, Homewood, IL: Richard D. Irwin.

Anthony, A. R. (1984), *The Hemodialysis Equipment and Disposable Industry*, Office of Technology Assessment, Congress of the United States.

Arenius, P. (2002), *Creation of Firm-Level Social Capital, its Exploitation, and the Process of Early Internationalization*, PhD Thesis, Helsinki University of Technology, Espoo.

Arnold, U. (1989), 'Global Sourcing – An Indispensable Element in Worldwide Competition', *International Management Review*, 29(4), 14–28.

Audretsch, D. B. (2002), *Entrepreneurship: A Survey of the Literature*, Prepared for the European Commission, Enterprise Directorate General, available at:europa.eu.intcommenterpriseentrepreneurshipgreen_paperliterature_survey_2002.pdf

Autio, E., Sapienza, H. J., and Almeida, J. G. (2000), 'Effects of age at entry. Knowledge intensity and imitability on international growth', *Academy of Management Journal*, 43(5), 909–24.

Autio, E., Yli-Renko, H. and Salonen, A. (1997), 'International growth of young technology based firms: Resource-based network model', *Journal of Enterprising Culture*.

Baden Fuller, C., and Stopford, J. (1991), 'Globalisation frustrated', *Strategic Management Journal*, 12, 493–507.

Bain, J. S. (1968), *Industrial Organization*, New York: Wiley.

Balabanis, G., and Katsikea, E. S. (2003), 'Being an entrepreneurial exporter: Does it pay?', *International Business Review*, 12, 233–52.

Barnett, W. P., Greve, H. R., and Park, D. Y. (1994), 'An evolutionary model of organizational performance', *Strategic Management Journal*, Winter Special Issue, 15, 11–28.

Barney, J. (1986), 'Strategic factor markets: Expectations, luck, and business strategy', *Management Science*, 32, 1231–41.

Barney, J. B. (1991), 'Firm resources and sustained competitive advantage', *Journal of Management*, 17, 99–120.

Bartlett, C. A. (1996), 'Building and Managing the Transnational: The New Organizational Challenge'. In Porter, M. (ed.), *Competition in Global Industries*, Boston: Harvard Business School Press.

Bartlett C. A. and Ghoshal S. (1990), *Managing across Borders: The Transnational Solution*, 2nd edn, Boston, MA: Harvard Business School Press.

Bartlett, C. A., and Ghoshal S. (1994), 'Changing the role of top management: Beyond strategy to purpose', *Harvard Business Review*, November–December, 79–88.

Bartlett, C. A., and Ghoshal, S. (1986), 'Tap your subsidiaries for global reach', *Harvard Business Review*, 64(6), 87–94.

Bartlett, C. A., and Ghoshal, S.(1998), *Managing across Borders: The Transnational Solution*, 2nd edn, Boston, MA: Harvard Business School Press.

Bartlett, C. A. and Ghoshal, S. (2000), *Transnational Management: Text, Cases and Readings in Cross-Border Management*, 3rd edn, Boston, MA: IrwinMcGraw-Hill.

Bateman, T. S. and Crant, J. M. (1993), 'The proactive component of organisational behaviour: A measure and correlates', *Journal of Organisational Behaviour*, 14(2).

Baum, J. A. C., and Haveman, H. A. (1997), 'Love thy neighbour? Differentiation and agglomeration in the Manhattan hotel industry, 1898–1990', *Administrative Science Quarterly*, 42, 304–38.

Beamish, Paul W. (1999), 'The role of alliances in international entrepreneurship'. In *International Entrepreneurship: Globalization and Emerging Businesses, Research in Global Strategic Management*, Vol. 7, Greenwich, CT: JAI Press, 43–61.

Beamish, W. and Makino, S. (1999). 'Characteristics and performance of international joint ventures with non-conventional ownership structures', *Journal of International Business Studies*, 29(4), 797–818.

Becattini G. (2000), *Distretti industriali e sviluppo locale*, Torino: Bollati Boringhieri.

Becherer, R. C. and Maurer, J. C. (1999), 'The proactive personality disposition and the entrepreneurial behaviour among small company presidents', *Journal of Small Business Management*, January.

Becker, G. S. (1976), *The Economic Approach to Human Behaviour*, Chicago: University of Chicago Press.

Bell, J. and Young, S. (1998), 'Towards an integrative framework of the internationalization of the firm'. In Hooley, G. J., Loveridge, R., and Wilson, D. (eds), *Internationalization: Process, Context, and Markets*, New York: St. Martin's Press, 529.

Bell, J. D. (1994), *The Role of Government in Small-Firm Internationalisation: A Comparative Study of Export Promotion in Finland, Ireland, and Norway, with Specific Reference to the Computer Software Industry*. Unpublished Ph.D. Thesis, University of Strathclyde, Glasgow.

Bell, J., McNaughton, R., and Young, S. (2001), 'Born-Again Global' firms – An extension to the 'Born Global Phenomenon', *Journal of International Management*, 7(3), 173–89.

Bengtsoon, L. (2004), 'Explaining Born Global: An organisational learning perspective on the internationalisation process', *International Journal of Globalisation and Small Business*, 1(1), 28–41.

Benito, G. (1997), 'Divestment of foreign production operations', *Journal of Applied Economics*, 29(10), 1365–77.

Benito, G. R. G., and Welch, L. S. (1994), 'Foreign market servicing: Beyond choice of entry mode', *Journal of International Marketing*, 2(2), 7–27.

Bilkey, W. J. and Tesar, G. (1977), 'The export behavior of smaller-sized Wisconsin manufacturing firms', *Journal of International Business Studies*, 8: 93–8.

Binks, M., and Vale, P. A. (1990), *Entrepreneurship and Economic Change*, London: McGraw-Hill.

Birkinshaw, J. (1997), 'Entrepreneurship in multinational corporations: The characteristics of subsidiary initiatives', *Strategic Management Journal*, 18, 207–29.

Birkinshaw, J. (1999), 'The determinants and consequences of subsidiary initiative in multinational corporations', *Entrepreneurship Theory and Practice*, 24(1), 9–36.

Birkinshaw, J. (2000), *Entrepreneurship in the Global Firm: Enterprise and Renewal*, London: Sage Publications.

Birkinshaw, J., and Morrison, A. (1995), 'Configurations of strategy an structure in multinational subsidiaries', *Journal of International Business Studies*, 26(4), 729–53.

Birkinshaw, J., Hood, N., and Jonsson, S. (1998), 'Building firm-specific advantages in multinational corporations: The role of subsidiary initiative', *Strategic Management Journal*, 19, 221–42.

Blomstermo, A., Eriksson, K., and Sharma, D. D. (2004), 'Domestic activity and knowledge development in the internationalization process of firms', *Journal of International Entrepreneurship*, 2(3), 239.

Blomstermo, A., Eriksson, K., Lindstrand, A., and Sharma, D. D. (2004), 'The perceived usefulness of network experiential knowledge in the internationalizing firm', *Journal of International Management*, 10(3), 355–73.

Bloodgood, J. M., Sapienza, H. J., and Almeida, J. G. (1996), 'The internationalization of new high-potential US ventures: Antecedents and outcomes', *Entrepreneurship Theory and Practis*, (Summer), 61–76.

Boettke, P. (1996), 'What is wrong with neoclassical economics (and what is still wrong with Austrian economics)'. In Foldvary, F. (ed.), *Beyond Neoclassical Economics: Heterodox Approaches to Economic Theory*, Cheltenham, UK and Lyme, NH: Elgar.

Bonaccorsi, A. (1992), 'On the relationship between firm size and export intensity', *Journal of International Business Studies*, 23(4), 605–35.

Bowles, S. and Gintis, H. (2000), 'Walrasian economics in retrospect', *The Quarterly Journal of Economics*, 115(4), 1411–39.

Brandenburger, A. M. and Nalebuff, B. J. (1998). 'The right game: Use game theory to shape strategy', *Harvard Business Review*, 73(4), 58–63.

Brown, P., and Bell, J. (2001), 'Industrial clusters and small firm internationalization'. In Taggart, J. H., Berry, M., and McDermott, M. (eds), *Multinationals in a New Era*, Basingstoke: Palgrave Macmillan, 10–27.

Brown, J. S. and Duguid, P. (2002), *The Social Life of Information*, 2nd edn, Boston, MA: Harvard Business School Press.

Bruno, A. V., and Tyebjee, T. T. (1982), 'The environment for entrepreneurship'. In Kent, C. A., Sexton, D. L., and Vesper K. H. (eds), *Encyclopedia of Entrepreneurship*, New York and Englewood Cliffs, CA: Prentice Hall, 288–307.

Brush, C. G. (1995), *Interational Entrepreneurship: The Effect of Firm Age on Motives for Internationalisation*, New York: Garland Publishing.

Buckley, P. J., and Casson, M. (1976), *The Future of the Multinational Enterprise*. London: Macmillan.

Burch, J. G. (1986), *Entrepreneurship*, New York: John Wiley & Sons.

Burgel, O. and Murray, G. C. (1998), 'The international activities of British start-up companies in high-technology industries: Differences between

internationalisers and non-internationalisers'. In Reynolds, P. D., Byrave, W. D., Carter, N. M., Manigart, S., Mason, C. M., Meyer, G., and Shaver, K., (eds), *Frontiers of Entrepreneurship Research*, Wellsley, MA: Babson College.

Busenitz, L. W., Gomez, C., and Spencer, J. W. (2000), 'Country institutional profiles: Unlocking entrepreneurial phenomena', *Academy of Management Journal*, 43(5), 994–1003.

Butos, W., and Koppl, R. (1999), 'Hayek and Kirzner at the Keynesian beauty contest', *Journal des Economists et des Etudes Humanines*, 9(23), 257–75.

Calof, J. L. (1994), 'The relationship between firm size and export behavior revisited', *Journal of International Business Studies*, 25(2), 367–87.

Calof, J., and Beamish, P. (1994), 'The right attitude for international success', *Business Quarterly*, Autumn, 105–110.

Calvelli, A. (1998), *Scelte d'impresa e mercati internazionali*, Torino: Giappichelli.

Campbell, A., and Goold, G. (1987), *Strategies and Styles: The Role of the Centre in Managing Diversified Corporations*, Oxford: Basic Blackwell.

Cantillon, R. (1755), *Essai sur la nature du commerce en general*, from Vaan Praag (1999), *Some Classic Views on Entrepreneurship*, London: Kluwer Publishers, p. 174 n. 3.

Cantwell J. A. (1995), 'The globalisation of technology: What remains of the product cycle model?', *Cambridge Journal of Economics*, 19, 155–74.

Capron L., and Hulland, J. (1999), 'Redeployment of brands, sales forces, and general marketing management expertise following horizontal acquisitions: A resource-based view', *Journal of Marketing*, 63, 41–54.

Carolan, E., and Griffin, R. (2005), Subsidiary strategy: Tales from an entrepreneurial subsidiary, *28th AIB-UK Chapter Conference Proceedings*, Bath.

Carpenter, M. A., and Fredrickson, J. W. (2001), 'Top management teams, global strategic posture, and the moderating role of uncertainty', *Academy of Management Journal*, 44(3), 533–46.

Carpenter, M. A., Sanders, W., and Gregersen, H. (2001), 'Bundling human capital with organizational context: The impact of international assignment experience on multinational firm performance and CEO pay', *Academy of Management Journal*, 44(3), 493–512.

Casson, M. (1982), *The Entrepreneur: An Economic Theory*, Robertson: Oxford.

Casson, M (1990), *Entrepreneurship*, Cheltenham: Edward Elgar.

Caves R. E. (1982), *Multinational Enterprise and Economic Analysis*, Cambridge: Cambridge University Press.

Caves R. E., and Pugel, T. (1980), 'Intraindustry differences in conduct an performance: viable strategies'. In Salomon Brothers Center for Study of Financial institutions, *U.S. Manufacturing Industries*, New York: New York University, Monograph Series in Financial Economics, n.1980–2.

Cavusgil, S. (1980), 'On the internationalisation process of firms,' *European Research*, 8, 273–81.

Cavusgil, S. T. (1984), 'Organisational characteristics associated with export activity', *Journal of Management studies*, 21(1), 3–22.

Cavusgil, S., Tamer, S. and Naor, J. (1987), 'Firm and management characteristics as discriminators for export behavior', *Journal of Business Research*, 15(3), 221–35.

Chetty, S., and Eriksson, K. (2002), 'Mutual commitment and experiential knowledge in mature international business relationships', *International Business Review*, 11(3), 305–24.

Chetty S., Eriksson K. and Hohenthal, J. (2002), 'A cross cultural comparison of collaborative experience in internationalising firms'. In A. Blomstermo and D. Sharma (eds), *Learning in The Internationalisation Process Of Firms*. Cheltenham, UK: Edward Elgar.

Choi, Y. B. (1993), *Paradigms and Conventions: Uncertainty, Decision Making, and Entrepreneurship*, Michigan: The University of Michigan Press.

Christensen C. M. (1999), *Innovation and the General Manager*, New York: McGraw-Hill Higher Education.

Coase, R. H. (1937), 'The nature of the firm', *Economica (NS)*, November, 386–405.

Cochran, D. S., and Dolan, J. (1984), 'Qualitative research: An alternative to quantitative research in communication', *The Journal of Business Communication*, 21(4), 25–33.

Cohen, W. M., and Levinthal, D. A. (1990), 'Absorptive capacity: A new perspective on learning and innovation', *Administrative Science Quarterly*, 35.

Coleman, J. C. (1988), 'Social capital in the creation of human capital', *American Journal of Sociology*, 94, 95–120.

Conner, K. R. (1991), 'A historical comparison of resource-based theory and five schools of thought within industrial organization economics: Do we have a new theory of the firm?', *Journal of Management*, 17(1), 121–54.

Conner, K. R., and Prahalad, C. K. (1996), 'A resource-based theory of the firm: Knowledge versus opportunism', *Organisational Science*, 7(5), 477–501.

Cooper R. G., and Kleinschmidt E. J. (1985), 'The impact of export strategy on export sales performance', *Journal of International Business Studies*, 16, 37–55.

Cooper, A. C., Gimeno-Gascon, F. J., and Woo, C. Y. (1994), 'Initial human and financial capital as predictors of new venture performance', *Journal of Business Venturing*, 9, 371–95.

Cooper, A. C., Woo C. Y., and Dunkelberg W. C. (1988), '"Entrepreneurs" perceived chances for success', *Journal of Business Venturing*, 3(2), 97–108.

Cope, J., and Watts, G. (2000), 'Learning by doing – An exploration of experience, critical incidents and reflection in entrepreneurial learning', *International Journal of Entrepreneurial Behaviour and Research*, 6(3), 104–24.

Coviello, N. E., and Munro, H. J. (1995), 'Growing the entrepreneurial firm: Networking for international market development', *European Journal of Marketing*, 29(7), 49–61.

Covin, J. G., and Slevin, D. P. (1989), 'Strategic management of small firms in hostile and benign environments', *Strategic Management Journal*, 10(1), 75–88.

Covin, J. G., and Slevin, D. P. (1991), 'A conceptual model of entrepreneurship as firm behaviour', *Entrepreneurship Theory and Practise*, Fall, 7–25.

Crossan, M. M., Lane, H. W., and White, R. E. (1999), 'An organizational learning framework: From intuition to institution', *Academy of Management Review*, 24(3), 522–37.

Czinkota, M. R., and Ronkainen, I. (1995), *International Marketing*, 4th edn, Forth Worth, TX: The Dryden Press.

de la Torre, J., and Moxon, R. W. (2001), 'E-commerce and global business: The impact of the information and communication technology revolution on the conduct of international business', *Journal of International Business Studies*, 32 (4), 12–25.

Daily, C. M., Certo, S. T., and Dalton, D. R. (2000), 'International experience in the executive suite: The path to prosperity?', *Strategic Management Journal*, 21, 515–23.

Dana, L. P, Etemad, H., and Wright, R. W. (1999), 'The impact of globalisation on SMEs', *Global Focus*, 11(84), 93–105.

Dana, L. P., and Wright, R. W. (2004), 'Emerging paradigms of international entrepreneurship'. In Dana, L. P. (ed.), *Handbook of Research on International Entrepreneurship*, Cheltenham, UK, and Northampton, MA: Edward Elgar.

Daneke, G. A. (1998), 'Beyond Schumpeter: Nonlinear economics and evolution of the US innovation system', *Journal of Socio-Economics*, 27(1), 97–115.

Deakins, D., and Freel, M. (1998), 'Entrepreneurial learning and the growth process in SMEs', *The Learning Organization*, 5(3), 144–55.

Deephouse, D. (2000), 'Media reputation as a strategic resource: An integration of mass communication and resource-based theories', *Journal of Management*, 26, 1091–1112.

Delany, E., and Molloy, E. (1998), *Strategic Thinking for Multinational Subsidiaries*, Dublin: M.D.L. Management Consultants.

Delmar, F., and Shane, S. (2001), 'Legitimating first: Organizing activities and the survival of new ventures', *Journal of Business Venturing*, 18(2), 189–216.

Demsetz, H. (1988), 'The theory of the firm revisited', *Journal of Economic Law*.

Denicolai, S., Palamara, G., and Zucchella, A. (2005), 'Drivers and dimensions of export performance', *8th Vaasa International Business Conference Proceedings*, University of Vaasa, Vaasa, 21–23 August, 2005.

Dess, G. G., and Robinson, R. B. (1984), 'Measuring organizational performance in the absence of objective measures: The case of privately held firms and conglomerate business units', *Strategic Management Journal*, 5, 265–73.

Dimitratos, P., Lioukas, S., and Carter S. (2004), 'The relationship between entrepreneurship and international performance: The importance of domestic environment', *International Business Review*, 13, 19–41.

Dimitratos, P. and Jones, M. V. (2005), 'Future directions for international entrepreneurship research', *International Business Review*.

Doz, Y. L., and Prahalad, C. K. (1984), 'Patterns of strategic control within multinational corporations', *Journal of International Business Studies*, Fall, 55–72.

Drucker, P. F. (1985), *Innovation and Entrepreneurship: Practice and Principles*, New York: Harper & Row.

Dubini, P., and Aldrich, H. (1991), 'Personal and extended networks are central to the entrepreneurial process', *Journal of Business Venturing*, 6, 305–13.

Dunning, J. H. (1977), 'Trade, location of economic activity and the MNE: A search for an eclectic approach'. In Ohlin, B., Hesselborn, P., and M. Wijkman (eds), *The International Allocation of Economic Activity*, New York: Holmes and Meier.

———. *International Production and the Multinational Enterprise*, London: George Allen & Unwin.

———. (1988), 'The eclectic paradigm of international production: A restatement and some possible extension', *Journal of International Business Studies*, 19(1), 1–32.

———. (1991), *Explaining International Production*, New York: Harper Collins Academic.

———. (1995), 'Reappraising the eclectic paradigm in an age of alliance capitalism', *Journal of International Business Studies*, 26(3).

———. (1998), 'Location and the multinational enterprise: A neglected factor?', *Journal of International Business Studies*, 29, 45–66.

Dunning, J. (2000), *Regions, Globalization and The Knowledge-Based Economy*, Oxford: Oxford University Press.

Dunning, J. and Wymbs, C. (2001), 'The challenge of electronic markets for international business theory', *International Journal of The Economics of Business*, 8(2), 123–45.

Dussauge, P., Garrette, B., and Mitchell, W. (2000), 'Learning from competing partners: Outcomes and durations of scale and link alliances in Europe, North America, and Asia', *Strategic Management Journal*, 21, 99–126.

Eisenhardt, K., and Martin, J. (2000), 'Dynamic capabilities: What are they?', *Strategic Management Journal*, 21(10–11), 1105–21, Special Issue.

Eisenhardt, K. M. (1989), 'Building theories from case study research', *Academy of Management Review*, 14(4), 532–50.

Eisenhardt, K. M. (1991), 'Better stories and better constructs: The case for rigor and comparative logic', *Academy of Management Review*, 16(3), 620–27.

Enright, M. (1998), 'Regional clusters and firms strategy'. In Chandler, A. D., Hangstrom, P., and Solvell, O. (eds), *The Dynamic Firm: The Role of Technology, Strategy, Organizations and Regions*, New York: New York University Press.

Eriksson, K., Johanson, J., Majkgard, A., and Sharma, D. D. (1997), 'Experiential knowledge and cost in the internationalization process', *Journal of International Business Studies*, 28, 2, 337–60.

Eriksson, K., Johanson, J., Majkgard, A., and Sharma, D. D. (2000), 'Effect of variation on knowledge accumulation in the internationalization process', *International Studies of Management and Organization*, 30, 1–26.

Eriksson, K., Majkgard, A., and Sharma, D. D. (2000), 'Path dependence and Knowledge development in the internationalization process', *Management International Review*, 40, 4.

Etemad, H. (2003), 'Managing relations: The essence of international entrepreneurship'. In Etemad, H., and Wright, R. (eds), *Globalisation and Entrepreneurshi: Policy and Strategy Perspectives*, Cheltenham, UK, and Northampton, MA: Edward Elgar.

Etemad, H. (2004), 'A typology'. In Dana, L. P. (ed.), *Handbook of Research on International Entrepreneurship*, Cheltenham, UK, and Northampton, MA: Edward Elgar.

EU Enterprise publications. (2002), *Observatory of European SMEs 2002: Annual Report*, European Commission.

Evans, D. S. and Jovanovic, B. (1989), 'An estimated model of entrepreneurial choice under liquidity constraints', *The Journal of Political Economy*.

Evans, J., Treadgold, A., and Mavondo, F. (2000), 'Psychic distance and the performance of international retailers: A suggested theoretical framework', *International Marketing Review*, 17(45), 373–91.

Fetter, R. B, Shin Y., Freeman J. L., Averill R. F., and Thompson, J. D. (1980), 'Case-mix definition by diagnosis-related groups', *Medical Care*, 18 (Suppl.), 1–53.

Ffowcs, W. J. (1997), 'Local clusters and local export growth', *New Zealand Strategic Management*, Summer, 24–9.

Finkelstein, S., and Hambrick, D. C. (1996), *Strategic Leadership: Top Executives and Their Effects on Organizations*, Minneapolis, MN: West Publishing.

Floyd, S. W., and Wooldridge, B. (1999), 'Knowledge creation and social networks in corporate entrepreneurship: the renewal of organisational capability', *Entrepreneurship Theory and Practice*, 23(3), 123–43.

Forsgren, M. (2002), 'The concept of learning in the Uppsala Internationalization Process Model: A critical review', *International Business Review*, 11(3).

Forsgren, M., Johanson, J., and Sharma, D. D. (2000), 'Development of MNC centers of excellence'. In Holm, U., and T. Pedersen (eds), *The Emergence and Impact of MNC Centers of Excellence*, Basingstoke: Palgrave Macmillan.

Fortis, M. (1998), *Il Made in Italy*, Bologna: Il Mulino.

Franko, L. (1876), *The European MNC*, Greenwich, CT: Greylock Press.

Fresenius Medical Care (2002), *Annual Report*, www.fmc-ag.com

Friedman, M. (1976), *Price Theory: A Provisional Text*, Chicago: Aldine.

Gabrielsson, M., Kirpalani, M., Dimitratos, P., Solberg, C. A. and Zucchella, A. (2006), 'Born globals'. Propsotions to help advance the discipline, panel, EIBA conference Fribourg.

Gaglio, C. M. (1997), 'Opportunity identification: Review, critique and suggested research directions'. In Katz, J. A. (ed.), *Advances in Entrepreneurship, Firm Emergence and Growth*, Vol. 3, Greenwich: CT: JAI Press, pp. 139–202.

Gambro (2002), *Annual Report*, www.gambro.com

Gartner, W. B. (1985), 'A conceptual framework for describing the phenomenon of New Venture creation', *The Academy of Management Review*.

Gartner, W. B. (1989), 'Who is an entrepreneur? is the wrong question', *Entrepreneurship Theory and Practice*, 13(4), 47–68.

Gartner, W. B. (1990), 'What are we talking about when we talk about entrepreneurship?', *Journal of Business Venturing*, 5, 15–25.

Ghoshal, S., and Bartlett, C. A. (1990), 'The multinational corporation as an interorganizational network', *Academy of Management Review*, 15, 603–25.

Ghoshal, S., and Nohria, N. (1997), *The Differentiated Network: Organizing Multinational Corporations for Value Creation*, San Francisco, CA: Jossey-Bass.

Gilad, B., and Levine, P. (1986), 'A behavioral model of entrepreneurial supply', *Journal of Small Business Management*, 24, 45–51.

Granovetter, M. (1973), 'The strength of the weak tie', *American Journal of Sociology*, 78, 1360–80.

Granovetter, M. (1985), 'Economic action and social structure: The problem of embeddedness', *American Journal of Sociology*, 91, 481–510.

Grant, R. M. (1991), 'The resource-based theory of competitive advantage', *California Management Review*, 33(3), 114–35.

———. (1996), 'Toward a knowledge-based theory of the firm', *Strategic Management Journal*, 17, 109–22.

Grant, Robert M., Jammine, A. P., and Thomas, H. (1988), 'Diversity, diversification, and profitability among British manufacturing companies, 1972–84', *Academy of Management Journal*, 31, 771–801.

Griffin, R. (1999), 'Power in and about the Irish subsidiary', *IAM conference*, Limerick.

Griffin, R. (2003), 'The loosely bound subsidiary: A case of subsidiary management buy out', *6th McGill Conference on International Entrepreneurship*, Derry.

Guba, E. G., and Lincon, Y. S. (1994), 'Paradigmatic controversies, contradictions and emerging confluences'. In N. K. Denzin and Y. S. Lincoln (eds), *Handbook of Qualitative Research*, 1st edn, Thousand Oaks, CA: Sage.

Gulati, R., and Gargiulo, M. (1999), 'Where do interorganizational networks come from?', *American Journal of Sociology*, 104 (5), 1439–93.

Gulati, R., Nohria, N., and Zaheer, A. (2000), 'Strategic networks', *Strategic Management Journal*, 21, 203–15.

Gunning, P. (1997), 'The theory of entrepreneurship in Austrian economics'. In W. Keizer et al. (eds), *Austrians in Debate*, London: Routledge.

Gupta, A. K., and Govindarjan, P. (2000), 'Knowledge flows within multinational corporations', *Strategic Management Journal*, 21, 473–96.

Guth, W., and Ginsberg, A. (1990), 'Introduction: corporate entrepreneurship', *Strategic Management Journal*, 11, 297–308.

Guth, W. D., and Taguiri, R: (1965), 'Personal values and corporate strategy', *Harvard Business Review*, 43(5), 123–32.

Hambrick, D. C. (1981a), 'Environment, strategy, and power within top management teams', *Administrative Science Quarterly*, 28(2), 253–76.

Hambrick, D. C. (1981b), 'Strategic awareness within top Management teams', *Strategic Management Journal*, 2, 263–79.

Hamel, G. and Prahalad, C. K. (1994), *Competing For The Future*, Boston, MA: Harvard Business School Press.

Hanks, S. H., Watson, C. J., Jansen, E., and Chandler, G. N. (1993), 'Tightening the life-cycle construct: A taxonomic study of growth stage configurations in high-technology organizations', *Entrepreneurship: Theory and Practice*, 18(2), 5–31.

Harper, D. (1996), *Entrepreneurship and the Market Process: An Enquiry into the Growth of Knowledge*, London: Routledge.

Harper, D. (1998), 'Institutional conditions for entrepreneurship', *Advances in Austrian Economics*, 5, 241–75.

Hart, Myra M., Brush, C., and Greene, P. (1999), 'From planning to growth and beyond: A cross industry analysis of entrepreneurial priorities'.

In W. Bygrave (ed.), *Frontiers of Entrepreneurship Research, 1998: Proceedings of the 18th Annual Entrepreneurship Research Conference*, Babson Park, Mass.: Babson College.

Harverston, P. D., Kedia, B. L., and Davis, P. S. (2000), 'Internationalisation of born globals and gradual globalising firms: The impact of the manager', *Advances in Competitiveness Research*, 8(1), 92–9.

Hayek, F. A. (1945), 'The use of knowledge in society', *American Economic Review*, 35(4), 519–30.

Hayek, F. A. (1948), *Individualism and Economic Order*, London, Routledge.

Hébert, R. F. and Link, A. N. (1989), 'In search of the meaning of entrepreneurship', *Small Business Economics*.

Hedlund, G. (1980), 'The role of foreign subsidiaries in strategic decision making in Swedish multinational corporations', *Strategic Management Journal*, 1, 23–6.

Hedlund, G. (1986), 'The hypermodern MNC: A heterarchy?', *Human Resource Management*, 25(1), 9–35.

Hennart, J.-F. (1982), *A Theory of Multinational Enterprise*, Ann Arbor, MI: UMI.

Hicks, J. (1939), *Value and Capital*, Oxford: Clarendon Press.

Hill, R. W., and Hillier, T. J. (1977), *Organisational Buying Behaviour*, London: MacMillan.

Hinttu, S., Forsman, M., and Kock, S. (2002), 'Mission impossible? Internationalization without Social Networks', Paper for the project LIIKE: GLOBAL – Sucessful Internationalization of SME, 1–22.

Hitt, M. A., Hoskinson, R. E., and Kim, H. (1997), 'International diversification: Effects on innovation and firm performance in product-diversified firms', *Academy of Management Journal*, 40 (4), 767–98.

Hitt, M. A., and Ireland, R. D. (1985), 'Corporate distinctive competence, strategy, industry, and performance', *Strategic Management Journal*, 6, 273–93.

Hitt, M. A., and Ireland, R. D. (2000), 'The intersection of entrepreneurship and strategic management research'. In D. L. Sexton and H. Landstrom (eds), *The Blackwell Handbook of Entrepreneurship*, Oxford: Blackwell, 45–63.

Hitt, M. A., Ireland, R. D., and R. E. Hoskinsson (1999), *Strategic Management*, Cincinnati, OH: South-Western.

Hitt, M. A., Ireland, R. D., and Lee, H. (2000), 'Technological learning, knowledge management, firm growth and performance: an introductory essay', *Journal of Engineering and Technology Management*, 17, 231–46.

Hitt, M. A., Ireland, R. D., Camp, S. M., and Sexton, D. L. (2001), 'Strategic entrepreneurship: Entrepreneurial strategies for wealth creation', *Strategic Management Journal*, 22, (special issue), 479–91.

Hitt, M. A., Ireland R. D., Camp S. M., and Sexton D. L. (2002), *Strategic Entrepreneurship: Creating a New Mindset*, Oxford: Blackwell.

Hitt, M. A., Keats, B. W., and DeMarie, S. (1998), 'Navigating in the new competitive landscape: Building strategic flexibility and competitive advantage in the twenty-first century', *Academy of Management Executive*, 12(4), 22–42.

Hodgson, G. M. (1993), Economics and Evolution: Bringing Life Back into Economics, Oxford: Polity Press.

Holmquist, C. (2003), 'Is the medium really the message? Moving perspective from the entrepreneurial actor to the entrepreneurial action', *New Movements in Entrepreneurship*, Cheltenham: Edward Elgar, 2003.

Holstein, W. J. (1992), 'Little companies, big exports', *Business Week*, 13 April, 70–2.

Hoskisson, R. E, Hitt, M. A., and Hill, C. W. L. (1993), 'Managerial incentives and investment in R&D in large multiproduct firms', *Organization Science*, 4, 325–41.

Huber, G. P. (1991), 'Organizational learning: The contributing processes and the literatures', *Organization Science*, 2(1).

Hymer, Stephen H. (1976), *The International Operations of National Firms: A Study of Direct Foreign Investment*, Cambridge, MA: The MIT Press.

Hyvarinen, L. (1990), 'Innovativeness and its indicators in small and medium-sized industrial enterprises', *International Small Business Journal*, 9(1), 65–79.

Ibeh, K. I. N. (2003), 'Toward a contingency framework of export entrepreneurship: Conceptualisations and empirical evidence', *Small Business Economics*, 20, 49–68.

Ibeh, K. I. N., and Young, S. (2001), 'Exporting as an entrepreneurial act: An empirical study of Nigerian firms', *European Journal of Marketing*, 35(56), 566–86.

Ibrahim, G., and Galt, V., (2002), 'Towards a theoretical synthesis of ethnic entrepreneurs'. In Kantarelis, D. (ed.), *Global Business and Economics Review –* Anthology, Working paper, University of Montreal, Montreal.

Ibrahim, Gamal, and Vyakarnam, S. (2003), 'Defining the Role of the Entrepreneur in Economic Thought: Limitations of Mainstream Economics,' *working paper*, Nottingham Business School.

Ietto-Gillies, G. (2005), *Transnational Firms and International Production. Concepts, Theories and Effects*, London: Edward Elgar.

Ireland, R. D., Hitt, M. A., Camp, S. M. and Sexton, D. L. (2001), 'Integrating entrepreneurship and strategic management actions to create firm wealth', *Academy of Management Executive*.

Italian Society of Nephrology, (2002), *Italian Registry of Dialysis and Transplant, Annual Report*, www.sin-ridt.orgsin-ridtsin-ridt.org.htm

Itami, H. (with T. W. Roehl) (1987), *Mobilizing Invisible Assets*, Cambridge, MA: Harvard University Press.

Jenks, L. H. (1950), 'Approaches to entrepreneurial personality', *Explorations in Entrepreneurial History*, 2, 91–9.

Johannisson B. (1994), 'Building a "glocal" strategy – internationalizing small firms through local networking', *39ème Conférence Mondiale de l'ICSB: Les PMEPMI et leur contribution au développement régional et international*, 27–29 juin, Strasbourg, 127–35.

Johannisson, B. (2000), 'Networking and entrepreneurial growth'. In Sexton, D. L., and Landstrom, H. (eds), *Handbook of Entrepreneurship*, Oxford: Blackwell, pp. 368–86.

Johanson, J., and Mattsson, L. G. (1987), *Internationalisation In Industrial Systems – A Network Approach Strategies in Global Competition*, Prince Bertil Symposium, Selected Papers, New York: Croom Helm, pp. 287–314.

Johanson, J., and Mattsson, L. G. (1988), 'Internationalization in industrial systems – a network approach'. In Hood, N., and Vahlne, J.-E. (eds), *Strategies in Global Competition*, New York: Croom Helm, pp. 287–314.

Johanson, J., and Vahlne, E. (1977), 'The internationalization process of the firm: A model of knowledge development and increasing foreign market commitment', *Journal of International Business Studies*, 8, 23–32.

Johanson, J., and J.-E. Vahlne (1990), 'The mechanism of internationalisation', International Marketing Review, 7(4), 11–25.

Johanson, J., and Vahlne, J.-E., (1992), 'Management of foreign market entry', *Scandinavian International Business Review*, 1(3), 9–27.

Johanson, J., and Vahlne, J.-E. (2003), 'Business relationship learning and commitment in the internationalization process', *Journal of International Entrepreneurship*, 1, 83–101.

Johanson, J., and Wiedersheim-Paul, F. (1975), 'The internationalization of the firm: Four Swedish cases', *Journal of Management Studies*, 12, 305–22.

Johnson H., (1970), 'The efficiency and welfare implication of the international corporation'. In, C. Kindleberger and D. Audretsch (eds), *The Multinational Corporation in the 1980s*, Cambridge, MA: MIT Press, pp. 35–56.

Jolly, V. K., Alahuta, M., and Jeannet J.-P. (1992), 'Challenging the incumbents: How high technology start-ups compete globally', *Journal of Strategic Ch'ange*, 1, 71–82.

Jones, M., and Coviello, N. E. (2005), 'Internationalization: Conceptualising an entrepreneurial process of behaviour in time', *Journal of International Business Studies*, 36, 284–303.

Kandsaami, S. (1998), 'Internationalization of small and medium sized born global firms: A conceptual model', *International Council for Small Business World Conference on Entrepreneurship, Proceedings*, Singapore.

Karagozoglu, N., and Lindell, M. (1998), 'Internationalization of small and medium-sized technology-based firms: An exploratory study', *Journal of Small Business Management*, 36(1), 44–59.

Keil, T., Autio, E., and Robertson, P. (1997), 'Embeddedness, power, control and innovation in the telecommunications sector', *Technology Analysis and Strategic Management*, 9(3), 299–316.

Khandawalla, P. N. (1987), 'Generators of pioneering-innovative management: Some Indian evidence', *Organization Studies*, 8(1), 39–59.

Kilby, P. (1971a), 'Hunting the heffalump'. In Kilby, P. (ed.), *Entrepreneurship and Economic Development*, New York: Free Press, 1–40.

Kilby, P. (1971b), *Entrepreneurship and Economic Development*, New York: Free Press.

Kirzner, I. M. (1973), *Competition and Entrepreneurship*, Chicago: University of Chicago Press.

———. (1979), *Perception, Opportunity, and Profit: Studies in the Theory of Entrepreneurship*, Chicago: University of Chicago Press.

———. (1992), *The Meaning of Market Process*, New York: Routledge.

———. (1997), 'Entrepreneurial discovery and the competitive market process: An Austrian approach', *Journal of Economic Literature*, 35, 60–85.

Knight, F. H. (1921), *Risk, Uncertainty and Profit*, Boston: Houghton Mifflin.

Knight, G. (2000), 'Entrepreneurship and marketing strategy: The SME under globalization', *Journal of International Marketing*.

Knight, G. A., (2001), 'Entrepreneurship and strategy in the international SME', *Journal of International Management*, 7(3), 155–71.

Knight G. A., and Cavusgil, T. (1995), 'The born global firm: A challenge to traditional internationalization theory', *Advances in International Marketing*, 8, 11–26.

Knight, G. A., and Cavusgil, V. (2004), 'Innovation, organizational capabilities, and the born-global firm', *Journal of International Business Studies*, 35, 124–41.

Knight, R. M. (1994), 'A longitudinal study of criteria used by venture capitalists in Canada', *Journal of Small Business and Entrepreneurship*.

Kobrin, S. (1991), 'An empirical analysis of the determinants of global integration', *Strategic Management Journal*, 12(17), 24–43.

Kogut, B., (1984), 'Normative observations on the international value-added chain and strategic groups', *Journal of International Business Studies*, 15(2), 151–67.

Kogut, B., and Zander, U. (1993), 'Knowledge of the firm and the evolutionary theory of multinational corporation', *Journal of International Business Studies*, 24(4), 625–46.

Kolb, H. (1994), *Experience as the Source of Learning and Development*, London: Prentice Hall.

Koolman, G. (1971), 'Say's conception of the role of the entrepreneur', *Economica New Series*, 38, 282–86.

Kotler, P., and Scott, W. G. (1993), *Marketing Management*, London: Prentice Hall.

Kuemmerle, W. (2002), 'Home base and knowledge management in international ventures', *Journal of Business Venturing*, 17, 99–122.

Kundu, S. K., and Katz, J. A. (2003), 'Born-international SMEs: BI-level impacts of resources and intentions', *Small Business Economics*, 20(1), 25–47.

Lado, A., Boyd, N., and Wright, P. (1992), 'A competency-based model of sustained competitive advantage: Toward a conceptual integration', *Journal of Management*, 18, 77–91.

Landström, H. (1999), 'The roots of entrepreneurship research', *New England Journal of Entrepreneurship*.

Larimo, J. (2001), 'Internationalization of SMEs – two case studies of Finnish Born Global Firms', *EIBA Conference Proceedings*, Paris.

Larsson, R. (1993), 'Case survey methodology: Quantitative analysis or patterns across case studies', *Academy of Management Journal*, 36(6), 1515–46.

Leamer, E. and Storper, M. (2001), 'The economic geography of the Internet age', *Journal of International Business Studies*, 32(4), 121–34.

Leonard-Barton, D., (1992), 'Core capabilities and core rigidities: A paradox in managing new product development', *Strategic Management Journal*, 13, 111–25.

Leonidou, L. C., and Katsikeas, C. S. (1996), 'The export development process: An integrative review of empirical models', *Journal of International Business Studies*, 27, 517–51.

Lesgold, A. (1988), 'Toward a theory of curriculum for use in designing intelligent instructional systems'. In Mandl, H., and Lesgold, A. (eds), *Learning Issues for Intelligent Tutoring Systems*, New York: Springer-Verlag.

Levinthal, D., and Myatt, J. (1994), 'Co-evolution of capabilities and industry: The evolution of mutual fund processing', *Strategic Management Journal*, Winter Special Issue, 15, 45–62.

Levitt, T. (1983), 'The globalisation of markets', *Harvard Business Review*, May–June, 92–102.

Li, H., and Atuahene-Gima, K. (2001), 'Product innovation strategy and the performance of new technology ventures in China', *Academy of Management Journal*, 44, 1123–34.

Liang, N., and A. Parkhe (1997), 'Importer behavior: The neglected counterpart of international exchange', *Journal of International Business Studies*, Fall, 495–529.

Lindmark, L. (1994), *Småföretagens Internationalization – En Nordisk Jämförande Studie*, Norway: Nordrefo.

Lindquist, M. (1991), *Infant Multinationals: The Internationalization of Young, Technology-Based Swedish Firms*, Stockholm, Diss: Stockholm School of Economics.

Ling-yee, L. (2004), 'An examination of the foreign market knowledge of exporting firms based in the people's Republic of China: Its determinants and effect on export intensity', *Industrial Marketing Management*, 33(7), 561–72.

Lorsch, J., and Allen, S. (1973), *Managing Diversity and Interdependence*, Cambridge, MA: Harvard University Press.

Lu, J. W., and Beamish, P. W. (2001), 'The internationalization and performance of SMEs', *Strategic Management Journal*, 22, 565–86.

Lumpkin, G. T., and Dess, G. G. (1996), 'Clarifying the entrepreneurial orientation construct and linking it to performance', *Academy of Management Review*, 21(1), 135–72.

Lüthje T., and Servais, P. (2005), 'Firms' international sourcing and intra-industry trade', *working paper* 2, Department of Business Research, University di Pavia.

Lydall, H. (1998), *A Critique of Orthodox Economics: An Alternative Model*, New York: St. Martin's Press.

Lye, A., and Hamilton, R. T. (2000), 'Search and performance in international exchange', *European Journal of Marketing*, 34(1), 176–89.

Maccarini, M. E., Scabini, P., and Zucchella, A. (2003), 'Internationalisation strategies in Italian district-based firms: Theoretical modelling and empirical evidence', *Paper Presented at theCconference on Cluster, Industrial Districts and Firms*, Modena, Italy, 12–13 September.

Maccarini, M. E., Scabini, P., and Zucchella, A. (2004), 'Co-location and business-specific issues in the internationalisation of SMEs: Their impact on the growth and on the international performance of Born Global firms', In *Recent European Research on SME Export Behaviour and Internationalization*, Proceedings of the University of Vaasa, Reports 111, Vaasa.

Maccarini, M. E., Palamara, G., Scabini, P., and Zucchella, A. (2004), 'International entrepreneurship and export performance', *30th EIBA Annual Conference*, 5–8 December 2004, Ljubljana, Slovenia.

Madhok, A. (1996), 'The organization of economic activity: Transaction costs, firm capabilities, and the nature of governance', *Organisational Science*, 7(5), 577–90.

Madsen, T. K., and Servais, P. (1997), 'The internationalization of Born Globals: An evolutionary process?', *International Business Review*, 6(6), 561–83.

Majkgard, A., and Sharma, D. D. (1998), 'Service quality by international relationships: Service firms in the global market'. In Rao, C. P. (ed.), *Globalization, Privatization and the Free Market Economy*, Westport, CT, and NewYork: Quorum Books.

Majocchi A. (2000), 'Are industrial clusters going international? The case of Italian SMEs in Romania', *working paper 12. Università dell'Insubria*, Varese.

Maleksadeh, A. and Nahavandi, A. (1985), 'Small business exporting. Misconceptions are abundant', *American Journal of Small Business*, 9(4), 7–14.

Malnight, T. W. (1996), 'The transition from decentralized to network-based MNC structures: An evolutionary perspective', *Journal of International Business Studies*, 27, 43–65.

Markusen, A. (1996), 'Sticky places in a slippery space: A typology of industrial districts', *Economic Geography*, 72, 293–313.

Marshall, C., and Rossman, G. B. (1999), *Designing Qualitative Research*, 3rd edn, London: Sage.

McClelland, D. C. (1971), 'Entrepreneurship and achievement motivation: Approaches to the science of socio-economic development'. *UNESCO*, Paris.

McDougall, P. P. (1989), 'International versus domestic entrepreneurship: New venture strategic behavior and industry structure', *Journal of Business Venturing*, 4, 387–99.

McDougall, P. P., and Oviatt, B. M. (1996), 'New venture internationalization, strategic change, and performance: A follow-up study', *Journal of Business Venturing*, 11(1), 23–42.

McDougall, P. P., and Oviatt, B. M. (1997), 'International entrepreneurship literature in the 1990s and directions for future research'. In Sexton, D. L., and Smilor, R. W. (eds), *Entrepreneurship 2000*, Chicago: Upstart Publishing, pp. 291–320.

McDougall, P. P., Oviatt, B. M., and Shrader, R. C. (2003), 'A comparison of international and domestic new ventures', *Journal of International Entrepreneurship*, 1, 59–82.

McDougall, P. P., Shane, S., and Oviatt, B. M. (1994), 'Explaining the formation of International New Ventures', *Journal of Business Venturing*, 9(6), 469–87.

McEvily, S., and Chakravarthy, B. (2002), 'The persistence of knowledge-based advantage: An empirical test for product performance and technological knowledge', *Strategic Management Journal*, 23, 285–305.

McEvily, B., and Zaheer, A. (1999), 'Bridging ties: A soure of firm hetereogeneity in competitive capabilities', *Strategic Management Journal*, 20, 1133–56.

McGee, J. E., and Peterson, M. (2000), 'Toward the development of measures of distinctive competencies among small independent retailers', *Journal of Small Business Management*, 38(2), 19–33.

McGrath, R. G., MacMillan, I. C., and Scheinberg, S. (1992), 'Elitist, risk-takers, and rugged individualists? An exploratory analysis of cultural differences between entrepreneurs and non-entrepreneurs', *Journal of Business Venturing*, 7(2), 115–35.

McGrath, R. G. and MacMillan, I. C. (2000), *The Entrepreneurial Mindset: Strategies for Continuously Creating Opportunity in an Age of Uncertainty*, Harvard: Harvard Business School Press.

McKinsey & Co. (1993) *Emerging Exporters: Australia's High Value-Added Manufacturing Exporters*, Melbourne: Australian Manufacturing Council.

Meyer, G. D., Neck, H. N., and Meeks, M. D. (2002), 'The entrepreneurship-strategic management interface'. In Hitt, M. A., Ireland, R. D., Camp, S. M., and Sexton, D. L. (eds), *Strategic Entrepreneurship: Creating a New Mindest*, Oxford: Blackwell Publishing, 19–45.

Miles, M. B., and Huberman, M. (1994), *Qualitative Data Analysis: An Expanded Sourcebook*, Thousand Oaks, CA: Sage.

Miles, R. E., and Snow, C. C. (1978), *Organizational Strategy, Structure, and Process*, New York: McGraw-Hill.

Miller, D. (1983), 'The correlates of entrepreneurship in three types of firms', *Management Science*, 29, 770–91.

Miller, D., and Friesen, P. H. (1978), 'Archetypes of strategy formulation', *Management Science*, 24(9), 921.

Miller, D., and Friesen, P. H. (1982), 'Innovation in conservative and entrepreneurial firms: Two models of strategic momentum', *Strategic Management Journal*, 3(1), 1–25.

Miller, D., and Shamsie, J. (1996), 'The resource-based view of the firm in two environments: The Hollywood film studio from 1936 to 1965', *Academy of Management Journal*, 39(3), 519–43.

Minniti, M., and Bygrave, W. (2001), 'A dynamic model of entrepreneurial learning', *Entrepreneurship Theory and Practice*, 25(3), 5–16.

Mises, L. Von (1949), *Human Action: A Treatise on Economics*, New Haven, CT: Yale University Press.

Mitchell, R. K., Smith, B., Seawright, K., and Morse, E. A. (2000), 'Cross-cultural cognitions and venture creation decision', *Academy of Management Journal*, 43, 974–993.

Moen, O. (2001), 'The Born Globals – a new generation of small European exporters', *International Marketing Review*, 19(2), 156–75.

Moen, ø. (2002), 'The relationship between firm, size, competitive advantages and export performance revisited', *International Small Business Journal*, 18(1).

Molloy, E. (1992), *Strategic Agenda for Subsidiary*. Kildare: AOMD.

Monczka, R., and Giunipero, L. C. (1984), 'International purchasing: Characteristics and implementation', *Journal of Purchasing and Materials Management*, Fall, 2–9.

Monczka, R., and Trent, R. (1991), 'Global sourcing: A development approach', *International Journal of Purchasing and Materials Management*, 27(2), 2–8.

Morris, M. H. (1998), *Entrepreneurial Intensity*, Westport, CT: Quorum Books.

Morris, M. H., and Lewis, P. S. (1995), 'The determinants of entrepreneurial activity: implications for marketing', *European Journal of Marketing*, 29(7), 31–48.

Morris, M. H., Kuratko, D. F. and Schindehutte, M. (2001), 'Towards integration: Understanding entrepreneurship through frameworks', *The International Journal of Entrepreneurship and Innovation*.

Morrow, J. F. (1988), 'International entrepreneurship: A new growth opportunity', *New Management*, 5(3), 59–60.

Nahapiet, J., and Ghoshal, S. (1998), 'Social capital, intellectual capital, and the organizational advantage', *Academy of Management Review*, 23, 242–66.

Nayyar, P. R. and Bantel, K. A. (1994), 'Competitive agility: A source of competitive advantage based on speed and variety', In P. Shrivastava, A. H. Huff and J. E. Dutton (eds), *Advances in Strategic Management: Resource-Based View Of The Firm*, Greenwich, CT: JAI Press.

Nelson R., and Winter, S., (1982), *An Evolutionary Theory of Economic Change*, Cambridge: MA: Harvard University Press.

Newman, H. (1978), 'Strategic groups and the structure-performance relationship', *Review of Economics and Statistics*, 60, 417–27.

Nonaka, I. (1994), 'A dynamic theory of organizational knowledge creation', *Organization Science*, 5(1), 14–36.

Nonaka, I., and Takeuchi, H. (1995), *The Knowledge Creating Company*, New York and Oxford: Oxford University Press.

Nooteboom, B. (2004), *Interfirm Collaboration, Learning and Networks: An Integrated Approach*, London: Routledge.

Norman, R., and Ramirez, R. (1993), 'From value chain to value constellation: Designing interactive strategy', *Harvard Business Review*, 71, 65–77.

Normann, R., and Ramirez, R. (1994), *Designing Interactive Strategy: From Value Chain to Value Constellation*, Chichester: John Wiley and Sons.

Obrecht, J. J. (2004), 'Entrepreneurial capabilities: A resource based systemic approach to international entrepreneurship'. In Dana, L. P. (ed.), *Handbook of Research on International Entrepreneurship*, Cheltenham, UK, and Northampton, MA: Edward Elgar.

Oviatt, B. M., and McDougall, P. P. (1994), 'Toward a theory of international new ventures', *Journal of International Business Studies*, 25(1), 45–64.

Oviatt, B. M., and McDougall, P. P. (1995), 'Global start-ups: Entrepreneurs on a worldwide stage', *Academy of Management Executive*, 9(2), 30–43.

Oviatt, B. M., and McDougall, P. P. (2000), 'International entrepreneurship: The intersection of two research paths', *Academy of Management Journal*, 43, 902–8.

Oviatt, B. M. and McDougall, P. P. (2003), 'Some fundamental issues in International Entrepreneurship', *Entrepreneurship Theory & Practice*.

Pareto, V. (1909), *Manuel de'economie politique*, Paris: Giard et Briére.

Pilotti L., and SEDITA – S. R. (2004), 'Human capital development in a complex learning system: The virtuous interaction between individuals, organizations and communities', *Working Paper n. 2005–17, Dipartimento di Scienze Economiche, Aziendali e Statistiche*, Università degli Studi di Milano.

Pedersen, T., Petersen, B., and Sharma, D. Deo, (2003), 'Knowledge transfer performance of multinational companies', *Management International Review*, 43(3), 69–90.

Petersen, B., Pedersen, T. and Sharma, D. D. (2002), 'The role of knowledge in firms' internationalisation process: Where, from and where to?'. In A. Blomstermo and D. Sharma (eds), *Learning in The Internationalisation Process Of Firms*. Cheltenham: Edward Elgar.

Penrose, E. T., (1959), *The Theory of the Growth of the Firm*, New York: John Wiley and Sons.

Penrose, E. T. (1995), *The Theory of the Growth of the Firm*, 3rd edn, New York: Oxford University Press.

Peteraf, M. A., (1993), 'The cornerstones of competitive advantage: A resource-based view', *Strategic Management Journal*, 14, 179–91.

Pfeffer, J., and Salancik, G. R. (1978), *The External Control of Organizations: A Resource Dependence Perspective*, New York: Harper & Row.

Polanyi, M. (1966), *The Tacit Dimension*, Garden City, NY: Anchor.

Porter, M. (1990), *The Competitive Advantage of Nations*, New York: Basic Books.

Porter, M. E. (1981), 'The contributions of industrial organization to strategic management', *Academy of Management Review*, 6(4), 609–20.

———. (1998), *On Competition*, Boston, MA: Harvard Business School Press.

Powell, W. (1990), 'Neither market nor hierarchy: Network forms of organization', *Research in Organizational Behavior*, 12, 295–337.

Prahalad, C. K. (1999), 'Transforming international governance: the challenge for multinational corporations', *Sloan Management Review*, Fall, 5–13.

Prahalad, C. K,. and Hamel, G. (1990), 'The core competence of the organisation', *Harvard Business Review*, May–June.

Preece S. B., Miles, G., and Baetz, M. C. (1998), 'Explaining the international intensity and global diversity of early stage technology based firms', *Journal of Business Venturing*, 14, 259–81.

Putnam R. D. (1993), *Making Democracy Work – Civic Traditions in Modern Italy*, Princeton, NJ: Princeton University Press.

Pyke F., Beccattini G., and Sengenberger, W. (1990), *Industrial Districts and Inter-Firm Cooperation in Italy*, Geneva: International Institute for Labour Studies.

Rao, H. (1994), 'The social construction of reputation: Certification contests, legitimation, and the survival of organisations in the American automobile industry: 1895–1912', *Strategic Management Journal*, 15 (Winter Special Issue), 29–44.

Rasmussen, E. S., Madsen, T. K. and Evangelista, F. (1999), *The Founding of Born Global Company in Denmark and Australia: Sense Making and Networking*, Odense University Proceedings, Odense: University of Southern Denmark.

Rasmussen, E. S., and Servais, P. (2002), 'Industrial districts, networks and Born Global firms'. In: Knudsen, T., Askegaard, S., and Jørgensen, N. (eds), *Perspectives on Marketing Relationships*, Købehavn: Thomson, pp. 125–48.

Reid, S. D. (1981), 'The decision-maker and export entry and expansion', *Journal of International Business Studies*, 12(2), 101–12.

Rennie, M. (1993), 'Global competitiveness: Born global', *McKinsey Quarterly*, 4, 45–52.

Reuber, A. R., and Fischer, E. (1997), 'The influence of the management team's international experience on the internationalization behavior of SMEs', *Journal of International Business Studies*, 28(4), 807–25.

Rialp, A., Rialp, J. and Knight, G. (2005), 'The Phenomenon of early internationalising firms: what do we know after a decade (1993–2003) of scientific inquiry?', *International Business Review*, 14, 147–66.

Rialp, J., and Knight, G. A. (2005), 'What do we know after a decade (1993–2003) of scientific inquiry?', *International Business Review*, 14(2).

Ricardo, D. ([1817] 1980), *Principles of Political Economy and Taxation*, London: Penguin.

Roth, K., and Morrison, A. (1997), 'Implementing global strategy: Characteristics of global subsidiary mandates', *Journal of International Business Studies*, 23, 715–36.

Roure, J. B., Keeley, R., and Keller, T. (1992), 'Venture capital strategies in Europe and the U.S: Adapting to the 1990s'. In Churchill, N. C. et al. (eds), *Frontiers of Entrepreneurship Research*, Babson Park, MA: Babson College, pp. 345–59.

Roy, D. A., and Simpson, C. L. (1981), 'Export attitudes of business executives in the smaller manufacturing firm', *Journal of Small Business Management*, 19, 16–22.

Rumelt, R. (1991), 'How much does industry matter?', *Strategic Management Journal*, 12, 167–186.

Rumelt, R. P. (1984), 'Toward a strategic theory of the firm'. In R. Lamb (ed.), *Competitive Strategic Management*, Englewood Cliffs, NJ: Prentice Hall, pp. 556–70.

Saarenketo, S., Puumalainen, K., Kuivalainen, O., and Kylaheiko, K. (2004), 'Dynamic knowledge-related learning processes in internationalizating high-tech SMEs', *International Journal of Production Economics*, 89(3), 363.

Sahlman, W. A., and Stevenson, H. H. (1991), 'Introduction'. In Sahlman, W. A., and Stevenson, H. H. (eds), *The Entrepreneurial Venture*, Boston, MA: McGraw Hill.

Saltman, R. B. (1992), *Single Source Financing System: A Solution for the United States*, JAMA, 268, 774–79.

Samiee, S., Walters P. G. B., and DuBois, F. L. (1993), 'Exporting as an innovative behaviour: An empirical investigation', *International Marketing Review*, 10(3), 5–25.

Samuelson, P. (1947), *Foundations of Economic Analysis*, Cambridge, MA: Harvard University Press.

Sapienza, H. J., Clercq, D. D., and Sandberg, W. R. (2005), 'Antecedents of international and domestic learning effort', *Journal of Business Venturing*, 20(4), 437.

Saxenian, A. (1994), *Regional Advantage: Culture and Competition in Silicon Valley and Route 128*, Cambridge, MA: Harvard Business Press.

Say, J-B. ([1803] 1971), *A Treatise on Political Economy*, New York: Augustus M. Kelley.

Schumpeter, J. A. (1934), *The Theory of Economic Development*, Cambride, MA: Harvard University Press. First published in German, 1912.

———. (1942), *Capitalism, Socialism and Democracy*. New York: Harper.

———. (1947), 'The creative response in economic history', *Journal of Economic History*, 7, 149–59.

————. (1950), *Capitalism, Socialism and Democracy*, 3rd edn, New York: Harper & Row.

Servais, P., Zucchella, A., MAccarini, M. E., and Palamara G. (2005) 'Relationship marketing from an international sourcing perspective: A study on early and late international firms', *8th Vaasa International Business Conference Proceedings*, University of Vaasa, Vaasa, 21–23 August, 2005.

Servais, P., and Jensen, J. M. (2001), 'The internationalization of industrial purchasing: The example of small Danish manufactures', *Advances in International Marketing*, 11, 227–54.

Servais, P. and Rasmussen, E. S. (2000), 'Different types of international new ventures', *Academy of International Business (AIB) Annual Meeting*.

Shane, S., and Venkataraman, S. (2000), 'The promise of entrepreneurship as a field of research', *Academy of Management Review*, 25(1).

Sharma, P., and Chrisman, J. J. (1999), 'Toward a reconciliation of the definitional issues in the field of corporate entrepreneurship', *Entrepreneurship Theory and Practice*, Spring, 11–27.

Shoham, A. (1988), 'Export performance: A conceptualization and empirical assessment', *Journal of international marketing*, 6(3), 59–81.

Simmonds K., and Smith, H. (1968), 'The first export order: A marketing innovation', *British Journal of Marketing*, 2, 93–100.

Sinkula, J. M. (1994), 'Market information processing and organizational learning', *Journal of Marketing*, 58, American Marketing Association.

Sisca, S., and Pizzarelli, F. (2002), 'Cost-benefit analysis and choice of dialysis treatment in Italy', *Dialysis and Transplantation*, 31(6).

Smart, D. T., and Conant, J. S. (1994), 'Entrepreneurial orientation, distinctive Marketing competencies and organizational performance', *Journal of Applied Business Research*, 10(3), 28–38.

Smith, A. ([1776] 1937), *An Inquiry Into the Nature and Causes of the Wealth of Nations*, New York: Modern Library.

Snow, C., and Thomas, J. B. (1994), 'Field research methods in strategic management: contributions to theory building and testing', *Journal of Management*, 31, 458–79.

Snow, C. C., Miles, R. E., and Coleman, H. J. (1992), 'Managing the 21st century network organisation', *Organisational Dynamics*, Winter.

Solow, R. (1956), 'A contribution to theory of economic growth', *Quarterly Journal of Economics*, 70, 65–94.

Solvell, O. and Zander, U. (1995), 'Organization of the dynamic multinational enterprise', *International Studies of Management and Organization*, 25(1–2), 17–38.

Sopas, L. (2001), 'Born exporting in regional clusters: Preliminary empirical evidence'. In Spender, J.-C. (1996), 'Making knowledge the basis of a dynamic theory of the firm', *Strategic Management Journal*, 17, 45–62.

Spender, J. C. (1996), 'Making knowledge the basis for a dynamic theory of the firm', *Strategic Management Journal*, 17, 45–62.

Starr, J. A., and MacMillan, I. C. (1990), 'Resource cooptation via social contracting: Resource acquisition strategies for new ventures', *Strategic Management Journal*, 11, 79–92.

Staum, M. S. (1987), 'The institute economist: From physiocracy to entrepreneurial capitalism', *History of Political Economy*, 19(4), 525–50.

Stampacchia, P. (2001), *L'impresa nel contesto globale – attività, risorse, configurazione*, Torino: Giappichelli.

Steensma, K., Marino, L., Weaver, M., and Dickson, P. (2000), 'The influence of national culture in the formation of technology alliances by entrepreneurial firms', *Academy of Management Journal*, 43, 951–73.

Stevenson, H. H. and Jarrillo, J. C. (1990), 'A paradigm of entrepreneurship: Entrepreneurial management', *Strategic Management Journal*.

Stopford, J., and Wells, L. (1972), *Managing the Multinational Enterprise: Organization of the Firm and Ownership of the Subsidiaries*, New York: Basic Books.

Storper, M. (1992), 'The limits to globalization: Technology districts and international trade', *Economic Geography*, 68, 60–93.

Sullivan, D. (1994), 'Measuring the degree of internationalization of a firm', *Journal of International Business Studies*, 25(2), 325–42.

Sullivan, T. J. (2001), *Method of Social Research*, Fort Worth, TX, and London: Harcourt College Publisher.

Taggart, J. H. (1996), 'Multinational manufacturing subsidiaries in Scotland: Strategic role and economic impact', *International Business Review*, 5(5), 447–68.

Taggart, J. H., Berry, M., and McDermott, M. (eds), *Multinational in a New Era: International Strategy and Management*, Basingstoke: Palrave Macmillan, pp. 29–46.

Takeuchi, H., and Porter, M. (1986), 'Three roles of international marketing in global strategy'. In Porter, M. (ed.), *Competition in Global Industries*, Boston, MA: Harvard Business School, pp. 111–46.

Tallman, S., and Li, J. (1996), 'Effects of international diversity and product diversity on the performance of multinational firms', *Academy of Management Journal*, 39, 179–96.

Teece, D. J. (1990), 'Contributions and impediments of economic analysis to the study of strategic management'. In Fredrickson, J. W. (ed.), *Perspectives on Strategic Management*, New York: Harper & Row.

Teece, D. J., Pisano, G., and Shuen, A. (1997), 'Dynamic capabilities and strategic management', *Strategic Management Journal*, 18, 509–33.

Tesar, G., and Moini, A. H. (1998), 'Longitudinal study of exporters and non exporters: A focus on smaller manufacturing enterprises', *International Business Review*, 7(3), 291–313.

Thomas, A. S., and Mueller, S. L. (2000), 'A case for comparative entrepreneurship: Assessing the relevance of culture', *Journal of International Business Studies*, 31, 287–301.

Thoumrungroje, A. and Tansuhaj, P. (2005), 'Entrepreneurial strategic posture, international diversification, and firm performance', *Multinational Business Review*.

Tieben, B., and Keizer, W. (1997), 'Introduction: Austrian economics in debate'. In Keizer, W., Tieben, B., and van-Zijp (eds), *Austrian Economics in Debate*, London and New York: Routledge.

Toyne, B. (1989), 'International exchange: A foundation for theory building in international business', *Journal of International Business Studies*, Spring, 1–17.

Turnbull, P. W., (1985), 'A challenge to the stages theory of the internationalization process'. In P. J. Rosson and S. D. Reid (eds), *Management Export Entry and Expansion*, New Yrok: Praeger, pp. 21–40.

UNCTAD, (2001), *Economic Development in Africa: Performance, Prospects and Policy Issues*, New York and Geneva: United Nations.

Urban S., and Vendemini, S. (1992), *European Strategic Alliances: Cooperative Corporate Strategies in the New Europe*, Oxford: Blackwell.

Uzzi, B. (1997), 'Social structure and competition in interfirm networks: The paradox of embeddedness', *Administrative Science Quarterly*, 42, 35–67.

Vancil, R. (1978), *Decentralization: Managerial Ambiguity by Design*, New York: Financial Executive Research Foundation.

Velo, D. (2000), 'La gouvernance dans un monde sans frontiers'. In Ricciardelli, M., Urban, S., and Nanopoulos, K. (eds), *Mondialisation et societes multiculturelles*, Paris: Presses Universitaires de France.

Venkataraman, S., (1997), 'The distinctive domain of entrepreneurship research', In Katz, J. A. (ed.), *Advances in Entrepreneurship, Firm Emergence and Growth*, Vol. 3., Greenwich, CT: JAI Press, pp. 119–38.

Venkatraman, N., and Ramanujam, V. (1986), 'Measurement of business performance in strategy research: A comparison of approaches', *Academy of Management Review*, 11, 801–14.

Vernon, R. (1966), 'International investment and international trade in the product cycle', *Quarterly Journal of Economics*, 80, 190–207.

Vernon, R. (1974), 'The location of industry'. In Dunning, J. H. (ed.), *Economic Analysis and the Multinational Enterprise*, London, Allen & Unwin, 89–114.

Vesper, K. (1990), 'Perspectives on entrepreneurship', *New Venture Strategies*.

Vienken, J., and Bowry, S. (2002), 'Quo vadis: Dialysis membrane?', *Artificial Organs*, 26(2), 152–59.

Volery, T. (2004), 'On field research methods for theory building and testing'. In Dana, L.-P. (ed.), *Handbook of Research on International Entrepreneurship*, Cheltenham, UK, Northampton, MA: Edward Elgar, pp. 781–92.

Walras, L. ([1874] 1926), *Eléments d'économie politique pure, Edition definitive, Paris: R. Pichon.*

Ward P., Bickford D. J., and Keong Leong, G. (1996), 'Configuration of manifacturing strategy, business strategy, enviroment and structure', *Journal of Management*, 22(4), 597–626.

Weick, K. E. (1995), *Sensemaking in Organizations*, Thousand Oaks, CA: Sage Publications.

Wernerfelt, B., (1984), 'A resource-based view of the firm', *Strategic Management Journal*, 5, 171–80.

Westhead, P., Wright, M., and Ucbasaran, D. (1998), 'The internationalization of new and small firms'. In Reynolds, P. D., Byrave, W. D., Carter, N. M., Manigart, S., Mason, C. M., Meyer, G. D., and Shaver, (eds), *Frontiers of Entrepreneurship Research*, Wellsley, MA: Babson College, pp. 464–77.

198 *References*

Westhead P., Wright, M., and Ucbasaran D. (2001), 'The internationalisation of new and small firms: A resource-based view', *Journal of Business Venturing*, 16, 333–58.

White, R. E., and Poynter, T. A. (1984), 'Strategies for foreign-owned subsidiaries in Canada', *Business Quarterly*, 49(2), 59–69.

Wickham, P. (1998), *Strategic Entrepreneurship*, London: Pitman Publishing.

Wiklund, J. (1999), 'The sustainability of the entrepreneurial orientation-performance relationship', *Entrepreneurship Theory and Practice*, 24(1), 37–48.

Wiklund, J., and Sheperd, D. (2003), 'Knowledge-based resources entrepreneurial orientation and the performance of small and medium-sized business', *Strategic Management Journal*, 24, 1307–14.

Williamson, O. E. (1975), *Markets and Hierarchies: Analysis and Antitrust Implications*, New York: Free Press.

Williamson, O. E. (1985), *The Economic Institutions of Capitalism*, New York: Free Press.

Wolff, J. A., and Pett, T. L. (2000), 'Internationalization of small firms: An examination of export competitive patterns, firm size, and export performance', *Journal of Small Business Management*, 4, 34–47.

Wright, R. W., and Ricks, D. A. (1994), 'Trends in international business research: Twenty-five years later', *Journal of International Business Studies*, 25(4), 687–701.

Yeoh, P., and Jeong, I. (1995), 'Contingency relationships between entrepreneurship, export channel structure, and environment', *European Journal of Marketing*, 29(8), 95–115.

Yeoh, P.-L. (2004), 'International learning: Antecedents and performance implications amongst newly internationalizing companies in an exporting context', *International Marketing Review*, 21(4), 511–35.

Yeung, H. W. C. (2002), *Entrepreneurship and the Internationalisation of Asian Firms: An Institutional Perspective*, Oxford: Edward Elgar.

Yin, R. K., (1989), *Case Study Research: Design and Methods*, rev. edn, Beverly Hills, CA: Sage Publications.

Yip, G. S. (2003), *Total Global Strategy*, Upper Saddle River and New York: Prentice Hall.

Yli-Renko, H., Autio, E., and Tontti, V. (2002), 'Social capital, knowledge and the international growth of technology-based new firms', *International Business Review*, 11(3), 279–304.

Young, S. (2004), 'Entrepreneurship in the multinational subsidiary', *Strathclyde International Business School*, 5 May 2004.

Young S., Hamill J., Wheeler, C., and Richard, D. (1989), *International Market Entry and Development*, Englewoods Cliffs, NJ: Prentice-Hall.

Young, S., Hood, N., and Hamill, J. (1988), *Foreign Multinationals and the British Economy*, London: Croom Helm.

Zacharakis, A. (1997), 'Entrepreneurial entry into foreign markets: A transaction cost perspective', *Entrepreneurship Theory and Practise*, 21(3), 23–39.

Zaheer, S. and Manrakhan, S., (2001), Concentration and dispersion in global industries: Remote electronic access and the location of economic activities', *Journal of International Business Studies*, 32(4), 134–45.

Zahra, S. A. (1991), 'Predictors and financial outcomes of corporate entrepreneurship: An exploratory study', *Journal of Business Venturing*, 6, 259–86.

Zahra, S. A. (1993), 'Conceptual model of entrepreneurship as firm behavior: A critique and extension', *Entrepreneurship: Theory and Practice*, 14(4), 5–21.

Zahra, S. A., and Covin, J. G. (1995), 'Contextual influences on the corporate entrepreneurship-performance relationship: A longitudinal analysis', *Journal of Business Venturing*, 10, 43–58.

Zahra, S. A., and Garvis, D. M. (2000), 'International corporate entrepreneurship: The moderating effect of international environmental hostility', *Journal of Business Venturing*, 15, 469–92.

Zahra, S. A., and George, G. (2002), 'International Entrepreneurship: The current status of the field and future research agenda'. In Hitt, M., Ireland, D., Sexton, D., and Camp, M. (eds), *Strategic Entrepreneurship: Creating an Integrated Mindset*, Strategic Management Series, Oxford: Blackwell Publishers, pp. 255–88.

Zahra, S., and Schulte, W. (1994), 'International Entrepreneurship: Beyond folklore and myth', *International Journal of Commerce and Management*, 4(12), 85–95.

Zahra S., Dharwadkar R., and George, G. (2000a), *Entrepreneurship in Multinational Subsidiaries: The Effects of Corporate and Local Environment Contexts*, available at: http:www.gatech.eduworkingpaper199999_00–27.pdf

Zahra, S. A., Ireland, D. R., and Hitt, M. A. (2000b), 'International expansion by new venture firms: International diversity, mode of market entry, technological learning and performance', *Academy of Management Journal*, 43(5), 925–50.

Zahra, S. A, Neubaum, D. O., and Huse, M., (1997), 'The effect of the environment on export performance among telecommunications new ventures', *Entrepreneurship Theory and Practice*, 22, 25–46.

Zikmund, W. G. (1997), *Business Research methods*, 5th edn, Forth Worth, TX: The Dryden Press.

Zollo, M., and Winter, S. G. (2002), 'Deliberate learning and the evolution of dynamic capabilities', *Organisational Science*, 13(3), 339–51.

Zucchella, A. (2001), 'The internationalisation of SMEs: Alternative hypotheses and empirical survey'. In Taggart, J. H., Berry M., and McDermott, M. (eds), *Multinationals in a New Era*, Basingstoke: Palgrave Macmillan, pp. 47–60.

Zucchella, A. (2002), 'Born global versus gradually internationalizing firms: An analysis based on the Italian case', *Paper Presented at the 28th EIBA Conference*, Athens.

Zucchella A. (2006), 'Local clusters dynamics: Trajectories of mature industrial districts between decline and multiple embeddedness', *Journal of Institutional Economics*, 2(1), 21–44.

Zucchella, A., and Maccarini, M. E., (1999), *I nuovi percorsi di internazionalizzazione*, Milan: Giuffrè.

Index

Agazzone, Stefania, 143
agglomeration, 94–6, 130
Aharoni, Y., 40
air-conditioning systems, 159–69
alertness, 62, 63, 66, 77, 133, 145
Alvarez, S., 67
aspirations, 126
asset ownership advantages, 36–7
assets, 36–7, 81–2, 88, 102
  see also resources
Austrian school, 60–5
autonomy, 117–18

Barney, J., 67
Barrera, Giuseppe, 143, 145–51
Barrera SRL, 143–52, 173
behaviour, 57
behavioural approaches, 29–30,
  39–52, 53–4
Bell, J., 52, 120, 168
Birkinshaw, J., 115, 116
Born-Again Global firms, 19, 119,
  144, 159–69
Born-Global firms
  case study, 143–52
  definitions, 2, 6
  description, 107–12
  entrepreneur's role, 127
  internationalization approaches,
    53, 54
  learning, 151–2
  social networks, 94
  and stage theory, 45
  studies of, 18
  see also International New
    Ventures (INVs)
Brush, C.G., 82
Buckley and Casson (1976), 35
business processes, 87–8, 126,
  128–9, 145–7, 155–7,
  162–5

business theory, 21–2, 52–5
Bygrave, W., 133

Caciolli, Roberto, 159, 160, 162,
  164, 165, 166, 167
Cantillon, R., 58, 64, 66, 77
capabilities, 85–9, 103, 125, 165–6, 174
capitalist's role, 65, 67
Carter, S., 19
case studies
  Barrera SRL, 143–52, 173
  Fresenius Medical Care Italy
    S.p.A., 144, 152–9, 173
  methodology, 137–43
  RC Group S.p.A., 144, 159–69, 173
Casson, M., 67
Cavusgil, V., 110
CEO's (Chief Executive Officer's)
  role, 76, 78
classical economic theory, 58–9
closed networks, 91
  see also networks
clusters, 94–6, 104, 112, 130–1
Coase, R.H., 34, 59–60
Cochran, D.S., 141
Coleman, J.C., 91
collaboration, 126, 129
communication, 10, 72–3
comparative advantage, 29
competence-based framework, 85
competences, 85–6, 122, 124–5
  see also skills
competitiveness, 114
complexity, 116
confidence, 71
contingency theory, 52
Cooper, A.C., 97
coordination, 129
corporate entrepreneurship, 112–19
costs, 31
Coviello, N.E., 8, 110, 112, 120

200